1995

G

T     W9-BAV-504

3 0301 00067986 6

# The Canadian Health Care System
## Lessons for the United States

# The Canadian Health Care System
# Lessons for the United States

**Edited by Susan Brown Eve, Betty Havens,
and Stanley R. Ingman**

LIBRARY
College of St. Francis
JOLIET, ILLINOIS

University Press of America, Inc.
Lanham • New York • London

Copyright © 1995 by
University Press of America,® Inc.
4720 Boston Way
Lanham, Maryland 20706

3 Henrietta Street
London, WC2E 8LU England

All rights reserved
Printed in the United States of America
British Cataloging in Publication Information Available

**Library of Congress Cataloging-in-Publication Data**

The Canadian health care system : lessons for the United States /
edited by Susan Brown Eve, Betty Havens, and Stanley R. Ingman.
p.   cm.
Originally published by the University of North Texas Center for
Texas Studies in 1994.
"Proceedings of the conference, 'The Canadian health care system,
lessons for the United States', held at the University of North Texas
Health Science Center, Fort Worth, Texas, April 2, 1993".
1. Medical care--Canada--Congresses. 2. Insurance, Health--Canada-
-Congresses. 3. Medical policy--Canada--Congresses. 4. Medical
care--United States--Congresses. 5. Insurance, Health--Congresses.
I. Eve, Susan Brown, II. Havens, Betty,  III. Ingman, Stanley R.
RA395.C3C38   1995       362.1'0971--dc20        95-19842 CIP

ISBN 0-7618-0005-0  (cloth: alk: paper)
ISBN 0-7618-0006-9  (pbk: alk: paper)

⊖™The paper used in this publication meets the minimum
requirements of American National Standard for Information
Sciences—Permanence of Paper for Printed Library Materials,

G
3 62.1
E 922

# Contents

155,529

# 2. Critical Perspectives ............................................ 137

Chapter

# 3. U.S. Needs and Directions ......................... 213

Chapter

# ACKNOWLEDGMENTS

The chapters in these proceedings were originally presented at Conference on the Canadian Health Care System: Lessons for the United States, held April 2, 1993 in Fort Worth, Texas. The primary funding for the conference was provided through grants from the Department of External Affairs and International Trade, Canada, and the Federation of North Texas Universities. Special thanks are due to J. E. B. Gibson, Consul General of the Canadian Consulate, Dallas, and Rosalind De Rolon for their assistance with developing the conference proposal. Mr. Gibson also gave the welcoming address for the conference. Dean Rollie Schafer, Dean of the Robert B. Toulouse Graduate School at the University of North Texas and Dean Lesley Thompson of the Graduate School at Texas Woman's University were generous in providing support from FNTU for the conference. This idea for the conference grew out of the work of one of the conference editors, Susan Brown Eve, in which she compared the use of health care services by older adults in Canada, Great Britain, and the United States. That research, which was presented as a part of this conference, was funded by a grant from the AARP Andrus Foundation. Additional funding for the conference was provided by the Texas Institute for Research and Education on Aging, of the University of North Texas and the University of North Texas Health Science Center, Stanley Ingman, Director. Daniel Johnson, Dean of the School of Community Service, provided strong support for the development of the North Texas Consortium for Health Research and Policy, which also co-sponsored this conference. Alfred F. Hurley, Chancellor of the University of North Texas and the University of North Texas Health Sciences Center, as well as Blaine Brownell, Provost and Vice President for Academic Affairs, also lent their support to the grant applications and to the conference.

The University of North Texas Health Science Center in Fort Worth generously donated space for the conference under the auspices of David Richards, D.O., President of UNTHSC. Benjamin Cohen, Vice President and Dean of Medicine, and his assistant, Gregory McQueen, assisted in getting continuing education credits for osteopathic physicians for the conference. Staff members at UNTHSC who were especially helpful include Nancy J. Popejoy, Program Director for Continuing Medical Education; Chuck Weatherall, TV Producer/Director of the Department of Biomedical Communications; and Ma'Lisa Laidlaw, News and Information Writer of the Office for Development.

CEU credit for allopathic physicians and nurses was obtained from the Division of Continuing Education at The University of Texas Southwestern Medical Center with the assistance of Ralph Anderson, M.D., Professor and Chair, and Robert Kinch, M.D., Professor, Department of Obstetrics and Gynecology, John Peter Smith Hospital in Fort Worth. Dr. Anderson's assistants, Kim McMillan and Leah Mitchell were meticulous and conscientious in assisting the conference organizers with the tedious details of this process and we are deeply grateful.

The American Association of Retired Persons provided volunteers to assist with registration and travel expenses for Betty Havens, who was then the Provincial Gerontologist of Manitoba and the Deputy Minister of Health. Additional assistance was provided by student volunteers in the federated doctoral programs in sociology at Texas Woman's University and the University of North Texas.

Preparation of these proceeding would not have been possible without the help of many staff members at the University of North Texas. James Lee, Ph.D., Director of the Center for Texas Studies, agreed to publish the original proceedings through the center. Jane Tanner, Ph.D., Director of Publications, performed miracles with messy manuscripts, turning them into beautiful copy. Dr. Tanner also did a superb job of preparing the manuscript for reprinting by University Press of America. Betty Griese, Director, and Rachel Dowdy, Coordinator, in the Data Entry Division of the UNT Computing Center provided major assistance retyping manuscripts when needed. The conference was administered Shirley White in the Center for Conference Management and Continuing Education, who calmly met all the deadlines, collected the money and paid the bills. Thanks are due to Fonda Gaynier, Secretary in the Department of Sociology and Social Work at UNT who kept us all organized and typed more mailing labels than we can count. Staff in the Texas Institute for Research and Education in Aging whose help is gratefully acknowledged include Ann Reban, Peggy Higgins, Xiaomei Pei, Jan Weaver, Elizabeth Tucker and Kay Branum.

Finally, there were many people who participated in the conference who did not submit a chapter for the conference proceedings. Participants who made formal presentations included Dennis Timbrell, M.D., CEO, Ontario Hospital Association and former provincial Minister of Health for Ontario; and David Low, M.D., President, University of Houston Health Science Center, Houston. Chairs of sessions and discussants included UNT/UNTHSC faculty Rose Rubin, Ph.D. Professor of Economics and Special Assistant to the Provost; Benjamin Cohen, D.O., Vice President and Dean; Janice Knebl, D.O., Professor of Geriatrics and Director, Geriatric Assessment and Planning Program; and Samuel T. Coleridge, D.O., Professor and Chair, Department of Family Medicine. Tim Philpot, CEO of John Peter Smith Hospital also served as a discussant. The chairs and discussants made a substantial contribution to the quality of the conference papers as the authors made their revisions and the editors wish to give them special thanks for this assistance.

# Section 1

## Introduction

# Introduction

This volume is the product of a conference on the Canadian health care system, held April 2, 1993, on the campus of the University of North Texas Health Sciences Center in Fort Worth. The purpose of the conference was to examine the Canadian health care system to determine if there were lessons that the United States could learn from the Canadian experience as the U. S. began to undertake the first serious attempt at health care reform in that country since 1965. The conference participants included a diverse group of health care professionals, health care policy makers, and behavioral and social scientists from the United States and Canada. The goal of the conference was to produce a document that would be as objective and value free as possible.

Robert L. Kane, M.D., the keynote speaker for the conference, holds an endowed chair in geriatrics at the University of Minnesota School of Public Health. In his opening chapter, "Canadian Lesson in Health Care Reform: Reading Between the Lines," he describes the Canadian health care system as a single payer system, administered by the provinces, with all provinces providing coverage for their citizens which abides by five common principals: portability across provinces, universal access to care, comprehensive coverage of hospital and medical services, public administer of provincial insurance plans, and no extra billing. Dr. Kane examines differences in the Canadian and American value systems which have produced differences in their systems for delivering health care. Americans are more committed to private entrepreneurship while Canadians are more accepting of a role for government in solving collective problems. He also explores differences in the size and complexity of the governmental units involved, level of technology, and the strength of interest groups in the health care sector as factors limiting the extent to which change in a health care system is possible. He concludes that the Canadian experience does suggest that it is possible to change the financing mechanisms to control costs and to improve access while leaving much of the existing delivery system intact.

In Chapter 2, "Financing Health Care in Canada," Frank Fedyck, of the Health Policy Division of Health and Welfare Canada, summarizes the major financial issues of the first four decades of the Canadian national health insurance. The federal government makes contributions to the provinces and territories to suport their health programs. Because of fiscal concerns at the national level, the federal per capita entitlements for health have been frozen at their 1989-90 levels. Mr. Fedyck presents an overview of health spending in Canada, and compares the patterns of Canadian spending to that of the U.S. Finally, Mr. Fedyck examines the cost control measures and pressures that the Canandian government is currently facing.

Betty Havens, then Assistant Deputy Minister of Continuing Care Programs and Provincial Gerontologist for Manitoba Health, presents an overview of the continuum of health and social services for the elderly in Manitoba. In the Canadian system, each of the ten provinces must adopt the basic minimum standards established by the federal government in order to receive its share of federal funds, but then has the autonomy to develop its own program, supplementing the core standards as the citizens of the province choose. The Manitoba continuing care program was established in 1974 and is a province wide, universal program that is provided at no cost to the consumer. Older persons requiring care are assessed to determine what their needs are and where and how these needs can be most adequately met. Coordinated health and community services are organized to avoid deterioration of the older persons and to maintain their health if it is determined that the most appropriate place for care is in the older person's own home in the community.

Eve, Pillai, Easterling, and Jones ("A Comparison of the Use of Health Care Services by Older Adults in the United States, Great Britain, and Canada") used comparable national surveys from the United States, Great Britain, and Canada to compare the accessibility of, and the predictors of, use of health care services— physicians, hospitals, home nursing services, and homemaker services. The effects of age and gender, health, income, and public and private insurance on the use of services were examined. The data used for the research were taken from the U. S. Health Interview Survey for 1984 (N=11,497), the British General Household Survey for 1985 (N=4156), and the Canadian General Health and Social Survey for 1985 (N=3130). Major findings of the study were that the British system was especially strong in the provision of home based services for older adults, including home visits from physicians and the provision of services from district nurses and homemakers, while the American and Canadian systems are especially strong in providing access to physicians in their offices and to hospital services. Based on this research, it was recommended that American and Canadian policy makers could benefit from an examination of the home services for the elderly in Britain while the British might benefit from an examination of the U. S. and Canadian methods of financing hospital care.

In Chapter 5, Dietz reports on the results of an analysis of the older adults with a physical or psychological disability included in the Health and Activity Limitation Study conducted by Statistics Canada in 1986–87. This research is important because it is the first major study of older adults who are disabled. There is not comparable dataset in the United States. In this research, she found that more than half of the older disabled adults had been hospitalized in the past year, 84 percent had seen a physician at least once in the past year, and over one-third had been visited by a home nurse in the past year. She used the Anderson and Newman health care services utilization framework to examine the predictors of use of health and social services. She found that activity limitations were generally the best predictors of use of hospital, physician and nursing services. Use of formal social services was related to Activity of Daily Living limitations and to low income. Use of informal social services was most strongly related to having a high income and to being married.

In Chapter 6, Easterling and Eve report on their research on the access to health and social services by older Canadians with developmental disabilities. Data were taken from the Canadian Health and Activity Limitation Survey, 1986–87 (n=640). Major findings were that nearly 70 percent of the disabled older adults had seen a physician in the past three months, one-third had been hospitalized in the past year with 14 percent having multiple hospitalizations, 14 percent had seen a nurse in the past three months, and more than 70 percent used prescription or nonprescription medicines in the past three months. While more than 40 percent of older disabled adults reported receiving help from non-family/non-neighbors, one-fourth to one-third of these older adults also reported that they needed help that they were not receiving, including preparing meals, grocery shopping, housework, heavy chores, personal finances, personal care, and taking short trips, taking long trips. In addition, approximately ten percent reported needing additional assistance with transportation. Thus, while there is much service being provided for this special population, much more is needed.

# Chapter 1

## Canadian Lessons in Health Care Reform
## Reading Between The Lines

*Robert L. Kane, MD*

### The art of the possible

The United States seems to have missed the chance to create an approach to providing some form of universal access to health care. The setback provides a time to regroup and rethink what ca and should be done. In the continuum of options, Canada represents a model somewhat to the left of center, but not at the extreme. It is not a national health service. Indeed, it is not even really a federally administered system. Rather, it is a collection of provincially operated programs, all of which abide by a set of common principles, which include portability across provinces, universal access, comprehensive coverage of hospital and medical services, administered publicly, and no extra billing. For purposes of American consideration, the Canadian approach can perhaps best be thought of as a single-payer system operated by small governmental units. After all, the largest Canadian province is smaller than many American states and the smallest is smaller than many American cities. In fact, the Canadian experience has demonstrated that it is feasible to operate a health care system with populations of less than a million people.

### Effects on quality

The Canadian health care system has been both praised and damned. Studies have been cited to show that care in Canada produces better (Roos, *et al.*, 1992) and worse (Roos, *et al.*, 1990) results than that in the United States. Some facts do seem clear, although the causal inferences are not always easy to determine. Canada uses more hospital care, but spends less than the United States on such care (Redelmeier and Fuchs, 1993). Canada has a lower ratio of specialists to generalist physicians and pays its doctors less (Fuchs and Hahn, 1990). Canadian infant mortality rates are lower than even white rates in the United States[1](Poullier, 1989). Canadians receive less technically intensive care with little, if any, diminution in outcomes (Rouleau, *et al.*, 1993; Zwanziger, *et al.* 1993; Roos, *et al.*, 1990; Anderson, *et al.*, 1989; Newhouse, *et al.* 1988).

7

## The Canadian health insurance program

As noted, the Canadian approach is provincially based. Although initially conceived as a partnership between the federal and provincial governments, it has evolved into a predominately provincial system with a fixed level of government support, comparable in the United States to a block grant. The size of this grant varies with the population and the wealth of the province. The province is then responsible for paying the costs of its health care program. In all provinces medical and hospital care are covered. Most provinces (all but two small ones) also cover long-term care. Canadian health insurance began with coverage for acute care only. In those provinces that opted to cover it, long-term care was covered later. Most provide some assistance for medications, often these are free or very inexpensive for elderly and poor persons.

It is also important to appreciate at the outset that the Canadian approach did not disrupt most of the health care system itself. Physicians are paid on a fee-for-services arrangement. Hospitals are operated by either private community boards or by community agencies. The pre-Medicare (Canada's name for its health care insurance system) medical structure was changed to some degree, however. Physicians in each province were paid on a negotiated fee schedule. Hospitals were generally paid on a global budget, a single sum expected to cover their operating costs for the year, adjusted annually for utilization. The introduction of Medicare also had some effects on existing structures. For example, the Veterans Administration medical system was no longer needed as a separate entity. In some provinces many of these facilities were converted into long-term care units.

## Different starting points

For purposes of extrapolating to the United States situation it is also important to appreciate that the two countries' medical care systems began from somewhat different points. Although the percent of GNP spent on health care was about the same in both countries when the Canadian reforms were introduced in the late 1960s, the patterns of care were somewhat different. Canada had (and still has) more hospital beds per capita and a substantially higher ratio of generalist physicians to specialists than in the United States.

Some would argue that there are important cultural differences as well. Whereas Americans seem to believe strongly in the virtues of private entrepreneurship, Canadians appear to have a greater tolerance for government and expect government to play a greater role in their lives. However, when one stops to consider how much of the American economy (including the private entrepreneurial sector) is tied directly or indirectly to government funding,[2] the differences in expectation may be more verbal than actual. Some observers have traced the differences in attitude back to the founding of the two countries, noting that many of the early emigrants to what became Canada came from those unwilling to be part of the American revolution. Whether the different traditions of the American west with its cowboys and violence and the Canadian north with its peace keeping Mounties really reflect national traits, there are differences in population behaviors such as homicide rates (Sloan, *et al.*, 1988). It is also true that Canada does not have the commitment to other expenditures, especially defense, that burdens the United States.

Undeniably, Canada is a smaller country in terms of population. While it does not have the heterogeneity of population found in the United States, it certainly does have enough cultural discord within its borders to threaten its continuation as a single entity.

## Implications of a single payer system

The Canadian approach to health care should be viewed less as a magic bullet than a potential target. Although a single payer system poses some potential problems, there are dramatic advantages as well. Indeed, some of both of these stem from the potential effectiveness of this approach. A single payer system has the capacity to control, or at least dramatically influence, the way health care is provided. As the only payer, it can set the rules, at least in terms of what will be paid for. Because it is ultimately responsible to the public, it cannot play too high a hand. Unfair actions that cause the providers to resist with cause will create public sympathy and lose public support for the system (and the government running it).[3] When other forms of payment for covered services are prohibited, as is the case in Canada in order to avoid creating a two-tiered system, control of payment provides an effective means to influence the distribution of care and hence to change the nature of the health care system. However, such power is not unbridled. Other groups, like physicians and hospitals, can take the government to court when they feel their sovereignty is being threatened. In a major suit in British Columbia some years ago, the provincial medical association challenged successfully the government's right to limit the distribution of specialists by creating a franchising system that would allow new practices to open in only undeserved areas.

Although the size of the potential saving is likely inflated, there is reason to expect that a single payer system can reduce administrative expenditures (Himmelstein and Woolhandler, 1986; Woolhandler and Himmelstein, 1991; Danzon, 1992; Barer and Evans, 1992). Certainly having a single set of forms and eliminating the need for marketing could save money. Here again, extrapolations from Canadian experience is tricky. Marketing might continue, if not by insurance companies then by provider groups, especially if some form of prepaid care were allowed as is now the case with American Medicare. The Canadians have never, for instance, established the oversight systems found in the United States within its Medicare program. There is nothing comparable to the American Peer Review Organization (PRO) program in Canada. Whether or not one believes that the PRO program is effective, most Americans believe that some sort of oversight system is needed to prevent exploitation either through underservice or overservice, depending on the incentives (Institute of Medicine, 1990).

Many Americans see in a single payer approach the threads of socialism. Competition is eliminated and hence the driving force for product improvement is removed. It is important to acknowledge the strongly held belief in the power of the marketplace that underlies much of American health care policy. At the moment there is greater trust in the power of Adam Smith's invisible hand than in the very visible hand of government. At the same time, one must appreciate that a governmentally operated insurance system does not eliminate competition. Rather it shifts the site of the playing field. Under the Canadian system, for example, providers can still compete for patients. The level that is eliminated is the competition among insurance companies. There is no reason to suspect that persons with free access and choice of provider would not select the one that offers the best quality and/or the best service. It is even possible that some people would opt for a prepaid package if that package provided additional benefits or offered some other incentives. Thus, a single payer system does not mean the end of competition, only the elimination of one set of middle men.

An important philosophical issue linked to a single payer system must be acknowledged: responsibility to the collective good and the right to protect one's own interests. On the surface, it would appear that Americans are strongly predisposed to the latter position. Certainly, popular expressions about the right to own guns and to buy what one can afford suggest that stance; but there is also evidence that American behavior is not so consistent, especially where it can be shown that another person's behavior can harm others. Thus, Americans are, for example, on the cutting edge of legislation that prohibits smoking in a variety of public places. Hirschman (Hirschman, 1978) has identified the consequences of an approach that permits some (usually the wealthiest) to opt out of social programs. The cost lies not simply in increasing the burden on those left behind but on removing from the debate those voices who would otherwise be the loudest when service was inadequate. Allowing them, in effect, to exit removes their voice and thus an important influence on quality. This situation pertains directly to a single payer approach if provisions are made to permit people to opt for other forms of care. To work, it must truly be a single payer. Detractors respond by suggesting that creating a monopoly undermines the potential for real choice and hence the incentive to provide better service.

## Managed Competition

Is it possible that competition is being used to hide another fear; namely, the ability of the government to gain greater control of professional practice? While some health care professionals may still harbor the illusion that they are independent practitioners, the growing trend in the United States is toward some form of organized practice. The real choice then is not between regulation/oversight and none but between regulation/oversight by government and regulation by corporation. There is no *a priori* reason to believe that private regulation will be kinder or gentler. Rather there will likely be less recourse to civil protections.

The image of managed competition with large corporate entities need provide solace to neither professional nor consumer. The strong philosophical underpinning for using private behemoths instead of government (or quasi-public) entities appears to rest on the belief that having several potential provider groups in an area will more likely assure quality. There is a presumption that people will choose wisely among competing programs in order to minimize their personal outlays. Leaving aside the problems of providing them with enough empirically derived information about the effectiveness of care delivered by each of these organizations, one may question the basic premise for such competition. In a country where competition between large corporations takes the form of buy-outs and schemes to control market share, to say nothing of misleading advertising, which tries to link one's product with all sorts of attractive if irrelevant images, what is the basis for presuming that competition produces the best service?

## Limits to extrapolation

The real problem in looking for medical care reform in the United States may lie in a crucial difference between Canada in the early 1970s (when it made its major changes) and the United States today, namely the strong influence of a wide variety of interest groups. Changing the American health care system means challenging what has become one of its major economic elements. Health care is now among the largest sectors of the American economy. Not surprisingly, it has spawned a huge number of interest groups, each dedicated to preserving or enlarging the piece of the pie its members have obtained. When one compares the potential for social reform today to the accomplishments of the Depression era, that earlier time takes on an attractive simplicity.

Likewise, Canada represents a different scale of activity. Not only were there fewer and less sophisticated medical and insurance establishments but there were only 10 provinces to grapple with. In some cases it was literally possible to buy out the dominant insurance provider and make them the operational agents (as government employees) for the new health program. In the United States today we have a plethora of organizations offering insurance products and representing various provider constituencies, to say nothing of the groups that purport to represent consumers and other interested parties.

The Canadians' lack of total commitment to entrepreneurism and competition is matched by a complementary reduction in enthusiasm for regulation. Although Canadian physicians are no more likely than their American counterparts to comply with expert recommendations about how to deliver care (Lomas, *et al.*, 1989) and there is equally wide variation in practice patterns Roos *et al.*, 1990; 1992) there exist no formal mechanisms to monitor and enforce quality comparable to the PROs. Even the provincial regulatory agencies appear to operate in a more consultative and cooperative mode than is the case in the United States.

Americans may differ from Canadians in another important respect. While they may not place as much faith in government, Americans do seem to consistently look for mechanistic solutions to social pressures. American policy often takes on a structure that was once referred to as a "domino theory," whereby one action inevitably leads to the next in a chain reaction. Much energy is spent looking for the place where leverage can most effectively be used to create the desired outcome. A series of theoretical models may be examined to find the best, usually the least obtrusive, solution. In contrast, the Canadian political style may be viewed as a series of approximations, wherein a policy goal is announced and steps taken toward it with the expectation that successive actions may be needed to refine the strategy. Part of this difference may be traced to the parliamentary system of government that provides more continuity and direct accountability than the American system of divided responsibility with its checks and balances.

**Payment reform or system change**

A basic question to be addressed in the debate over changing the American health insurance system is whether the goal is simply (not so simple actually) to provide a means to control costs and increase access or to change the basic health care system. Much of the discussion around options seems to imply that changing the payment system will change the underlying system. There is good reason to believe this, because much of the current system is, in fact, designed around payment devices. Even the service designations reflect funding sources.

Nonetheless, changing the methods of financing and payment may not bring about the reforms in the system that some seek. The Canadian experience suggests that it is possible to dramatically change the financing of health care and improve access while leaving much of the delivery system intact.[4]

There is similarly good reason to believe that the Canadian single payer approach may not be a panacea to control the rapidly escalating costs of care, a major motivator for changing the health care system. Although a single payer approach provides a means to control some important elements of cost, it does not guarantee they will be used or that they will work. The American search for a mechanism may be frustrated. There is active debate as to whether the Canadian Medicare can be credited with controlling the costs of care. The claims of Canadian success, usually expressed as comparative percentages of GNP spent on health care (Evans, 1992; GAO, 1992), are countered with accusations that the differences are narrowing or that the measures are biased because of different rates of growth in GNP (Danzon, 1992).

**Potential for system reform**

Having a single payer offers an opportunity to take steps to influence costs, but these steps require political will. Most of the analyses of rising costs attribute the bulk of the increase to a growth in technology. Not everyone agrees on the value of this technology. There is no question that technology of almost every form is more available in the United States than in Canada. America has more expensive machines and performs more procedures per capita than Canada, often by orders of magnitude. Technology advocates point to this discrepancy with pride and suggest that Canadians must queue up for services while Americans (at least insured Americans) can gain instant access to such care (whether they need it or not). They point to Canadians coming to the United States for treatment they cannot get in Canada. Technology critics point to the lower mortality rates in Canada, especially among the young as proof that access to primary care may be more effective in improving health than access to high technology. Even Americans have become concerned over the wide variation in the use of technology and are becoming concerned that availability may stimulate use without compensatory benefit. In response to accusations of border crossing, the technology critics compare the United States to a wealthy person captivated by gadgets. Would not his neighbors be better advised to borrow his tools (even rent them) rather than buy a set for themselves when they are already so often idle or underused? They argue further that the so-called long waits for care are more illusionary than real and do not affect acute needs.

Certainly being the main payer of care allows the government to shape the way care is provided. The United States has seen some of this effect in the implementation of the

Prospective Payment System for hospitals under Medicare. PPS has dramatically changed the way hospitals do business and has motivated hospitals to reconfigure themselves. Likewise, the recently introduced RBRVS for paying doctors under Medicare will likely affect their practices as well. Were the government to become the single payer instead of a dominant payer, its effects could be even more widespread.

**Possible changes**

What sorts of changes might be indicated? One of the factors influencing the active use of technology is the number of specialists trained to use the technology. By changing the balance between specialists and generalists, the government could curb technology while it also changed the way it paid for such procedures. Although direct franchising on certain types of specialists might not be viewed as legal, government incentives such as loan forgiveness for generalists or higher pay rates might induce some medical graduates to opt for this course. A more direct route would be to address the financing of post-graduate medical training. Today Medicare supports a substantial amount of such training and the other insurance payers do as well. Medicare provides specific supplements to its hospital rates for this purpose[5] as well as paying directly for physician services that are provided (or assisted) by house staff. These payments support the training of all types of physicians, not just those that benefit Medicare patients. By placing limits on the types of support for various types of physician training, the government could dramatically affect the future supply of these specialists. Of course, such actions mean taking responsibility for predicting accurately the future need for these specialists and forecasting can be treacherous (Sunshine, *et al.*, 1992; Schwartz and Mendelson, 1990; Bowman, 1989; Singer, 1989). Nonetheless, if the goal is limiting technology growth, such a step is indicated. To the extent that hospitals rely on house staff as cheap labor they may opt to fund them themselves, but they would have to do so out of limited operating budgets that would reduce costs elsewhere. Moreover, professional societies might then become more actively motivated to place caps on the number of authorized training slots available.

Canada has not solved the problem of coordinating care. Because it did not tamper extensively with the structure of the medical care system, the separate zones of responsibility remain largely intact. The actual administrative responsibility for acute and long-term care lies in the same ministry in most but not all provinces. Several provinces house all or part of long-term care in a ministry other than health.

Partly by design and partly by incentive, Canadian hospitals have shifted a substantial part of their excess capacity to long-term care. Under a global budget long-term patients are desirable because they provide utilization but cost less per day. At the same time, converting beds to care for such patients meets a demographic need while effectively removing beds from the acute care pool without encountering strong political opposition. This merging of acute and chronic care provides some coordination of services for discharged acute care patients but still leaves the interface between acute and chronic care largely unattended. With growing numbers of older persons, who are heavier users of hospital care, a better mechanism for linking hospital and post-hospital care is needed. The changes in hospital behavior after PPS suggest that their actions in discharging patients "quicker and sicker" (Kahn, *et al.*, 1990) places a heavier burden on the post-hospital system. (Shaughnessy and Kramer, 1990) Some means of assuring that hospital discharges are made in the patients' rather than solely the hospitals' interests is needed.

A single payer system provides the means, if not necessarily the motive, to improve the quality of care. The experience under Medicare suggests that it is possible to use data collected systematically across all provides to gain insights into the factors associated with better care and the extent to which these are met among different providers (Shaughnessy and Kramer, 1990). It is likewise possible under such a system to monitor outcomes of care and to make appropriate adjustments for differences in patient characteristics before interpreting these results.

**Potential for change**

Much of the continuing escalation in health care costs can be ascribed to the heavy use of expensive technologies and Americans may be described as technology addicts. What then are the prospects for treating this addiction? It is certainly easier to restrict further growth than to give up what one has already grown accustomed to, but there is even some reason to believe that Americans may be able and willing to reduce at least some of their dependence on expensive technology. The rising concerns about health care costs have prompted studies of small area variation, which demonstrate widely discrepant rates of technology use for what seem to be fairly comparable populations with no obvious correlation with improved outcomes (Wennberg and Gittelsohn, 1982, Wennberg, *et al.*, 1987). These findings have been interpreted as evidence of overuse and there is growing support for the search for ways to control such excesses, including the development of guidelines about the appropriate use of procedures.

Additional optimism about possibilities of basic behavior change come from other observations about American health practices. Consumer empowerment may create a different set of appetites. There is some suggestion that when consumers of medical are given complete information about the benefits and risks of various procedures, many opt for more conservative care (Kasper, *et al.*, 1992). In other areas, Americans have shown a remarkable capacity to give up pleasurable behaviors in the pursuit of better health. Marked reductions in cigarette smoking and fat consumption suggest that with good information Americans may be willing to give up technology if it can be shown to be bad for them.

On the other hand, Americans are highly susceptible to advertising. If providers of care continue to profit from increased use of technology, they will be tempted to encourage its consumption as with other goods. If the information presented is misleading, the results could be serious. A combination of revised market incentives and better dissemination of valid information will be needed.

## Notes

[1]However, it is noteworthy that life expectancy at age 65 is not higher in Canada compared to the United States. Interestingly, the elderly are the one group in the United States protected by some form of universal health insurance.

[2]The economic impact of federal reductions in defense spending indicate the heavy level of economic dependency on government spending in the United States, to say nothing of the many other areas where supports and subsidies have been critical.

[3]Public support may work in unexpected ways, as the physicians in Ontario discovered when they went on strike several years ago against the prohibition on extra-billing and discovered little public support for their position. As a result the stake was short-lived and unsuccessful.

[4]The extent of the perceived intactness will undoubted vary with the observer.

[5]Actually two different forms, an indirect and direct graduate medical education supplement.

## References

Anderson, G. M.; Newhouse, J. P. and Roos, L. L. 1989. Hospital care for elderly patients with diseases of the circulatory system: A comparison of hospital use in the United States and Canada. *New England Journal of Medicine* 23:321(21):1443–8.

Barer, M. J. and Evans, R. G. 1992. Interpreting Canada: models, mind-sets, and myths. *Inquiry* 11:44–61.

Bowman, M. A. 1989. Family physicians: Supply and demand. *Public Health Reports-Hyattsville* 104(3):286–293.

Danzon, P. M. 1992. Hidden overhead costs: Is Canada's system really less expensive? *Inquiry* 11:21–43.

Evans, R. G. 1992. The Canadian health-care financing and delivery system: Its experience and lessons for other nations. *Yale Law & Policy Review* 10:362–96.

Fuchs, V. R. and Hahn, J. S. 1990. How does Canada do it? A comparison of expenditures for physician's services in the United States and Canada. *New England Journal of Medicine* 323:884–90.

General Accounting Office. 1992. *Canadian health insurance: Estimating costs and savings for the United States*. United States General Accounting Office. (GAO/HRD-92-83).

Himmelstein, D. U. and Woolhandler, S. 1986. Cost without benefit: Administrative waste in U. S. health care. *New England Journal of Medicine* 314:441–5.

Hirschman, A. 1978. Exit, voice and loyalty: *Responses to the decline in firms, organizations and states*. Cambridge, MA: Harvard University Press.

Institute of Medicine. 1990. *Medicare: a strategy for quality assurance*. Washington, D.C.: National Academy Press.

Kahn, K. L.; Rubenstein, L. V.; Draper, D.; Kosecoff, J., *et al*. 1990. The effects of the DRG-based prospective payment system on quality of care for hospitalized Medicare patients: an introduction to the series. *Journal of the American Medical Association* 264:1953–5.

Kasper, J. F.; Mulley, A. G. and Wennberg, J. E. 1992. Developing shared decision-making programs to improve the quality of health care. *Quality Review Bulletin* 18:183–90.

Lomas, J.; Anderson, G. M.; Domnick-Pierre, K.; Vayda, E., *et al*. 1989. Do practice guidelines guide practice? The effect of a consensus statement on the practice of physicians. *New England Journal of Medicine* 321:1306-11.

Newhouse, J. P.; Anderson, G. and Roos, L. L. 1988. Hospital spending in the United States and Canada: A comparison. *Health Affairs*(Millwood) 7(5):6-16.

Poullier, J. P. 1989. Compendium of health care expenditures and other data. *Health Care Finance Review* (Annual Supplement):111–92. Table 58.

Redelmeier, D. A. and Fuchs, V. R. 1993. Hospital expenditures in the United States and Canada. *The New England Journal of Medicine* 328:772–8.

Roos, L. L.; Fisher, E. S.; Brazauskas, R.; Sharp, S. M.,*et al*. 1992. Health and surgical outcomes in Canada and the United States. *Health Affairs* 11:56-72.

Roos, L. L.; Fisher, E. S.; Sharp, S. M.; Newhouse, J. P.; Anderson, G.; Bubolz, T. A. 1990. Postsurgical mortality in Manitoba and New England. *Journal of the American Medical Association*, 263.

Rouleau, J. L.; Move, L. A.; Pfeffer, M. A.; Arnold, J. M. O., *et al*. 1993. A comparison of management patterns after acute myocardial infarction in Canada and the United States. *The New England Journal of Medicine* 328:779–84.

Schwartz, W. B. and Mendelson, D. N. 1990. No evidence of an emerging physician surplus: An analysis of change in physicians' work load and income. *Journal of the American Medical Association* 263(4):557–560.

Shaughnessy, P. W. and Kramer, A. M. 1990. The increased needs of patients in nursing homes and patients receiving home health care. *New England Journal of Medicine*. 332:21–7.

Singer, A.M. 1989. Projections of physician supply and demand: A summary of HRSA and AMA studies. *Academic Medicine* 64(5):235–240.

Sloan, J. H.; Kellerman, A. L.; Reay, D. T.; Ferris, J. S.,*et al*. 1988. Handgun regulations, crime, assaults, and homicide: a tale of two cities. *New England Journal of Medicine* 319:1256–62.

Sunshine, J. H.; Evans, R. G. and Chan, W. C. 1992. How accurate was GMENAC?—A retrospective review of supply projections for diagnostic radiologists. *Radiology* 182(2);365–368.

Wennberg, J. E. and Gittelsohn, A. 1982. Variations in medical care among small areas. *Scientific American* 246:120–35.

Wennberg, J. E.; Freeman, J. L. and Culp, W. J. 1987. Are hospital services rationed in New Haven or over-utilized in Boston? *The Lancet* May 23:1185–9.

Woolhandler, S. and Himmelstein, D. U. 1991. The deteriorating administrative efficiency of the US health care system. *New England Journal of Medicine* 324:1253–8.

Zwanziger, J.; Anderson, G. M.; Haber, S. G.; Thorpe, K. E. and Newhouse, J. P. 1993. Comparison of hospital costs in California, New York, and Canada. *Health Affairs* (Millwood) Summer;12(2):130–9.

# Chapter 2

## Financing Health Care in Canada

*Frank C. Fedyk*[1]
*HealthPolicy Division*
*Health Canada*

This paper provides an overview of the Canadian health care system and how it is financed. The paper examines the various stages of health policy development and the financing mechanisms used to support the organization and delivery of health care services to Canadians. Health funding remains a challenge for governments as deficits/debts have increased such that provinces are looking for ways to contain health expenditures and eliminate inefficiencies while continuing to provide a high quality of services at a price society can afford.

The cost control measures and pressures facing Canada as the health system goes through a period of renewal and transition are discussed. A common goal is to spend existing resources wisely while responding to pressures to spend more on health brought about by population aging and other factors. The challenge is to provide Canadians with affordable health care while pursuing a health renewal agenda that both improves quality of care and contains costs.

### Health Care System Overview[2]

To provide a context for how Canada finances its health care system, it is necessary to understand the history and nature of that system. Canada's health care system is a mixed private/public system. It is best described as an interlocking set of ten provincial and two territorial health insurance schemes. Each is universal and publicly funded.

The system is referred to as a system of national health care insurance in that national standards are set at the federal level. This confederate structure results from the constitutional assignment of jurisdictional responsibility over health care to the provinces and territories.

[1]Health Policy Division, Health Canada, Brooke Claxton Building, Room 1009A, Ottawa, Ontario, Canada K1A 0K9. The views and opinions are those of the author and should not be attributed to the Department of National Health and Welfare.

Health is primarily a provincial responsibility, with the federal government using its spending power to set national principles and conditions for payment of federal contributions in support of the provincial plans. The federal government also provides health services directly to Registered Indians, the military, and other special groups.

The beginning of Canada's public health insurance dates back to the late 1940s, when the province of Saskatchewan introduced the first publicly funded insurance program for hospital services. This was followed by the federal government offering to cooperate with the provinces in the mid-1950s to "cost-share," on roughly a 50-50 basis, hospital and diagnostic services. By 1961, all ten provinces and two territories had introduced public insurance plans that provided universal coverage for at least inpatient hospital care.

Public financed medical care insurance followed in the 1960s. Through the Medical Care Act of 1966, the federal and provincial/territorial governments covered the costs of provincial medical care services. This legislation contained the five national principles which characterize the present Canadian health system: universal coverage, comprehensive service coverage, reasonable access, portability of coverage, and public administration of insurance plans.

By the mid-1970s, the federal and provincial governments came to view conditional cost-sharing arrangements as no longer appropriate. Cost-sharing arrangements, which had been successful in establishing reasonably comparable health insurance programs and levels of services across the country, were no longer imperative for "established" health programs. For a number of reasons—including the desire for increased flexibility by the provinces to direct federal contributions to community-based health services such as home care services—alternative federal/provincial health financing arrangements were introduced in 1977.

Established Programs Financing (EPF) did not change the national conditions for insured health services, but it did combine federal contributions to the provinces in support of "established" hospital insurance and medical care services with contributions in support of post-secondary education (see description of EPF below). Federal contributions were de-linked from actual provincial expenditures in these areas and paid in the form of a "block" transfer (involving a tax transfer and cash payment), the value of which was based on the national per capita expenditures in the base year (1975–76). The equal per capita entitlement is escalated according to population changes and growth in the economy.[3]

An unconditional per capita cash transfer for Extended Health Care Services (EHCS) was also included in the EPF financial arrangements. This transfer for EHCS contributes to the health aspects of residential long-term care, including nursing home care and community-based extended health care, specifically home care and ambulatory care.

EPF remains the main program by which the federal government contributes to the health insurance programs of the provinces. However, the switch to "block" funding was not completely smooth. Because funds were no longer tied to specific programs, the provinces gained the flexibility to invest in alternate approaches to health such as community health centers or to expand supplementary health benefits such as prescription drug plans for seniors or dental care for children. The transition to block funding was not without difficulties.

In 1979, the Hall Commission was appointed to review health services in the country. The Commission reported that health care in Canada was very good but that extra billing by doctors and hospital user fees were threatening access to care. In response, the Parliament of Canada, with the support of all political parties, passed the Canada Health Act, which provides for an automatic dollar-for-dollar penalty if any province permits user charges or extra billing for insured health services. The Act states that the primary objective of Canadian health care policy is to protect, promote, and restore physical and mental well-being of the residents of Canada and to facilitate reasonable access to health services without financial or other barriers.

## Established Programs Financing (EPF)[4]

### Brief Overview

Under EPF, the federal government makes equal per capita contributions to provinces to assist in financing insured health services, extended health care services, and post-secondary education. The contributions are a combination of cash and tax transfers which were estimated at $20.8 billion for 1992–93. Provinces can use these funds to finance their responsibilities in the areas of health and post-secondary education according to their priorities. The health portion is subject to the provisions of the Canada Health Act. The Secretary of State is required to report annually to Parliament on federal and provincial support to post-secondary education.

### History

EPF was introduced in 1977 as a result of the replacement of cost-sharing of insured hospital and medical services with a formula-based method on uniform per capita block transfers to all provinces. The original transfer consisted of
- a "basic" cash contribution that was equal per capita in all provinces and represented 50% of the total entitlement;
- an equalized tax transfer whose per capita value varied among provinces;

- a residual cash "top-up" designed initially to bring all provinces to the same total entitlement per capita; and
- in the case of Quebec, an 8.5 personal income tax point abatement (which the province had been receiving since 1964), whose value was subtracted from that province's entitlement to the "basic" cash contribution.

Since 1982, seven revisions to the formula/indexation have been introduced. For the period 1990–91 to 1994–95, EPF transfers are frozen at their 1989–90 levels.

The main advantages to the provinces of switching to block funding was increased flexibility and less federal intrusion. The federal government, on the other hand, benefited from a clarified federal role and more predictability with respect to what its funding commitment would be.

### How EPF Works

Each province's total per capita entitlement is the same. Entitlement equals the national average per capita federal contributions to cost-shared programs in fiscal year 1975–76. Per capita entitlement is escalated to the current year by a formula that takes into account growth in the economy, as measured by changes in GNP per capita. Current per capita value to provinces of tax transfers (which consisted of the transfer of 13.5 personal income tax and 1 corporate tax point to the provinces) and associated equalization is calculated. These tax transfers are subtracted from total entitlement, and the remainder (times the population of the province) is paid to each province in cash:

$$\text{Total entitlement - Tax Transfer value} = \text{Cash Payment}$$

Under a 1964 agreement, Quebec chose to receive an additional tax transfer with respect to hospital insurance. The current value of this amount is deducted from Quebec's entitlement to determine its cash payment.

The per capita entitlement value remains fixed until 1994–95. Total contributions to the provinces continue to grow with provincial population (about 1% per annum).

### Funds Available through EPF

EPF transfers ($20.8 billion in fiscal year 1992-93) account for 52% of total federal transfers to the provinces and EPF transfers at $14.8 billion represent approximately 30% of provincial health expenditures. EPF is a general-purpose transfer (i.e., unconditional in the sense that the federal contribution is not conditional upon specified provincial expenditures). However, the funds provided under EPF for medically necessary hospital and medical services are conditional upon the national principles in the Canada Health Act (universality, comprehensiveness, portability, accessibility, and public administration).

### Financing of Health Care in Canada

**Financing**

The overriding principle which has characterized the evolution of Canada's health care system is that all Canadians, irrespective of age, income, or socioeconomic or health status, should have "reasonable" access to necessary hospital and medical services on a prepaid basis. Accordingly, the system has been largely financed through a graduated, progressive income system. Although most provinces have, at some point of time over the past 35 years, financed part of the cost of hospital and/or medical care programs through premiums, at no time did premium revenue account for more than one-third of provincial program costs. In addition to using general tax revenues to finance health care, provinces have used a variety of other tax-based mechanisms specifically targeted for health care, including payroll taxes and sales taxes. However, these were not directly linked to individual consumption of health care services.

The financing of the system primarily through general, progressive taxation eliminates the direct link between receipt of necessary health care services and payment for those services, and ensures that the system is financed on an equitable basis according to ability to pay. Even in those provinces where premiums are used as one source of funding (i.e., British Columbia and Alberta), premium assistance for those with low incomes is available to protect their income sufficiency.

With the exception of a surge of physician extra-billing and hospital user charges in the mid-1980s, private funding of health care has been restricted largely to health services and goods which are considered supplementary to medically necessary services. These goods include dental services, eyeglasses, and out-of-hospital prescription drugs. However, even as regards these latter categories, many provinces have extended coverage under provincial plans to some, or all, segments of the population, usually children and seniors.

**Organization**

*Hospitals*

Canadian hospitals are, for the most part, nonprofit entities whose operations are guided by community boards of trustees. Most are owned by voluntary organizations, municipal/provincial authorities, and—to a lesser degree—by religious orders. Less than 5% of all Canadian hospitals are privately owned, most of these operating in the long-term care field. Both the number of beds per 1,000 population and the number of hospitals have remained fairly constant throughout the past two decades, reflecting the early development of infrastructure in this area.

During the 1970s and 1980s, hospital financing underwent a conversion from a system where most public hospitals received payments from provincial governments based on a line-by-line budget review to a system of global budgeting (annual prospective payments for operating costs). The advantages of global budgets include increased flexibility for hospital administrators to respond to local population needs in operating their facilities, enhanced planning capability through predictability of funding, and cost containment.

An important feature of Canada's approach to hospital budgeting is the separation of operating expenses and capital spending. Although the funding of capital acquisitions varies considerably across provinces, common features include prior approval of the provincial Ministry of Health, based on a needs assessment, and the compulsory participation of municipal governments and/or privately raised funds (10% to 40%). Because the authority to approve an expansion rests with the agency that will have to cover ongoing operating costs, approval is not given lightly.

*Physicians*

General practitioners are regarded as the gate-keepers of the Canadian health care system. They are generally the initial point of contact for patients within the health care system, they control referrals to specialists and admissions to hospitals, and they determine the need for and prescribe any testing, treatment, or drug therapy which they deem to be medically necessary. Canadian physicians benefit from a high degree of professional autonomy.

Canada has experienced a tremendous growth in medical personnel. In 1975, there were 1.72 physicians per 1,000 population; by 1988, this ratio had increased to a level of 2.22 physicians per 1,000. The number of physicians became a major focus of provincial concern in the late 1980s and 1990s as provincial medical schools were turning out doctors at a rate for a population growth that Canada did not achieve. In short, Canada had planned for a population to physician ratio for a population of 30 million, when in fact, Canada's population was only about 26 million.

Within Canada's health system, most physicians work as independent practitioners on a fee-for-service basis and submit their claims to provincial health insurance plans for payment. Patients are generally free to choose their primary care physicians and a limited number of specialists, such as pediatricians, obstetricians, and ophthalmologists.

Fee schedules are negotiated periodically between provincial governments and medical associations. Although the focus of fee negotiations is on the overall percentage increase to be applied to the existing schedule, medical associations are generally free to reallocate spending among general practitioners and specialists.

## Health Access without Financial Barriers

Canada prides itself on the fact that its health care system offers free and reasonable access (on uniform terms and conditions) to quality health care services for all its residents. It is an accomplishment that is noteworthy, particularly in light of the nation's size and geographic diversity. That is not to say, however, that this significant achievement came easily. In fact, the building of the nation's health care system spans four decades, and although free and reasonable access on uniform terms and conditions has always been a primary objective throughout the system's evolution, the degree of accessibility has varied over the years.

Health care financing has played a crucial role in the building of a national health insurance system that offers universal accessibility to medically necessary services. Cost-sharing between the federal and provincial governments was instrumental in the initial development and expansion of hospital and medical services at the national level. After basic health care services were in place across the nation, the primary federal-provincial health financing mechanism was changed from cost-sharing to block-funding. This, however, would later give rise to new concerns with respect to financial barriers to access.

## Access to Hospital Services

In 1956, the federal government, seeking to encourage the development of hospital insurance programs in all provinces, offered to cost-share hospital and diagnostic services on roughly a 50/50 basis. The enabling legislation, the Hospital Insurance and Diagnostic Services Act (HIDS Act), was passed in 1957. By 1961, all ten provinces and the two territories had signed agreements establishing public insurance plans that provided universal coverage for at least inpatient hospital care, and that qualified for cost-sharing.

## Access to Medical Services

The 1966 Medical Care Act enabled the federal government to enter into conditional cost-sharing arrangements, again on roughly a 50/50 basis, covering provincial medical care services. This legislation embodied what were to become the five national principles or standards which characterize the present Canadian health care system: universal coverage, comprehensive service coverage, reasonable access, port-

*155; 529*

**LIBRARY**
College of St. Francis
JOLIET, ILLINOIS

ability of coverage, and public administration of insurance plans. Within two and half years of the Medical Care Act's passage, all provinces had established qualifying medical care insurance plans which provided coverage for all medically necessary physician services. Similar plans were in place in the two territories by 1972. Thus, by that year the goal of national health insurance in Canada had materialized.

**Financial Barriers to Access**

In 1977, the federal-provincial transfer mechanism was changed from cost-sharing to block-funding. This change in financing arrangements did not alter the national principles or standards that the provincial health insurance plans were expected to meet under the HIDS Act and Medical Care Act, but did make the enforceability of those conditions much more difficult, if not practicable as the transfer to the province was no longer directly linked to the terms and conditions of federal legislation. This led to future problems regarding accessibility to medically necessary health care services in the 1980s. Of particular concern were patient user fees in the form of hospital user charges and extra-billing by physicians. Clustering of extra-billing within certain specialties and in some geographical locations was impeding patient access.

To address this concern, the Canada Health Act was passed unanimously by the Federal Parliament in 1984, after encountering much opposition from organized medicine and the provinces. It replaced the HIDS Act and the Medical Care Act, consolidating their provisions within one piece of updated legislation. The Act embodies the same five national standards or principles that had appeared in the HIDS Act and the Medical Care Act (see Table 1):

These standards are set out as criteria which provincial health insurance plans must meet in order for a province to qualify for its full federal cash health transfers (the federal contribution is made up of a cash portion as well as a tax transfer).

The Act contains an enforcement mechanism intended to improve the federal government's ability to enforce the criteria. It includes strong provisions to discourage provinces from allowing user fees for medically necessary hospital and medical services through mandatory financial penalties. The Canada Health Act also extended the principle of universality to mean 100% of provincial residents (formerly the principle of universality was considered to have been met if 95% of the provincial residents were insured). The legislation remains in force and has never been amended.

## Table 1
### *Canada Health Act, 1984*

The five standards that all provincial health insurance plans must satisfy for full federal cash contributions for insured health services:

> *Universality*—Each plan must cover all residents of the province who are eligible for coverage after a minimum period of residency of not more than three months on uniform terms and conditions.
>
> *Comprehensiveness*—The health care insurance plan of a province must insure all insured health services provided by hospitals, medical practitioners, or dentists, and where the law of the province so permits, similar or additional services rendered by other health care practitioners.
>
> *Accessibility*—Provincial health insurance plans must provide reasonable access to necessary hospital and physician care without financial barriers. No one may be discriminated against on the basis of income, age, or health status.
>
> *Portability*—Residents are entitled to coverage when they are temporarily absent from their home province or when moving to another one. All provinces have some limits on coverage for services provided outside Canada and require prior approval for non-emergency out-of-province services.
>
> *Public Administration*—The insurance plan must be administered on a non-profit basis by a public authority responsible to the provincial government

*Canada Health Act*, 1984, Office Consolidation, Minister of Supply and Services Canada, January 1986.

## National Health Expenditures

### Spending Levels

In 1991, health spending in Canada totalled an estimated $66.8 billion (US $56.9 billion). Canada spent US $2,110 per capita for health care in 1991 (C $2,474), while the United States spent $2,817, about 34% more.[5]

In 1971, Canada and the United States were spending about the same percentage of their gross domestic product (GDP) on health care, 7.5% and 7.6%, respectively.

By 1991, the share of Canada's GDP spent on health care had risen to 9.9% while U.S. spending had reached 13.2% (U.S. Department of Health and Human Services, 1993).[6]

## Source of Funding

The major source of funds for health care in Canada is the public sector, accounting for 72% of funding in 1991. Within the public sector, the provinces and territories are the major funder (46% of total expenditures), with the federal share amounting to 24% of total expenditures and local government and workers' compensation accounting for only 1% of total expenditures, respectively.

Growth of private sector expenses has increased over the last few years from about 25% throughout the 1980s to 28% of total expenditures by 1991. Private expenditures include various uninsured and privately insured services provided by physicians, dentists, and other specialists, as well as non-funded institutional care costs, drugs, and appliances.

## Expenditure Category

Health institutions (i.e., hospitals and other facilities such as nursing homes and chronic care facilities) remain the main expense category, accounting for almost one half of total expenditures (39.1% for hospitals in 1991 and 10% for other institutions). Physician services (15.2%) and drugs (13.8%) are the next two largest expense categories.

Expenditures on drugs have exhibited the highest level of growth among categories of health care expenditures over the last few years, increasing by 10.5% from 1990 to 1991. Expenditures on "other institutions," "other health professionals," and "physicians' services" increased slightly faster than total outlays (at 8.7%, 8.0%, and 6.5%, respectively), whereas "hospital-related" and "other" health expenditures increased at a slightly slower rate (5.7% and 5.5%, respectively). Capital expenditures declined by 7.4% from 1990 to 1991.

## Long-Term Trends

Over the past decade, health expenditures by source of funds indicate that the federal share declined from approximately one-third of total expenditures (i.e., 2.6% federal direct plus 30.3% in transfers to provinces) in 1980 to about one-fourth (24.4%) in 1991. On the other hand, the combined share of provincial and local expenditures on health increased from 41% in 1980 to 46.8% in 1991. Private expenses increased from 25.3% of total expenditures in 1980 to 27.8% in 1991.

Health expenditures in constant dollars indicate that annual increases (in 1986 dollars) have been moderating over the last few years. The annual rate of real increase, after reaching 5.4% in 1987, declined to 2.5% for 1991. The trend in constant per capita health expenditures is similar—the annual rate of increase in real per capita health expenditures (in 1986 dollars) fell from 4.5% in 1987 to 1.1% in 1991.

## Current Financial Challenges

*Premiums*

From a public finance perspective, health care premiums in Canada are regarded as a regressive means of financing a health system. Although premium financing is not contrary to the Canada Health Act,[7] the linking of premium payment to entitlement to coverage is deemed by most to be inconsistent with the principle of universality. Most provinces have, at some time during the development of their health care systems, relied upon premiums as a source of financing. By the beginning of the 1980s, however, all jurisdictions except for three provinces and one territory had abandoned this method in favor of full financing through tax revenues. At the end of the 1980s, only two jurisdictions were using premiums to help finance health care programs.

*Special Groups*

Although universal health insurance has provided reasonable access to necessary health care for all Canadians, it has not resulted in equal health status levels. Lower socioeconomic groups, those living in remote regions of the country, and certain ethnic or cultural groups do not appear to have benefited to the same extent as the majority of Canadians. Although this is not technically a health care access issue, it does require a more targeted approach to the delivery of health services defined in a broad sense.

## Cost Control

Controlling health care costs has been a perennial issue in Canada. As is the case in many industrialized countries, cost control has taken on more importance over the course of the last decade. During the 1980s, slower economic growth combined with continued high growth in health expenditures increased the ratio of health expenditures over GDP from 7.4% in 1980 to 9.9% in 1991.

Canada has adopted an array of approaches to the problem of containing health costs. To a large extent, the existence of sole-source financing (i.e., each provincial government is the major funder of all publicly financed health services) has equipped Canada with a potentially potent cost-control mechanism. Because virtually all public health care expenditures are channeled through a single budget in each province, provinces have been able to use broad-based controls relating to operating budgets for hospitals, capital/technology acquisition, and fee/salary negotiations for health care workers as means of controlling health costs. Sole-source funding has also provided for the efficient, low-cost administration of health insurance programs.

**System-Wide Controls**

Apart from the sole-source financing feature which is an inherent part of Canada's health care system, two other significant system-wide measures have been used to contain overall health spending. The first relates to the high-inflation period following the OPEC crisis in the mid-1970s, at which time the federal government instituted a national wage and price control program. Because labor costs are such a major element in the overall health budget, this program was very effective in lowering the rate of increase in health costs between 1975 and 1978. This was to be only a short-term remedy, however, as labor costs rebounded in the early 1980s to catch up with lost purchasing power.

The second system-wide measure relates to federal-provincial health care financing. During the 1980s, the federal government amended fiscal arrangements four times to limit the growth of health transfers to the provinces. These measures were undertaken in an effort to stem the growth of federal spending in the face of a mounting public debt. Provinces opposed the unilateral actions of the federal government, claiming that the proportion of total provincial health expenditures that had to be covered by their own-source revenue had thus increased from 57% in 1980 to 65% in 1990.

**Institutional Sector**

Expenditures on acute, chronic, and rehabilitative care services in institutions account for approximately 50% of total health expenditures in Canada. Key cost-control measures in this area include
   • prospective global budgets for hospitals ;
   • bulk purchasing of drugs, disposable needles, and other items acquired in large quantities;
   • consolidating or contracting-out "hotel" services;
   • regionalization/rationalization of specialty services; and
   • private-sector management of hospitals;
More recently, efforts have focused on reducing the system's reliance on high-cost institutional services while promoting the use of less expensive and more appropriate forms of care at the community level. Examples of initiatives in this area in-

clude home care programs, extramural hospitals (inpatient services provided in the home), and independent health care facilities. Alternative funding methods for hospitals, focusing on intensity of resource use, are also being examined.

## Physician Services

Faced with yearly increases in medical care expenditures averaging more than 10% over the decade, most of the provinces began to introduce utilization controls and capping during fee negotiations with their physicians toward the end of the 1980s (the province of Quebec introduced capping of physicians salaries in 1976). Today, virtually all provinces have formal or informal utilization/capping formulas for medical care expenditures.

A coordinated national approach to managing physician human resources has recently been adopted. Key elements of this strategy include the reduction of medical school enrollments and postgraduate medical training positions by 10%, and the development and implementation of national clinical guidelines with an emphasis on health outcomes research. Although the vast majority of Canadian physicians are paid on a fee-for-service basis, efforts are now underway to determine the feasibility of alternative remuneration methods for physicians.

## Assessment

Although system-wide measures have proven effective over the short run, the Canadian experience indicates that sustained reductions in the rate of increase in health spending are difficult to achieve in the longer term. Sector specific measures have proven to be somewhat more effective, but it remains to be seen whether they will be adequate to contain costs while at the same time ensuring appropriateness of care. As more emphasis is placed on technology assessment and quality assurance, the role of health care financing may have to be reassessed to better support the system's shift toward health outcomes.

## The Reform Process

Health care systems are dynamic in that they must respond to the changing health needs of populations and adapt to advances in treatment methods and practices. As can be ascertained from the preceding section, Canada's approach to health care reform acknowledges the limited effectiveness of market forces in health care and rejects such policies as managed competition and the creation of internal markets. Rather, Canada is managing the cost-containment reform process by using the single-payer control afforded by provincial governments as principal payers of health care and by focusing on quality assurance. A vital component of this approach is enhanced coop- eration among governments, providers, and consumers.

Meeting the twin objectives of quality care and universal access within the con- text of slow economic growth and fiscal restraint which is characteristic of the late 1980s and early 1990s requires a delicate balance among the interests of governments (as payers), health care providers, and individual consumers (both as taxpayers and patients). Although the relationship between governments and health care providers has traditionally been adversarial, the participation of providers and representatives of consumers in a recently formed, broad-based coalition reflects a growing consen- sus on the need to preserve and improve the existing system while striving toward a broader vision of health. Given the inevitability of further cost containment and sub- stantive reform in the Canadian health care system, the constructive involvement of stakeholders can only be regarded as a considerable asset.

Nonetheless, the Canadian health care system carries with it a tremendous mo- mentum. The system has evolved over four decades and is firmly entrenched in the minds and souls of Canadians. "Health" and "health care" remain synonymous for the vast majority, a political reality which has often frustrated efforts to reorient the sys- tem. The emergence of a cost-control agenda in the context of a national health insur- ance system such as Canada's focuses attention on health service rationing, waiting lists, and availability of new technologies (the U.S. health reform debate has also contributed to this perception). The principal hurdle facing governments in Canada, however, is to educate the general public that the purpose of cost containment is to preserve the very essence of Canada's health care system by ensuring that health dollars are spent in areas where they are most likely to be of benefit to the health of Canadians.

The pressures facing Canada's health care system are well known: intensity of servicing for an aging population, human resource management, new technologies, and public expectations. There is a broad consensus as to the need to enhance activi- ties in the areas of technology assessment, quality assurance, and public education, and—where appropriate and possible—to coordinate these activities at the national level. Similarly, there is much agreement on the need to bolster efforts in dealing with other determinants of health, focus on health outcomes, and establish health goals.

The evolving partnership among the federal governments, provincial governments, and stakeholders will likely be an important factor in the success of these necessary reforms, although economic and fiscal conditions will continue to be determining factors with regard to the speed with which governments can respond to these chal- lenges.

## CONCLUSION

With the fundamental issue of access now largely resolved, quality assurance and cost control have now become the primary focus of attention within Canada's health care system. Preservation of the underlying principles of Canada's medicare system, as embodied in the Canada Health Act, is seen to be inextricably linked to the effective management of the health care system through cost effectiveness, appropriateness of care, and positive health outcomes.

As the more pragmatic concerns of containing costs are addressed, and as economic conditions improve, attention is likely to be redirected to longer-term considerations. Efficiency gains achieved in the financing and delivery of (curative) health care could be utilized to enhance activities in the areas of health promotion and disease prevention and ultimately, other determinants of health such as education, housing and the environment. Additional efforts in these areas could also result in a narrowing of the gap in health status between the richest and poorest segments of Canadian society. It remains to be seen, however, whether financing instruments currently in place are adequate to support such a shift.

### Notes

[2]Summary from the *OECD Health Care Reform Project: National Paper* (Health and Welfare, 1992). Other documents that provide an overview of Canada's health system and its financing include Canadian Embassy, 1993, *Health Care in Canada*, Washington, D.C., and Health and Welfare, July 1992. Background paper on Health Care Access and Financing in Canada, at the Four Nations Social Policy Conference at Penn State University, September 15–17, 1992.

[3]As part of the federal government deficit reduction plan, per capita EPF transfers to the provinces are frozen at the 1989–90 per capita level until 1994–95. The federal government has initiated a review of the system of federal-provincial transfers. The purpose of the review is to adapt the transfers to the economic and fiscal circumstances of the 1990s and to examine whether they can be made more effective in addressing the national needs and priorities of Canadians (Department of Finance, 1990). *The 1990 Federal Budget*, tabled in the House of Commons by the Honorable Michael H. Wilson, Minister of Finance, February 20, 1990. The last in-depth examination of federal transfers to the provinces was conducted in the early 1980s. See House of Commons, August 1981, *Fiscal Federalism in Canada*. Report of the Parliamentary Task Force on Federal-Provincial Fiscal Arrangements.

[4]For a complete description of Established Programs Financing, see Department of Finance, 1992, *Established Programs Financing 1992–93*; and Department of Finance, February, 1991, *Federal Transfers to the Provinces: Questions and Answers*.

[5]For further details on spending levels by category of expense and source of fund, see Health and Welfare, February 1993, *Health Expenditure in Canada: Fact Sheets*.

[6]U.S. Department of Health and Human Services, January 1993, *United States Health Spending, 1991*. HH News, p. 2.

[7]For an explanation of the definition of premiums in the context of Canadian health financing, see Minister of Supply and Services Canada, January 1986, *Canada Health Act, 1984*; and Minister of Supply and Services, February 1993, *Canada Health Act Annual Report, 1991–92*.

## References

Canadian Embassy. 1993. *Health care in Canada*. Washington, DC.

Department of Finance. 1990. *The 1990 federal budget*. Ottawa: House of Commons.

Department of Finance. 1991. *Federal transfers to the provinces: questions and answers*. Ottawa: House of Commons.

Department of Finance. 1992. *Established programs financing 1992–93*. Ottawa: House of Commons.

Health and Welfare. June, 1992. *OECD health care reform project: national paper, Canada*.

Health and Welfare. July, 1992. *Background paper on health care access and financing in Canada: the Four Nations Social Policy Conference at Penn State University, September 15–17, 1992*.

Health and Welfare. February, 1993. *Health expenditures in Canada: fact sheets*.

House of Commons. 1981. *Fiscal federalism in Canada*. Report of the Parliamentary Task Force on Federal-Provincial Fiscal Arrangements.

Minister of Supply and Services Canada. January, 1986. *Canada Health Act, 1984*. Office Consolidation Copy.

Minister of Supply and Services Canada. February, 1993. *Canada health act annual report*.

U.S. Department of Health and Human Services. 1993. *United States health spending—1991*. *HH news*, p. 2.

# Chapter 3

## The Long-Term Care of Frail Elderly People
### Canada's National Report
Prepared for the OECD

*Betty Havens*
*Centre on Aging, University of Manitoba*
*Formerly Assistant Deputy Minister of Continuing Care Programs*
*and Provincial Gerontologist, Manitoba Health*

## INTRODUCTION

The Social Policy Working Group of the Organization of Economic Co-operation and Development (OECD) identified **The Long-term Care of Frail Elderly People** as an agenda item for the December, 1992 meeting of Social Policy Ministers. To that end, the 24 member nations of the OECD have been invited to participate in a study on the long-term care of frail elderly persons. A framework has been developed by the OECD Secretariat, in consultation with subject matter experts from member countries, for the preparation of "national profiles," which are to provide a comprehensive, but comparable, overview on long-term care of frail older persons in each OECD country.

The purpose of this paper is to describe and assess the long-term care (ltc) of frail older Canadians during the past three decades and to discuss the direction of reform for the 1990s and beyond. In accordance with the common framework developed for the national papers, this paper has five main sections. Chapter One deals with the demographic changes in the population over the last three decades and provides a projection of the number of older Canadians into the future. The chapter also describes the major policy and program developments in the care of frail older persons in Canada since the 1960s. In order to provide a proper context for the development of ltc programming Chapter One begins with a brief review of the development and evolution of Canada's national health insurance system.

Chapter Two describes the main services and cash benefits that are available to frail older persons in Canada at both the national and provincial level. Without going into detail about the level of programming in each province, the chapter attempts to illustrate the range of services and programming that is available across the country.

Chapter Three deals with the various co-ordination mechanisms that have been developed to formulate and  manage ltc policies and programmes in Canada. Again, given the provincial responsibility of health programming in Canada the mechanisms reflect both provincial autonomy as well as the need for national standards and coordination where appropriate.

Chapter Four examines the financial aspects of long term care in Canada, both from a public policy perspective (i.e., federal and provincial roles and responsibilities) and private sector perspective (i.e., individual out-of-pocket expenses, co-payments or user fees and third-party insurance).

The final chapter deals with the future direction of long term car reform and programming in Canada. This chapter attempts to balance the desire of older Canadians to remain independent and in their own community for as long as possible and the costs to society in meeting the long-term care needs of frail persons in a cost-effective and efficient manner. The various reform pressures and processes of the provinces/territories are briefly discussed to illustrate how Canada is providing a full continuum of care for frail older persons.

## DEVELOPMENT OF LONG-TERM CARE IN CANADA

### Background on Canada's Health Care System

To provide a context for ltc programming in Canada it is necessary to understand the nature of Canada's health care system (OECD Health Care Reform Project, 1992). The Canadian health care system is best described as an interlocking set of 10 provincial and 2 territorial health insurance schemes. Each is universal and publicly-funded. The system is referred to as a system of national health care insurance in that national standards are set at the federal level. This confederate structure results from the constitutional assignment of jurisdictional responsibility over health care to the provinces and territories.

The beginning of Canada's public health insurance dates back to the late 1940s when the province of Saskatchewan introduced the first publicly-funded insurance program for hospital services. This was followed with the federal government offering to cooperate with the provinces in the mid-50s to "cost-share," on roughly a 50/50 basis, hospital and diagnostic services. By 1961, all ten provinces and two territories had introduced public insurance plans that provided universal coverage for at least in-patient hospital care.

Public financed medical care insurance followed in the 1960s. Through the *Medical Care Act, 1966* the federal and provincial/territorial governments covered the costs of provincial medical care services. This legislation contained the five national principles which characterize the present Canadian health system: universal coverage, comprehensive service coverage, reasonable access, portability of coverage and public administration of insurance plans.

By the mid-70s, the federal and provincial governments came to view conditional cost-sharing arrangements as no longer appropriate. Cost-sharing arrangements, which had been successful in establishing reasonably comparable health insurance programs and levels of services across the country, were no longer imperative for "established" health programs. For a number of reasons—including the desire for increased flexibility by the provinces to direct federal contributions to community-based health services—alternative federal/provincial health financing arrangements were introduced in 1977. Established Programs Financing (EPF) did not change the national conditions for insured health services, but did combine federal contributions to the provinces in support of "established" hospital insurance and medical care services with contributions in support of post-secondary education. Federal contributions were de-linked from actual provincial expenditures in these areas and paid in the form of a "block" transfer (which involved a tax transfer and cash payment), the value of which was based on the national per capita expenditures in the base year (1975–76). The equal per capita entitlement is escalated according to population changes and Gross National Product (GNP) growth. (As part of the federal government deficit reduction plan per capita EPF transfers to the provinces are frozen at the 1989–90 per capita level until 1994–95. The federal government has initiated a review of the system of federal-provincial transfers. The purpose of the review is to adapt the transfers to the economic and fiscal circumstances of the 1990s and to examine whether they can be made more effective in addressing the national needs and priorities of Canadians.)

An unconditional per capita cash transfer for Extended Health Care Services (EHCS) was also included in the EPF financial arrangements. The unconditional per capita cash transfer for EHCS contributes to the health aspects of residential long-term care, including nursing home care and community-based extended health care, specifically home care and ambulatory care.

Under these financing arrangements the federal share of total health expenditures has declined from 32.9% in 1980 to 26.7% in 1990, while the provincial share of total expenditures has increased from 39.4% to 43.9% respectively (Policy, Planning & Information Branch, 1992).

**Definition of Long-term Care/Continuing Care**

There is no universally accepted, or applied, definition of ltc in the Canadian health care system. Consequently, long-term care has come to have many different meanings depending on the circumstances in which it is being applied. From a health programming perspective the most common definition is the one proposed by the Federal, Provincial and Territorial Subcommittee on Long-Term Care (SCLTC):

> **long-term care** represents a range of services, delivered in the community and institutions, that addresses the health, social, and personal care needs of individuals who have never developed or have lost some ability to look after themselves. Services many be provided on a continuous or intermittent basis, for a long time or for an indefinite period. Services are provided in the least restrictive environment possible. The objective is to promote functional independence and to improve the quality of life. The primary target groups for long-term care services are those with functional limitations due to chronic illness, terminal illness, physical disability, or mental disability (Federal, Provincial, & Territorial Subcommittee on Long Term Care, 1988).

Recent initiatives in the ltc field include the introduction of the concept of **continuing care** (cc). Continuing care addresses issues from a global perspective relating to all aspects of health and social service systems. Consequently, the F/P/T Subcommittee on Continuing Care (SCCC), which replaced the F/P/T Subcommittee on Long-Term Care, has approached ltc planning in the context of a continuing care system, which is multifaceted and combines both health and social services. Continuing care is an amalgamation of diverse categories of services which are integrated by an overall system of service delivery. Continuing care is not a type of care service, but a system of service delivery. Major components of a continuing care system include supportive community services such as meals-on-wheels services, adult day care, group homes, homemaker services, home nursing care, community physiotherapy and occupational therapy, assessment and treatment centers, day hospitals, nursing homes and chronic care hospitals (Federal, Provincial & Territorial Subcommittee on Continuing Care, 1992).

In this context, the range and type of long-term care services and programs provided in Canada applies to more than frail older Canadians and includes a wide range of services. However, because of the high incidence of chronic illness and functional disability among older Canadians (approximately one-half of all Canadians aged 65 years old and over reported a disability in 1986. Approximately 46%

of the people aged 65 or older in Canada, a total of 1,221,995 individuals, have some form of disability. Approximately 84% of (1,026,915) seniors with disabilities live in households and the remaining 16% (195,080) reside in institutions.) one can readily understand how frail seniors are in fact major consumers of ltc/cc services (Statistics Canada, 1990).

Most researchers also agree that the package of ltc services important to remain independent, and for healthy aging, extends well beyond medical and health care to include social and economic supports such as living arrangements, transportation services and income security benefits (Marshall, 1989).

Another aspect of ltc/cc for frail older persons to be considered is the interaction between formal and informal ltc/cc. In Canada, a number of researchers and surveys indicate that the majority of ltc/cc is provided to frail older persons from the informal sector, not through the formal system and if one wishes to talk about the development of ltc in Canada it is necessary to acknowledge this important role (The results from the 1991 Health and Activity Limitation Survey indicate that disability among the population aged 65 and over was 46.3% in 1991) (Statistics Canada, 1985).

**Population Aging**

The speed of population aging continues to quicken in Canada, as in most other OECD countries. In 1961, approximately 1.4 million Canadians or 7.6% of the population were aged 65 or over. By 1991, some 3.2 million Canadians were aged 65 or over and represented 11.6 percent of the total population. Over the next 30 years the "seniors boom" will be such that some 6.3 million individuals are expected to be age 65 or over in 2021, as more than one-in-five Canadians will be a senior.

**Number, Percentage of Canadian Population Aged 65 or Over
1961 to 2021**

| Year | Number (000's) | Percentage of Total Population (%) |
|---|---|---|
| 1961 | 1,391 | 7.6 |
| 1981 | 2,361 | 10.7 |
| 199 | 13,170 | 11.6 |
| 2001p | 3,942 | 13.7 |
| 2021p | 6,342 | 20.4 |

p - projected.
Source: Selected Census and other Statistics Canada publications.

Not only is Canada's senior population increasing but the largest increase in the senior population is expected to be among individuals aged 85 or over. In 1991, approximately 283,000 individuals were aged 85 or over. By the year 2021, the number of Canadians aged 85 or over is expected to increase by about three-fold (825,000) and account for 13% of the total population aged 65 and over.

**Number and Percent Distribution of Senior Population, Canada 1991 and 2021**

| Age Group | 1991 (000's) | % Dist'n | 2021p (000's) | % Dist'n |
|-----------|--------------|----------|---------------|----------|
| 65 or over | 3,170 | 100 | 6,342 | 100 |
| 65-74 | 1,895 | 60 | 3,622 | 57 |
| 75-84 | 992 | 31 | 1,895 | 30 |
| 85 or over | 283 | 9 | 825 | 13 |

p - projected.
Source:Selected Census and other Statistics Canada publications.

**Definition of Frail Senior**

Not only is it difficult to arrive at a consensus on what services and programs constitute ltc/cc it is as equally difficult to agree on what constitutes frailty among older persons. Using the OECD definition of frail elderly, that is "people aged 65 and over who are suffering from a chronic illness or from some other condition, physical or mental, which causes some long term loss of function," suggests that ltc/cc services should include any use of the full range of health and social services available to this segment of the population.

Canada's 1986 Health and Activity Limitation Survey (HALS) identified a senior (individual aged 65 and over) as being disabled or "frail" according to functional limitation. A modified version of the "Activities of Daily Living" questions of the World Health Organization *International Classification of Impairments, Disabilities and Handicaps* was applied to identify disabled seniors. Older individuals were not considered disabled if they used a technical aid and that aid completely eliminated the limitation, e.g., an individual who uses a hearing aid and states that he has no limitation when using the aid would not be included in the HALS data base. The concept of time was also used as an additional parameter to Canada's Health and Activity Limitation Survey. The limitation had to be of a minimum six months duration, i.e., has lasted or is expected to last six months or more.

## Policy Development of Ltc Services for Seniors

The development of ltc services has been gradual and evolutionary like the rest of Canada's health care system over the last 30 years. The 1960s and 1970s were a time of rapid growth in ltc programming. Again the trend was to begin with the construction of ltc facilities, including chronic care hospitals, other residential facilities such as homes for the aged and nursing homes. The institutional sector of ltc was developed rapidly such that by the beginning of the 1980s the ratio of ltc beds per 1000 population aged 65 years old and over was about 7 beds per 1000 persons 65 or over.

The change in federal contributions in support of health programs (i.e, from "cost-sharing" to "block-funding") was also a recognition that pressures for community-based services, including home care were increasing in response to the desire of individuals to remain in their own homes. The movement of some frail aged persons from institutions to the community was facilitated by the provinces developing community-based initiatives. For example, in the early 1980s, New Brunswick introduced the "hospital without walls" or "extramural hospital" in order to deal with the early discharge of patients and to provide in-home health and social services in the most cost-effective manner.

Interest in and the development of community-based ltc in the past decade also grew because of concern about health care costs. Provincial funding agencies supported the development of community-based health services, such as home care for frail persons, because of the desire to allocate limited budgets as effectively as possible while maintaining, if not improving, health care and quality.

Like the concept of ltc, there is no universally accepted definition of home care. Home care comprises health services provided in the home; but the range of services offered varies across the country and as such home care can consist of a comprehensive package of home care/support services at one end of the spectrum to only a few home care services at the other end of the spectrum.

Home care has developed differently in different regions of Canada. In most cases home care began with smaller, urban programs through voluntary agencies such as the Victorian Order of Nurses. Some provinces developed comprehensive, government-organized home care in the 1970s, while others followed suit in the 1980s. Today, all provinces and territories support home care services, but there is no common approach to how services are delivered or financed. It is expected that pressure for home care services will continue to increase in order to respond to the care needs of recipients and caregivers. For example, an important element of today's home care programming involves respite care for informal caregivers as up to one-third of individuals aged 85 years old or over may be suffering from some form of cognitive impairment or dementia. Similarly, palliative care is also becoming a more common home care service.

The balance of the 1990s are expected to remain a period of health cost containment and improved efficiency as the economic realities are such that no government can sustain unlimited growth in health expenditures. In all jurisdictions it is generally believed sufficient resources are devoted to health care and what is required is ways to ensure the quality of care while achieving cost-savings and efficiencies in the system. To that end, many provinces are pursuing policies designed to reform ltc services. The objectives of many of the health reform measures are to support frail seniors to remain in their own communities for as long as possible and to provide a range of services necessary for the individual to remain independent and to age healthfully.

## PROGRAMS, BENEFITS, AND SERVICES FOR LTC OF THE FRAIL ELDERLY

### Introduction

The concept of ltc for frail seniors encompasses care in the home or the community and care in a public or private institution. The range of services included in the ltc package could span the full spectrum of social, health, economic, personal, and support services. While most of these services are delivered by provincial/territorial governments in Canada, some are provided by the federal government and others have been developed by volunteer and non-profit organizations.

There is no shortage of approaches to ltc programming, services and benefits available to the estimated 1.2 million frail older Canadians. Given the dynamic nature of the Canadian health care system programs have been developed over a number of years, with evolution being gradual and continuous over the last three decades.

### Provincial Programs and Services

Given that health is under provincial jurisdiction ltc/cc services, benefits and supports provided to Canadians are primarily administered by the provinces and delivered at the community level across the country. In general, at least some ltc/cc services are available and accessible to all residents through a variety of settings (in the recipient's home, in the community or through institutional facilities such as special care homes, nursing homes, extended care centres or chronic care hospitals).

Approximately 50% of ltc facilities are privately owned and administered in Canada, which is in sharp contrast to hospitals where only 5% are privately owned. The 50% of ltc facilities in the public sector are primarily administered and operated at the local community level by voluntary, non-profit boards of directors.

There are three basic types of institutional facilities for ltc. The first type of facility accommodates individuals who are fully mobile and require only light personal care support and/or full homemaking services. These ltc facilities are commonly referred to as retirement homes, lodges, manors, hostels, rest homes or homes for the aged. The second type, which includes nursing homes or special care homes, is for individuals who are mobile but require personal care, nursing supervision and may require some medical supervision. Establishments with the most intensive, 24-hour nursing care and medical supervision, are known as extended care or chronic care facilities. Many of the residents in nursing homes and extended care facilities are bed-ridden (National Advisory Council on Aging, 1991).

According to Statistics Canada estimates, Canada has approximately 193,000 ltc beds of which approximately 25,000 are in short-term general hospitals and 168,000 are in nursing homes for long-term chronic care. The per capita ltc beds per 1000 population was 6.3 for nursing homes beds in 1989, down from 6.5 beds per 1000 population in 1984 (Statistics Canada, 1988; 1989; 1990).

Ltc/cc services and systems are increasingly being viewed as a package of care designed to provide the full range of services to meet the changing health care needs of the recipient. Providing the range of ltc/cc services in a continuum allows ltc recipients to "age in place," and facilitate the transition of providing care in the home to care in a facility, where necessary. To "age in place" is a phrase that is commonly used in ltc to refer to providing the level and range of health and support services that enables the recipient to remain in his/her home for as long possible. For example, provincial home care services provide assistance with activities of daily living (such as personal care, meal preparation and cleaning), which often enables an aging or disabled individual to remain healthy and independent in his/her home. The majority of Canadians are able to age in place because of the extent of support services available from the community. Over the past five years there has been a noticeable increase in the average age of individuals who are admitted to ltc institutions. (Ontario and other provinces report that the average age of admission to ltc facilities is now over 80 years. Manitoba, for example, has reported that the average age at admission has been over age 80 since 1984 and the average age for admission for 1992 is expected to be over age 85). In fact, the average length of stay and the intensity of care in a ltc facility is increasing (Ministry of Community & Social Services, 1991).

Thus, a wide range of ltc programs and benefits are available to Canadians residing in the 10 provinces and two territories of Canada. Part of the mandate of the Federal, Provincial and Territorial Subcommittee on Continuing Care is to prepare a comprehensive review of existing institution-based, community-based and home-based adult long-term care services in Canada. The most recent *Description of Long-Term Care Services in Provinces and Territories of Canada* was released in September, 1991. This report provides a comprehensive description of the ltc programs and services provided by the provinces and territories in institutions, in the home and in the community, including adult day care.

Manitoba, for example, supports the maintenance of independent living for their young disabled and seniors through programs like:

> *Home Care* — provides a range of direct and indirect care in the home based on need (e.g. personal care, nursing care, therapy, Meals-on-wheels, etc.).
>
> *Manitoba Home Care Equipment/Supply Program* — provides medical equipment and supplies to physically disabled residents.
>
> *Support Services to Seniors* — supports projects sponsored by communities to meet everyday living needs of seniors in these communities.
>
> *Adult Day Care* — provides clients the opportunity to participate in individual or group activities in a support environment and receive a nutritious meal in a social setting.
>
> *Respite Care* — provides respite to caring family members through short-term admissions of clients to a Personal Care Home.

In addition, several provincial programs, such as Saskatchewan's Aids to Independent Living (SAIL) provide aids and services to handicapped and disabled residents living in their province. SAIL, for instance, offers the free loan and repair of mobility and environmental aids and financial assistance for home and vehicle modifications.

### Access to LTC Services

Canada's health and social security programs are a reflection of strong public support for improving the health and well-being of all Canadians. Many of

Canada's publicly-financed programs address the issue of ltc. While some of Canada's social programs are provided directly by the federal government, most are delivered by provincial governments.

Ltc, in some jurisdictions of Canada, is now organized as a system of service delivery based on a **coordinated continuum of care** model. The overall objective of the various stakeholders within this system (e.g., governments, local communities, service providers, family members and the care recipient) is to be able to provide the continuum of care necessary to allow the individual to maintain his/her independence for as long as possible. This is done through access to the full range of health care and social support services available from the community. Institutionalization is now, for most funding bodies and care recipients, the choice of last resort.

Given the universal nature of Canada's health care system access to ltc services is based on need rather than ability to pay. Priority for either home care, other community-based ltc services, or for ltc in a special care facility is not determined by ability to pay.

For individuals considered permanent residents in ltc facilities, all provinces have a per diem fee system to contribute to the cost of accommodation. The per diem rate schedule is usually set as a percentage of the maximum benefit an eligible individual could expect to receive from Canada's elderly benefit system. For example, in 1991 British Columbia's per diem charge for residents in residential care facilities was approximately 85% of the maximum Old Age Security (OAS) and Guaranteed Income Supplement (GIS) benefit. In 1991, the maximum monthly benefit from OAS and GIS for a single recipient was approximately $810. Thus, after deduction of the per diem fee a ltc resident in receipt of maximum monthly OAS/GIS benefits was left with a comfort allowance of about $120 per month.

The development of community-based alternatives to institutional ltc remains a priority for provincial ministries of health in the 1990s as governments implement health reform agendas that focus on cost-effectiveness and efficiency. Organizationally, cost-savings and improved provision of community-based health services have been achieved in most provinces through the implementation of a single point of entry/access system.

Where it has been implemented the establishment of a single point of entry for ltc services has enabled those provinces to optimize the utilization of community-based health and support services. The single point of entry approach is based on the operating principle that, whatever level of client care is necessary, to the extent possible, non-institutional services will be used as the first option in the ltc system. The major components of the single point of entry system are an integrated access system through referral, an assessment process, case coordination ensuring access to home health and support services, as well as entry into ltc facilities, and reassessment.

Another innovation, developed as part of an integrated system of community level health services for seniors in one province, is the "Quick Response Team." The Victoria Health Project uses Quick Response Teams to avert admissions of seniors to hospital, by providing recuperative support at home. The patient retains his/her sense of independence, and the need for permanent institutional care can be substantially delayed.

Policy-makers, major service providers and ltc consumers have all accepted this fundamental need to shift the emphasis away from high-priced institutional care to community-based care. Over the last decade (and in some western provinces for longer) the thrust of ltc policy/program development has been to reallocate existing resources, coupled with some new resources, to the development of community services that keep ltc recipients out of institutions for as long as possible. Not only are these and other community support services such as adult day care and caregiver respite services able to reduce the cost of ltc but also greatly enhance the quality of life of recipients and caregivers.

**Federal Programs and Services**

The federal government, while not directly responsible for ltc health care services, also supports the ltc needs of frail older persons through a number of federal programs, tax benefits and other activities of various departments. (The federal government does have jurisdictional responsibility for the provision of health services to Indians on reserves, the Inuit and the armed forces).

Tax assistance through the personal income tax program includes the provision of a **Disability Tax Credit**. The value of the tax credit has been increasing over the past few years and eligibility for the Disability Tax Credit has been broadened to include all Canadians with severe disabilities. The benefit is also transferable to a family member.

The federal government has also expanded the list of items eligible for the **Medical Expense Tax Credit** to include disability-specific items that promote independence. In particular, the 1991 federal budget broadened tax assistance to those disabled taxpayers or their families who incur part-time attendant care expenses (including the costs of respite care). Specifically, for disabled Canadians (which includes frail seniors), up to $5,000 of part-time attendant care expenses which are not otherwise deductible in computing income now qualify for the

Medical Expense Tax Credit. This provision took effect for the 1991 and subsequent tax years. This provision is available by, or on behalf of, a disabled person who qualifies for the Disability Tax Credit in respect of an attendant who is not related to the disabled person. This measure is to assist families to care for disabled individuals at home and to promote greater independence for disabled Canadians who wish to live on their own. The Department of Finance estimates that this measure will benefit 35,000 Canadian households at a cost of $20 million per year.

Among the expenses now eligible for the Medical Expense Tax Credit are specially trained service animals that assist individuals with a severe and prolonged impairment; and modifications to the home which enable a person with a severe and permanent mobility restriction (e.g., those with multiple sclerosis or cerebral palsy) to gain access to the home or rooms within (this extension became effective for 1991 and extended the previous provision which applied only to those confined to a wheelchair).

Increased **Canada Pension Plan** (CPP) disability benefits also assist disabled Canadians. The maximum CPP disability benefit was $8,925 in 1991, which by providing a minimum guaranteed income for recipients of CPP disability benefits improves the financial situation of disabled/frail, non-senior Canadians. (For both the Canada Pension Plan and Quebec Pension Plan a disability pension is paid to a person with a severe or prolonged mental or physical disability, who meets the minimum contributory requirements of the program. The pension consists of a flat-rate portion plus an earnings-related portion equal to 75% of the retirement pension which would be payable if the person were 65 years of age. Benefits continue until the death of the beneficiary or until the beneficiary ceases to be disabled, reaches age 65 (at which time CPP/QPP retirement pension is payable), or begins receiving a retirement pension between the ages of 60 and 65 years. Under QPP, benefits also cease to be payable if the beneficiary performs remunerative employment for more than three months). (Health & Welfare Canada, 1991).

Housing services and programs from Canada Mortgage and Housing Corporation (CMHC) such as the Residential Rehabilitation Program for the Disabled (RRAP-D) provides financial assistance to assist disabled persons, many of whom are seniors, modify their home/apartment in order to increase mobility and enable the person to remain autonomous. In addition, through its research and demonstration activities CMHC supports the development of new and innovative housing options for persons with disabilities and provides a wide array of information booklets such as *Maintaining Seniors Independence: A Guide to Home Adaptation*.

The Status of Disabled Persons Secretariat has also been established within the federal government. Given that many of the disabled population are frail seniors with a physical or mental disability the Department of the Secretary of State has assigned a high priority to research and information-sharing activities. The Secretary of State has also supported a national survey on volunteer activity which, among many other issues, documents the extent and nature of care being provided to frail older Canadians in private households (Statistics Canada, 1987).

Health and Welfare Canada's Seniors Independence Research Program (SIRP) and Seniors Independence Program (SIP) have also identified the ltc of frail seniors as a priority. For example, SIRP is supporting research on conditions affecting the health of frail seniors. A major national and regional study have been initiated on Alzheimer's and other dementias known as the Canadian Study on Health and Aging. Research has also been supported on osteoporosis and on support for informal caregivers.

Finally, the Seniors Independence Program aims to improve the quality of life and independence of seniors. SIP's three objectives are: to encourage seniors to get involved in planning and carrying out projects that affect their quality of life and independence; to encourage seniors and others to provide services in their communities; and to support high risk groups such as disadvantaged frail seniors.

## COORDINATION OF CARE

Various co-ordination mechanisms have been developed to formulate and manage ltc policies and programs in Canada. For example, through the Conference of Federal, Provincial and Territorial (F/P/T) Deputy Ministers of Health a number of F/P/T advisory committees and/or task forces have been established over the years to develop national standards, strategies and information to assist in the development and planning of ltc services.

The Subcommittee on Long-Term Care, which has been recently renamed the Subcommittee on Continuing Care, has been in existence for many years and has taken steps to establish a strategic direction for ltc/cc services in Canada through its various activities. Its recent publication *Future Directions in Continuing Care* identifies six major trends that are expected to have an impact on future policy directions for ltc programming (see Chapter five).

In addition, a number of F/P/T committees serve to establish common terminology for ltc services and produces a number of educational and/or clinical guidelines and national overviews on provincial services for frail seniors including an assessment of home care and *Description of Continuing Care Services in Provinces and Territories*.

In September, 1992 a restructuring of the F/P/T advisory committee structure was implemented through the consolidation of all committees into four new policy committees dealing with: 1) Population Health; 2) Health Human Resources; 3) Health Services; and 4) Health Information.

All advisory committees will now report to the Conference of Deputy Ministers of Health through a liaison Deputy Minister, thereby ensuring that matters of policy and program direction are dealt within the F/P/T deputy minster forum.

## FUNDING OF CARE

**Financing of LTC**

For the most part, ltc services, like other health and social support services in Canada, are financed from general tax revenues. The federal contributions for insured health services, including support for extended health care services, are provided through *Established Programs Financing* (EPF). In 1992–93, total federal health transfers to the provinces will be $14.8 billion, of which $1.4 billion is for Extended Health Care Services. Federal health contributions come from the Consolidated Revenue Fund which derives its revenues through the federal tax system.

The provinces also, by and large, fund ltc services from general tax revenues. The level of care in each type of ltc facility differs from province to province. However, rather than continuing to fund ltc facilities based on the type of facility or type of bed, some provinces have introduced new funding mechanisms based on the residents' care requirements. (Historically, governmental financing of ltc has been fragmented, coming from a variety of sources. For instance, Insured Health Services cover physician services, acute and chronic care and rehabilitation but not rehabilitation services for ltc; Extended Health Care Services financing funds levels I and II facility-based services, professional home nursing care and ambulatory care; and the Canada Assistance Plan makes contributions in support of special care facilities and home support services.) While some provinces, such as Manitoba, have funded ltc facilities based on residents' care requirements since the 1970s the shift from institutional based classification to patient level of need classification of funding has been gradual. British Columbia and Saskatchewan introduced patient care level funding for institutional ltc in the 1980s. Nevertheless, some provinces continue to fund institutional based ltc according to the classification of the facility.

Funding according to care needs responds to the fact that individuals who are seeking admission to ltc facilities are older and have more complex care and service requirements. Alberta, for example, introduced a new patient classification-based funding system for all nursing homes and auxiliary hospitals operating in the province in 1989. All ltc facility residents were classified in the fall of 1988 using the Alberta Patient Classification Form for Long-Term Care Facilities. Under this model facility residents are reassessed/reclassified annually and ltc facilities are funded on the basis of their residents' care requirements.

User fees for health care have been discouraged by financial penalties of the *Canada Health Act*. (The change in financing arrangements [i.e., the introduction of EPF in 1977] made the enforceability of the conditions of the *Hospital Insurance and Diagnostic Services Act* (HIDS) and *Medical Care Act* much more difficult. The early 1980s were a time of problems with respect to access to medically necessary services. Of particular concern were patient user fees in the form of hospital user charges and extra-billing by physicians. To address this concern, the *Canada Health Act* was passed by the federal Parliament in 1984.) Consequently, for medically necessary health-related services, including ltc insured health care services, no charges accrue to the recipient. However, as noted earlier a monthly accommodation fee is paid by permanent residents in ltc facilities. Residents may also be charged for additional services (such as laundry, telephone, cable television, etc.) and up-graded accommodation (semi-private, private room) in those provinces where single rooms are not the standard type of accommodation.

Many of Canada's nursing homes operate on a for-profit basis. Residents in these facilities, as those in not-for-profit ltc facilities, do not have to pay for nursing and personal care services (the facility receives subsidies from the province). This is consistent with the principle of universal access to health services which is one of the fundamental principles of Canada's publicly insured health care system.

The private sector, in addition to its investment in ltc facilities and their operation also provides other ltc services such as private health insurance to cover a number of supplementary services and the supply of ltc equipment and operating supplies.

Canada's ltc system is a major recipient of individual, service organization, and corporate donations. Many ltc facilities have been provided gifts of special equipment from individuals and organizations. In addition, a number of community groups raise funds in support of the construction or renovation of nursing homes or other types of ltc facilities.

Canada is also dependent on the voluntary contributions of informal caregivers, who provide care in the recipient's homes, in the community and in ltc facilities. Informal care is a very important and essential element of the quality of life for ltc recipients. Informal care covers the full range of care services—personal care, transportation to doctor's appointments, shopping and support in/around the home (meal preparation, cleaning and yard work). (The National Advisory Council on Aging reported that most of the support needed by seniors is given by their families. Long-term care programs are intended to complement self-care and family care [*Expressions*, 1991].)

In 1990, the most recent year for which data are available Canada spent approximately $62 billion on health care. Of this amount, an estimated $7.2 billion or 11.6% was in support of two main health care expenditures related to ltc (i.e., Long-term Care Institutions $6.6 billion and Home Care $575 million). Both of these categories of health expenditures have experienced considerable growth in the 1980s, with annual increases for community-based home care services in excess of 15% since the mid-1980's. The rate of increase in expenditures for institutional ltc, on the other hand, has been restrained and in more recent years even declined in some provinces.

The average per diem cost of chronic care is less than the average per diem cost for acute care. Given that approximately 20 percent of all acute care hospital beds are assigned to chronic care expenditures, about one-fifth of hospital expenditures could be allocated to ltc. In other words, Canada is likely spending in the order of $12 billion annually on ltc.

## POLICY ISSUES FOR TOMORROW

A series of national issues facing Canada in the area of ltc have been identified by ltc planners and decision-makers (Federal, Provincial & Territorial Subcommittee on Continuing Care, 1992). There are six major trends that are expected to have an impact on the future policy direction for ltc programming: **demographic aging; changes in health status, sociological trends, economic conditions, service trends,** and **the integration of/between continuing care systems**.

Among **demographic trends** is the fact that the over 65 population is the fastest growing segment of the population, with those aged 85 or over increasing at three times the rate of annual increases in the total population. Similarly, because of the longer life expectancy of women (19 years for women at age 65 compared to 15 years at age 65 for men) women outnumber men 2 to 1 in the over 85 age group. Ltc programming will also need to continue to respond to the multi-cultural and Aboriginal nature of Canadian society as well as the increasing numbers of severely disabled (physically and/or developmentally handicapped) children and adults.

**Health status** trends will also affect ltc programming in Canada. While health promotion, disability postponement, illness prevention and active living programming have flourished in the last 15 years major ltc challenges include the increasing prevalence of chronic illness, especially dementias and other mental health problems among the elderly (the prevalence of dementia may be as high as one-in-three for persons aged 85 or over); increased longevity coupled with the rising prevalence of activity limitation/disability in the population (in 1991 46% of the population aged 65 or over had a chronic health problem) and the special support needs linked to new diseases such as AIDS. Prolongation of life through the use of high technology and the specific ltc needs of paediatric disabled children are also emerging health trends.

One **sociological change** that could have an impact on ltc issues is the availability of informal caregivers now that women are entering the work force in greater numbers. Other sociological changes relevant to ltc/cc programming include recent trends related to family size, occupation mix, participatory expectations of recipients in decision-making, lifestyle choices (risk taking) and demand for optimal care.

**Economic circumstances and conditions** also effect ltc programming. All levels of government agree that Canada is allocating sufficient resources to health care (9.5% of GNP or $2321 per capita in 1990). Responses to the changing health needs of Canadians must be dealt with through reforms to the existing systems, in a cost-effective manner.

**Service trends** also need to be considered and are related to timeliness and appropriateness of sites of care, professional and para-professional levels of provider, acceptable or optimal quality and standards, and efficiency of treatment modalities.

**The interaction** between health and social policy is also a challenge. The connection between health and income security; affordable, functional housing; transportation; research and scientific development; and health promotion/disease prevention are all major strategic issues for ltc policy development into the 21st century.

The demand for ltc services and programming is expected to grow at a faster rate than most other segments of Canada's health care system, particularly in community-based care and services. A potential decline in the anticipated availability of informal caregivers will have to be addressed. A range of options and choices will have to be considered to support informal caregivers, including flexible work arrangements for employed caregivers, and expansion of formal support policies and services, and increasing the pool of volunteer caregivers through efforts known as "seniors helping seniors."

Future policy direction for ltc/cc is expected to continue the shift away from institutional ltc to the coordination of community-level care systems and the promotion of self-care. Home care, home support and community-based health/ social support services are still in their infancy with their budgets frequently deemed as discretionary expenditures. As such, not all ltc services and systems are uniformly available or accessible across Canada.

Another policy challenge is the fact the current funding mechanisms for the ltc system are not conducive to a well integrated system. Existing funding maintains a fragmentation of social and health services. As a result, most ltc services and systems tend to be biased in favour of higher cost institutional services and higher cost professional services in the community. Finally, the actual transfer of resources to lower-cost, non-medical services has been slow in many jurisdictions.

However, the projected increase in the senior population (from 11.6% of the population in 1991 to over 20% of the population in 30 years) is forcing governments to re-examine the funding mechanisms for the delivery of ltc support services. Most of the provincial health reviews completed over the last decade have identified inefficiencies in the health care sector and have focused on redirecting health care resources toward community-based care alternatives.

To assist the development of new policy directions for ltc the Federal/ Provincial/Territorial Subcommittee on Continuing Care has recommended that such services be guided by fifteen principles (Federal, Provincial & Territorial Subcommittee on Continuing Care, 1991). These guiding principles call for policies and programs that maximize the autonomy and independence of individuals, coupled with the design of individual services that respond to the changing health and social needs of the individual.

CONCLUSION

Canada faces a number of challenges and opportunities in responding to the changing ltc needs of its frail senior population. The federal and provincial/ territorial governments are committed to developing new partnerships with health providers and consumers to effectively deal with the ltc requirements of older Canadians.

Demographic aging of the population and other socio-economic conditions are having a substantial impact on ltc/cc in Canada. Not only does the public expect a wider spectrum of ltc/cc services, but provinces must contain health care cost while maintaining and improving the quality of care. Fortunately, ministries of health have an action plan and are working in partnership with all ltc/cc partners to direct resources in a fiscally and socially responsible manner.

## References

*Expressions.* 1991. Summer, 7 (3).

Federal/Provincial/Territorial Subcommittee on Continuing Care. 1992. Future directions in continuing care. *Health and welfare Canada,* September.

Federal, Provincial and Territorial Subcommittee on Long Term Care. Description of long term care services in provinces and territories of Canada. 1988. *Health and welfare Canada,* August.

*Health and Welfare Canada.* 1991. Basic facts on social security programs, January.

Marshall models for community-based long term care: an analytic review. 1989. *Health and welfare Canada.*

Ministry of Community and Social Services. 1991. *Redirection of long-term care and support services in Ontario: a public consultation paper.* Ministry of Health and Ministry of Citizenship, October, 31.

National Advisory Council of Aging. 1991. *At home: in the community or in an institution?* Summer, 7 (3).

OECD Health Care Reform Project. 1992. National paper Canada. *Health and Welfare Canada,* June.

Policy, Planning and Information Branch. 1992. Health expenditures in Canada: fact sheets. *Health and Welfare Canada,* March.

*Statistics Canada.* 1985. General social survey.

*Statistics Canada.* 1987. National survey of volunteer activity, Fall.

*Statistics Canada.* 1988–89 and 1989–90. Annual return of residential care facilities.

*Statistics Canada.* 1988–89 and 1989–90. Hospital statistics: preliminary report. Catalogue 82-003S, Quarterly.

*Statistics Canada.* 1990. Barriers confronting seniors with disabilities in Canada. 1986 health and activity limitations survey, August, Catalogue 82–615:1.

*Statistics Canada.* 1992. *The Daily,* October 13.

# Chapter 4

## Use of Health Care Services by Older Adults in the United States, Great Britain and Canada[1]

*Susan Brown Eve, Ph.D.*
Department of Sociology and Social Work
University of North Texas

*Vijayan Pillai, Ph.D.*
Department of Sociology and Social Work
University of North Texas

*Calvin Henry Easterling, Ph.D.*
Department of Behavioral Science
Oral Roberts University

*John D. Jones, Ph.D.*
Office of Institutional Research and Planning
Midwestern State University

### INTRODUCTION

The major objectives of this research are to compare the accessibility of, and the predictors of use of health care services for older adults in the United States; Great Britain, including England, Scotland and Wales; and Canada, using comparable available survey data from the three countries. This research has important policy implications. Like all industrialized countries, the United States, Great Britain and Canada are experiencing an aging of their populations, a trend which demographers predict will last into the next century when approximately 20 percent of the population of all three countries will be 65 years of age or older. This increase in the proportion of the population is already creating social and political pressures in all three countries to shift national resources to programs that provide for the elderly and away from programs that provide for the welfare of younger members of the population. Increases in the proportion of the populations over 65 years of age will increase the need for health and social services for the older adult population.

[1]This research was funded in part by grants from the AARP Andrus Foundation and from Faculty Research Funds of the University of North Texas.

In comparison with Great Britain and Canada, the United States has tended to rely relatively more on individual, rather than government, solutions to social problems, particularly in the area of health care services (Hollingsworth, 1986; Starr, 1982). Thus, the shift in national priorities from the young to the elderly has the potential in the U.S. to lead to intergenerational conflict. However, a recent survey by the American Association of Retired Persons found that the overwhelming majority of young and middle-aged adults in the U.S. support increased spending for social programs for older adults. There are many factors influencing this change of philosophy among the U.S. public. A major factor is that most women now find it necessary to work to help support their families, and therefore, have less time than they may have had in the past to care for elderly relatives. Other factors include the increased geographic mobility of the American family which makes it less feasible to care for older relatives than in the past. While there is increasing popular support for government solutions to the problems of older people and their families, research suggests that the government programs that were designed to help older people increase their access to  health care resources, particularly as those programs were modified in the 1980s, have not been without their problems. Thus, the purpose of this research is to examine the British experience with the National Health Service, and the Canadian experience with National Health Insurance, to determine what lessons there might be in those experiences for the U.S. as it attempts to revise its health care delivery system to meet the increased needs for health care services for older people in a way that is, at the same time, fiscally responsible.

Data for older adults in the U.S. will be taken from the National Center for Health Statistics' national Health Interview Surveys for 1984 (NCHS, 1986). Data for older adults in Great Britain will be taken from the Office of Population Censuses and Surveys' national General Household Survey for 1985 (OPCS, 1987). Data for Canada will be taken from Statistics Canada's General Health and Social Survey for 1985 (Statistics Canada, 1987). Each of these three datasets include a special supplement on the aging population of that country.

**Theoretical Framework**

The theoretical framework used for the research will be the health care services utilization framework developed by Andersen and Newman (1973). There are three major types of predictor variables in the health care services utilization framework. First, are the *need variables*, including objective and subjective evaluations of health status. Second, are the *enabling variables* consisting of family level variables, including income, public and private health insurance coverage, and access to transportation; as well as community level measures of availability of health care services, usually measured using proxy measures such as urban/rural residence and region of country of residence. Third, are the *predisposing variables* which include demographic characteristics, social structure characteristics and health belief variables. This research will focus particularly on the effects of the need and enabling variables since past research has shown them to be most predictive of use of health care services.

The major variables in this model for which comparable measures are available in the three countries are presented in Figure 1. The dependent variables that will be analyzed are the use of hospitals, physicians, home nurses and homemaker services,

**Fig. 1. List of Comparable Variables Available for
U.S. (HIS), British (GHS) and Canadian (GHSS) Datasets**

| VARIABLES | HIS 1984 | GHS 1985 | GSS 1985 |
|---|---|---|---|
| *Use of Health Care Services* | | | |
| Consulted with doctor in past yr. | X | X | X |
| Home vist with doctor in past yr. | | X | |
| Hospitalized in past yr. | X | X | X |
| Use of nurses | X | X | X |
| Use of homemakers | X | X | X |
| | | | |
| *Need Variables* | | | |
| Self-assessed health status | X | X | X |
| | | | |
| *Enabling Variables* | | | |
| Family/household income | X | | X |
| Medicare coverage | X | | |
| Medicaid coverage | X | | |
| Private insurance coverage | X | | |
| | | | |
| *Predisposing Variables* | | | |
| Age | X | X | X |
| Sex | X | X | X |

since comparable data are available from all three countries. The first major hypothesis of this research is that older adults in Great Britain and Canada will have greater access to physician, hospital, nursing and homemaker services than will older adults in the U.S. The second hypothesis is that the predisposing variables will be related to the use of health care services in similar ways in the three countries: specifically, use of all services will increase with age in all three countries; older women will tend to use the services of physicians, home nurses, and homemakers more than older men; and older men will tend to have the greatest use of hospitals. The third hypothesis is that the need variable, health status, will have a positive effect on the use of health care services in all three countries, with those in greatest need using the most care, although the patterns of access to care are expected to differ. This hypothesis is expected because all three health care systems are designed to assure that those older people who need health care will have access to that care. However, each system has somewhat different priorities and these priorities can be expected to result in differential access to services among the systems. The fourth hypothesis is that the enabling variables will have the most pronounced effect on use of all health care services in the United States. Unfortunately, this hypothesis can only be tested by comparing the U.S. with Canada because of lack of comparable data in Great Britain. Specifically, increases in income in the United States will tend to increase the use of physician services, home nurses and homemakers, while hospital services, which are more adequately protected by Medicare and Medicaid, will not be as affected by income. In addition, use of health care services by older adults in the United States will be greater when the older adults are covered by one of the two major public health insurance programs, Medicare or Medicaid, or by supplementary private insurance.

## REVIEW OF LITERATURE

The major objectives of this research are to compare (1) the accessibility, and (2) the predictors of health care services utilization among older adults in the United States, Great Britain, and Canada. While the majority of older adults in industrialized countries are reasonably healthy and, therefore, capable of leading independent lives, there are many older people with intensive health care needs, including especially those with multiple chronic conditions that account for the large proportions of the health care budgets of all three countries that are devoted to care of the elderly. The United States and Great Britain represent two extremes on a continuum of types of health care financing systems for the elderly. Great Britain provides health care services to the elderly through the National Health Service which is available to all citizens regardless of age or income. The underlying public policy assumption of the British system is that integrating the elderly into the national system is both more efficient and involves less risk of segregating the elderly from the general welfare of the younger citizens in the country. The British NHS has been modified to take into account the special circumstances of the elderly, especially their low income and the more demanding nature of their health care problems. For example, pensioners can obtain prescription medicines without an additional charge and general practitioners are paid a higher additional fee for treating patients over 65 (Nusberg, 1984; Roemer, 1985).

**United States**

In the United States, health care services for the elderly are financed through a combination of government programs and private insurance. Medicare is a type of national health insurance developed especially for older adults. It is funded primarily through contributions from employees and employers, as well as by retired people themselves through monthly premiums. More recently, the program has been supplemented through general tax revenues. Medicare is not a comprehensive program however. Medicare currently has a complicated system of deductibles and coinsurance payments and excludes many health services that are covered by the NHS in Great Britain. The result is that only 40–50 percent of the health care expenses of older adults are covered by Medicare in the U.S. The basic emphasis of the Medicare system is on individual responsibility, especially for routine care.

In addition to Medicare, the U.S. also has a program called Medicaid that is funded jointly by the federal government and the individual states. The program was developed especially to help certain categories of low income people gain access to health care services. Eligibility and coverage vary from state to state but for those older adults who qualify, Medicaid will pay Medicare deductibles and co-insurance payments and will pay for some of the health care services not covered by Medicare. However, Medicaid coverage does not assure equal access to health care services since private physicians and private hospitals (either nonprofit or proprietary) may choose whether or not to accept Medicaid payment. Private insurance, (so-called Medigap insurance) is also used to supplement Medicare coverage for those older people who can afford these policies. Such coverage is not widespread because of the costs involved. In 1984, only 7 percent of the health care costs of older adults in the U.S. were paid for by private insurance.

In the United States, the major policy issue in the delivery of health care services, and therefore, in the policy oriented health care services research in the 1960s and early 1970s, was accessibility of health care, especially for vulnerable groups like the poor and the elderly (Davis and Schoen, 1978; Kane, *et al.*, 1976). However, in the late 1970s and 1980s the dominant issue has been containment of costs of health care (Davis, *et al.*, 1990; Davis and Rowland, 1984; Ginsburg and Moon, 1984; Hadley, 1984; Hsiao and Kelly, 1984; Long and Smeeding, 1984; Luft, 1984; Sapolsky, *et al.*, 1981). Reforms designed to cut the cost of health care services may have also had the effect of decreasing the accessibility of health care for older adults, especially the poor. Thus, the efforts at cost containment in the 1980s have led to concerns that accessibility may once again be problematic, especially for poorer older adults (Bayer, *et al.*, 1983; Burt and Pittman, 1985; Davis and Millman, 1983; Estes, *et al.*, 1983; Eve, 1982, 1984, 1988a, 1988b; Eve and Friedsam 1979, 1980; Martin and Eve, 1984; Palmer and Sawhill, 1982; Yaggy, 1984). Since health and resources decline with age, the problems of health care accessibility also increase with age and cause the greatest problems for the "oldest-old," those 85 years of age and older (Manton and Soldo, 1985; Soldo and Manton, 1985; Minaker and Rowe, 1985). Furthermore, Estes, *et al.* (1984) have demonstrated that even with Medicare and Medicaid, when health status is controlled, income continues to be positively related to use of physicians among older adults whose health status is only fair or poor.

**Great Britain**

In the case of Great Britain, the existence of a virtually free National Health Service should make health care services more accessible for all groups of elderly when age, income and health are controlled. However, researchers in that country have raised questions about the adequacy of the health care services, about whether the consumers are as knowledgeable as they should be of benefits and how to obtain them, about whether the health care services are equitably distributed in the country, and about whether coverage of health care needs is sufficiently comprehensive. In fact, there was increasing controversy over these issues in Great Britain in the 1980s (Brown, 1979; Butler and Vaile, 1984; Goodman, 1980; Hollingsworth, 1986; Klein, 1983; Townsend and Davidson, 1982; Walters, 1980). However, research has shown that in spite of criticism of the welfare state in general, and the NHS in particular, the NHS continues to have strong popular support. One study, for example, found that 89 percent of the population supported continued or even increased spending for the Service (Taylor-Goobey, 1983). A number of studies have addressed the problems of older people in gaining access to health care services in the 1980s (Barker, 1987; Hedley, *et al.*, 1986; Jeffreys, 1983; Odam, 1987; Read, 1982; Vetter, *et al.*, 1984; Vetter, *et al.*, 1985; Vetter, *et al.*, 1987; Victor and Vetter, 1985, 1987). Using data from the 1980 General Household Survey, Victor and Vetter (1986) examined the links between poverty, disability and the use of health and social services among the elderly. They found no significant differences in use of health services, including physicians, between the poor and nonpoor elderly when level of disability was controlled.

## Canada

The underlying philosophy of the Canadian system is equal access for all people to medically necessary health care (Hatcher, *et al.*, 1984; Roemer, 1985). The national health care system in Canada is a federated structure. By 1960, all ten Canadian provinces had developed universal hospital insurance programs as a result of a program of federal grants-in-aid that covered about 50% of the costs, subject to federal requirements of universal access, comprehensiveness of benefits, public administration and portability between provinces. By 1971, all provinces had also adopted universal medical insurance programs in which physicians are generally paid on a fee-for-service basis according to negotiated fee schedules which vary by province. The Canadian system has been more successful in holding down health care costs than has the U.S. At the same time, the system provides a high level of health care, with days of hospital care per thousand in the population and number of physician visits per year substantially higher than in the U.S. In addition, longitudinal research has documented that differences between income classes changed to favor the poor in Canada when universal insurance was introduced. Nevertheless, some provinces continue to require that the patient pay a fee at the time service is rendered for ambulatory medical care, and, even though these expenses may be reimbursed later on, they may reduce access to health care services for some low income older adults (Nusberg, 1985).

### Comparisons of the Three Countries

Each form of health care coverage has its own advantages and disadvantages. While the major hypothesis of this research is that health care is more accessible to older adults in Great Britain and Canada, it is also important to carefully examine the effects of age, sex, income and health within each of the three countries (Nusberg, 1984; Abel-Smith, 1983).

While there are many studies that have examined the use of health care services in the United States, and others that have examined the use of health care services in Great Britain, there are very few studies that have focused on a comparison of the use of health care services by older adults in the two countries. One exception is the classic study by Ethel Shanas and her colleagues which compared samples of older people in the U.S., Great Britain and Denmark (Shanas, *et al.* 1968). That study, however, focused on many issues related to quality of life of older people, not just health care and, thus, did not treat health care in great depth. More recent studies have not been found that have made the comparisons that will be made in this research. Comparison of the use of health care services in the three countries would be interesting from a theoretical perspective because Great Britain, Canada and the U.S. have such different health care delivery systems and yet find themselves facing very similar health care policy issues related to the older adult population (Crichton, 1981).


## RESEARCH METHODOLOGY

This research used comparable datasets from the U.S. for 1984, from Great Britain for 1985, and from Canada for 1985. Data for the U.S. were taken from the national Health Interview Surveys for 1984, (NCHS, 1986). The HIS, conducted by the national Center for Health Statistics, a division of the U.S. Public Health Service, is an ongoing survey of a nationally representative sample of approximately 116,000 individuals, 11,497 of whom are over the age of 65. The HIS has been extensively field tested to establish the reliability and validity of the interview questionnaire.

Data for older adults in Great Britain are available from the General Household Survey, a continuous ongoing survey of a sample of the general non-institutionalized population. Approximately 32,000 people in 14,000 households in Great Britain, are surveyed each year by the Office of Population Censuses and Surveys (OPCS, 1986). Fourteen percent of the sample, or 4,156 respondents, are aged 65 years or over. The GHS has been extensively field tested to insure reliability and validity.

In 1985, the General Social Survey was initiated by Statistics Canada (Statistics Canada, 1987). That year, the data were collected with special emphasis on health and the elderly. A national sample of all noninstitutionalized persons 15 years of age and older living in all ten provinces were interviewed. People aged 65 and over were over-sampled. Data were collected from approximately 13,000 people, 3130 of whom were older adults. Studies of reliability and validity were conducted to insure that the data are as accurate as possible.

Two of the greatest methodological problems in doing secondary analysis of preexisting datasets is that not all variables are measured that the researchers would have liked, and not all variables are measured exactly as the researchers would preferred. This problem is compounded in this research by using data from three different sources, the American National Center for Health Statistics, the British Office of Population Censuses and Surveys, and Statistics Canada. These different agencies ask similar questions in different ways and include different response categories to questions. Furthermore, because of differences in culture and in the health care delivery systems in the three countries, it does not always make sense to ask exactly parallel questions, and, even where it does, the questions may not have the same meaning in one country as in another (Plfanz and Schach, 1976). The operational definitions of variables which are measured in comparable ways and which have comparable meanings in all three countries are summarized in Figure 1.

Inspection of Figure 1 reveals that there are comparable measures of the major dependent variables (use of physicians, hospitals, nurses, and homemakers) as well as of the major categories of predictors variables including age, sex, and health status. Comparable measures of income were only available for Canada and the United States. In addition, measures of coverage by Medicare, Medicaid and private health insurance were available in the U.S. These measures will be discussed in more detail with the presentation of results below.

Research findings are presented in Figures 1 through 24. Missing data was not a significant problem in these datasets, except for the measures of annual income for the United States and Canada. Results using these variables are presented in Figures 18 through 21. For the U.S. data, there was missing data for 1895 of the 11,497 respondents. For the Canadian data, there was missing data for 853 of the 3130 respondents. For all other variables in all three datasets missing cases are less than 50 and have a negligible effect on the results reported. Missing data are not reported to keep the figures as simple as possible.

## RESULTS

The difference of means of the health care service utilization variables were used to test the hypothesis that health care services are more accessible for older adults in Great Britain and Canada than for older adults in the United States. The results of the t-tests for the differences of means are discussed below.

The comparable measure of physician utilization available for the three countries is whether or not the older adult saw a physician in his office in the past year. As shown in Figure 2, more than 80 percent of older adults in the U.S. had seen a physician in the past year, as had older Canadians in 1985, compared to only 57 percent of older adults in Britain in 1985 ($p<.01$). However, nearly one-third of the older Britons reported seeing a physician in their home in the past year—an option which is virtually unavailable in the U.S. Two-thirds of older adults in Britain had seen a physician either in the office or at home in the past year in 1985.

There was only one comparable measure of hospital utilization in the past year available for all three countries—whether or not the respondents were hospitalized. Figure 3 shows that nearly 20 percent of the older Americans and older Canadians had been hospitalized in the past year compared to only 11 percent of older Britons ($p<.01$).

There were two measures of health related social services available in the datasets—use of visiting nurses/district nurses/personal care nurses, and use of homemaker/home help services. In the U.S., older adults were asked if they had used these services in the past year; in Canada, they were asked if they were currently using them; and in Britain, they were asked if they had used the service in the past month. As shown in Figure 4, only 2.9 percent of older adults in the U.S. reported using a visiting nurse in the past year in 1984, compared to 4.5 percent of older Britons in 1985 who reported seeing a district nurse in the past month (p<.01). Less than one percent of older Canadians reported currently using a nurse for personal care in 1985 (p.01). Reference to Figure 5 shows that only 1.5 percent of older Americans had used a homemaker service in the past year in 1984, compared to nearly six percent of older Canadians who reported current use, and nearly nine percent of older Britons who had used home help in the past month (p<.01).

Thus, the first research hypothesis was not confirmed for all comparable measures of health care services utilization. Older Americans and Canadians were much more likely to have seen a physician for an office visit—a percentage difference of 15 percent when the U.S. and Great Britain are compared and 17 percent when the comparison is between Great Britain and Canada. However, older Britons were the only group who had visits from physicians in their home. Older Americans and older Canadians were twice as likely to have been hospitalized. Older Britons were much more likely to have had a visit from a nurse in their home, and to have used a home help. Older Canadians were much more likely than older Americans to have used homemaker services. Thus, the patterns of use of health care services is more complex than originally hypothesized. The Americans and Canadians are very similar in terms of use of physicians and hospital, and the British, while providing fewer expensive physician and hospital visits overall, provide more home visits from physicians, nurses and home helps.

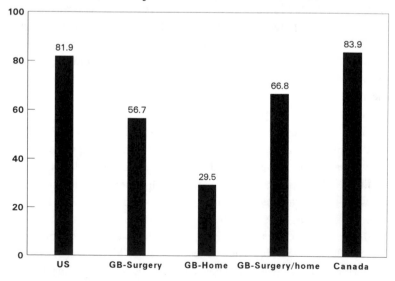

## Fig. 2. Percent of Older People with Physician Visit in Past Year

N = 11,497/U.S.; 4156/GB; 3130/Can.

## Fig. 3. Percent of Older People Hospitalized in Past Year

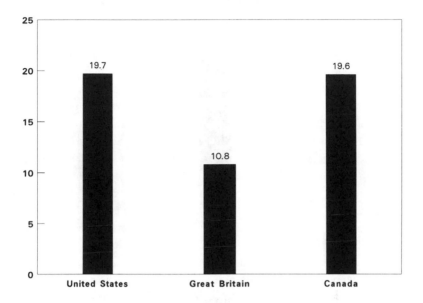

## Fig. 4. Percent of Older People with a Home Visit from a Nurse

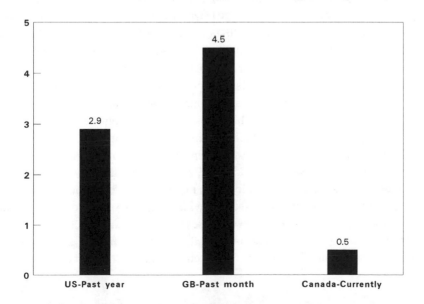

## Fig. 5. Percent of Older People
## with Homemaker Visit

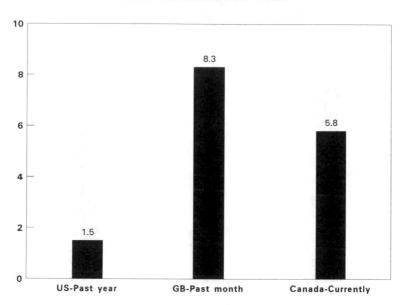

Having examined the data for the first hypothesis, the use of health care services was additionally examined inside each country to determine how use of the services was affected by age and sex (Hypothesis 2), health status (Hypothesis 3), and income and public and private insurance coverage (Hypothesis 4). The results of the analyses of variance within age groups (65–74 years, 75–84 years and 85 years or older in the United States and Britain; 65–69 years, 70–74 years, 75–79 years, and 80+years) are presented below in Figure 6 for comparisons of the use of physician services , in Figure 7 for comparisons of the use of hospitals , in Figure 8 for comparisons of the use of home nursing services , in Figure 9 for comparisons of the use of homemaker services. Among the older Americans, having been hospitalized, having seen a visiting nurse, and having used a homemaker service, all increased with age (p<.05 in all cases). Percent of older Americans who had seen a physician in the past year increased from the 65–74 year-old category, to the 75 to 84 category, but then decreased slightly. Among older Britons, having seen a physician in his surgery decreased with age while having seen a physician at home increased with age (p<.05). Use of hospitals also increased with age (p<.05). Use of district nurses and home helps all tended to increase with age (p<.05). For older Canadians in 1985, the percent seeing a physician increased up through the age groups 75 to 79 and then declined slightly. The percent having been hospitalized, the percent seeing a personal care nurse and the percent using a homemaker all increased with age.

The differences in the patterns of use of health care services are clear and very marked. In the U.S. and Canada, the percent having an office visit with a physician is very high—more than 80 percent—for all the older age groups, increasing only slightly into the oldest age groups, while office visits decline sharply and home visits increase sharply with age in Britain. In Britain, less than 40 percent of the oldest-old adults have had an office visit with a physician in the past year, but nearly 60 percent have had a home visit. The older adults in the U.S. are the most likely to be hospitalized at all ages, and the likelihood of being hospitalized increases with age. One-fourth of the 85 year old and older adults were hospitalized in the U.S. in the past year. Older Canadians are only slightly less likely to be hospitalized and that likelihood also increases with age. Older Britons, by contrast, are only about half as likely to be hospitalized and increases with age are less dramatic. The percent of the 85+ population with a hospitalization is only 15 percent. Use of visiting nurses, and homemakers increases with age in all three countries but the contrast between the very modest increases in the U.S. and Canada and the large increases in Britain is noteworthy. In the U.S. in 1984, seven percent of the oldest-old had seen a visiting nurse, and five percent had used a homemaker service *in the past year*. By contrast in Britain, 18 percent of the oldest-old had seen a district

## Fig. 6. Percent of Older People with Physician Visit in Past Year by Age

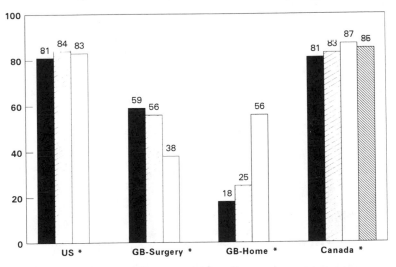

■ 65-74 US&GB;65-9 Ca　☐ 75-84 US&GB;70-4 Ca　☐ 85 + US&GB;75-79 Ca　▨ 80 + Canada

\* p < .05

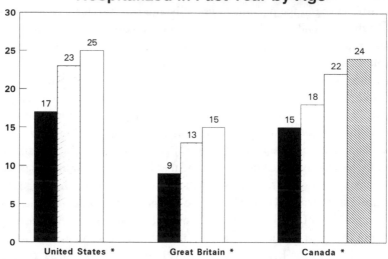

## Fig. 7. Percent of Older People Hospitalized in Past Year by Age

■ 65-74 US&GB;65-9 Ca   □ 75-84 US&GB;70-4 Ca   □ 85+ US&GB;75-9 Ca   ▨ 80+ Canada

* P < .05

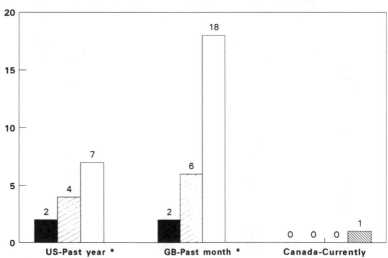

## Fig. 8. Percent of Older People with a Home Visit from a Nurse by Age

■ 65-74 US&GB;65-9 Ca   □ 75-84 US&GB;70-4 Ca   □ 85+ US&GB;75-79 Ca   ▨ 80+ Canada

* P < .05

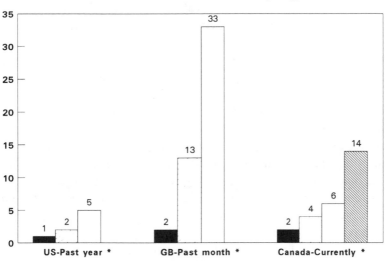

## Fig. 9. Percent of Older People with Homemaker Visit by Age

■ 65-74 US&GB;65-9 Ca　☐ 75-84 US&GB;70-4 Ca　☐ 85 + US&GB;75-9 Ca　▨ 80 + Canada

\* p < .05

nurse, and 33 percent had used a homemaker service *in the past month* in 1984. Also in contrast to the United States, 14 percent of the oldest-old in Canada were currently using homemaker services, although oldest-old Americans were more likely to have used a visiting nurse. Thus, the prediction in Hypothesis 2 that use of services would increase with age, is confirmed in all three countries for all health care services except use of physicians, although there are significant inter-country differences in the strength of the effect of age.

　　Analyses of variance of sex by use of the health care services, presented in Figures 10, 11, 12 and 13, reveal that, in the U.S., older women were significantly (p<.05) more likely to have seen a physician, to have used a visiting nurse service, and to have used a homemaker service. In 1984, older men were not significantly more likely to have been hospitalized, as is usually observed. Among the older Britons, older women were significantly more likely to have seen a physician at home, to have seen a district nurse, and to have used a home help service (p<.05 for the three variables). Older men were more likely to have seen a physician in his office and to have been hospitalized (p<.05). For older Canadians, older women were significantly more likely to have seen a physician in the past year, less likely to have been hospitalized, and more likely to have used a homemaker service. Thus, the prediction from Hypothesis 2, that older men would tend to use hospital services more than older women, and that older women would tend to use the other health care services the most, is generally found to be true.

The effect of health status on use of health care services is presented in Figures 14 through 17. In all three countries, the very clear and significant trend is for use of each of the four services to be greatest for those in the poorest health, as predicted in Hypothesis 3. Thus, in spite of the very significant differences in the three health care systems, all are effective in making care accessible to those who need it most. The patterns of use of health care services by health status once again show clearly that the U.S. and Canadian systems are both most effective in making hospital care and office based physician care accessible, while the British system is more effective in making home based care from physicians, nurses and homemakers accessible.

Results of the analyses of variance of the utilization measures by family income in the U.S., and by household income in Canada, are presented in Figures 18, 19, 20, and 21. No comparable measure of household income was available for Great Britain. In the U.S., income is not significantly related to having seen a physician in the past year, or to having been hospitalized, but is significantly inversely related to having seen a visiting nurse, and to having used a homemaker service ($p<.05$ in all cases). These findings are contrary to the prediction in Hypothesis 4, that use of health care services would increase with income among older adults in the United States. In Canada, household income was significantly inversely related to having been hospitalized in

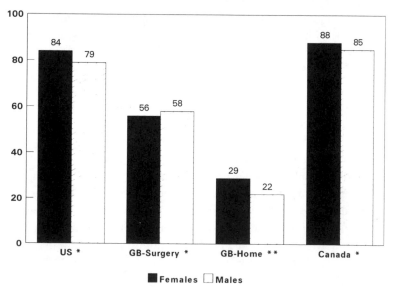

## Fig. 10. Percent of Older People with a Physician Visit in Past Year by Gender

* $p<.05$; ** $p<.10$

## Fig. 11. Percent of Older People Hospitalized in Past Year by Gender

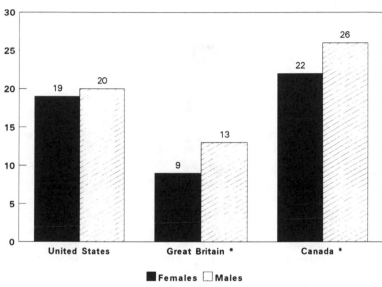

* p < .05

## Fig. 12. Percent of Older People with Nurse Home Visit by Gender

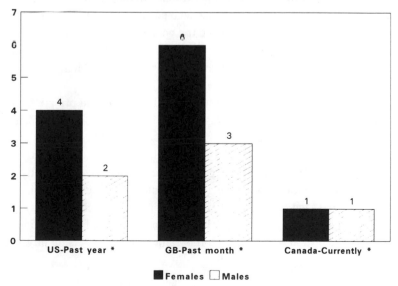

* p < .05

## Fig. 13. Percent of Older People with Homemaker Visit by Gender

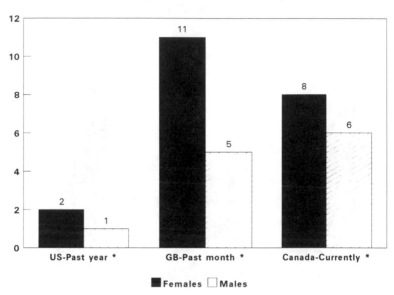

Females ☐ Males

* p < .05

the past year, but none of the other relationships were significant. Thus, in the U.S. and Canada, the existing health care financing mechanisms appear to have been successful in making hospital care accessible to those who need the care the most, those with low incomes who are also most likely to have the poorest health. It is interesting that use of visiting nurse services and homemaker services is inversely related to income in the United States. These services appear to be best insured (by Medicaid) for the low income elderly in the U.S.

The effects of Medicare coverage, Medicaid coverage and private health insurance coverage are presented in Figures 22, 23, and 24 respectively. These effects provide some insight into the effect of income on use of services among older adults in the United States found above. Use of physician services is significantly increased by all three types of coverage, while use of hospital services is significantly increased only by the two public forms of insurance. This pattern indicates that public insurance (both Medicare and Medicaid) is most effective in providing access to hospital care so that supplemental private insurance for hospital care provides little additional access. However, private insurance remains an important factor in accessing physician care.

## Fig. 14. Percent of Older People with Physician Visit in Past Year by Health

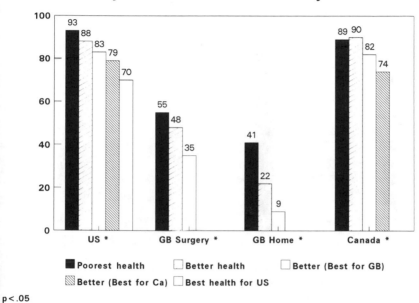

* p < .05

## Fig. 15. Percent of Older People with Hospital Visit in Past Year by Health

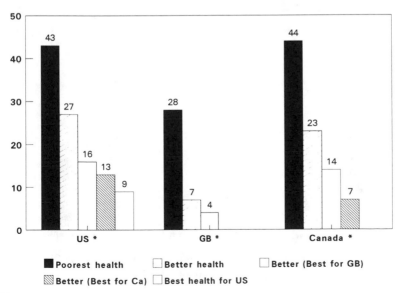

* p < .05

## Fig. 16. Percent of Older People with Home Nurse Visit by Health

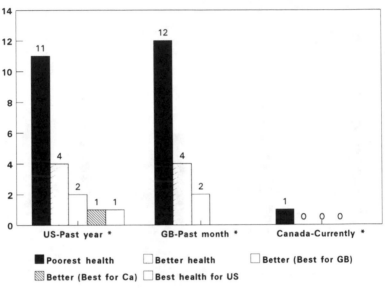

## Fig. 17. Percent of Older People with Homemaker Visit by Health

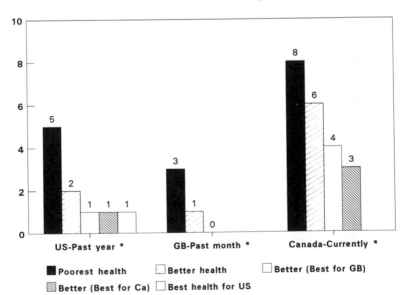

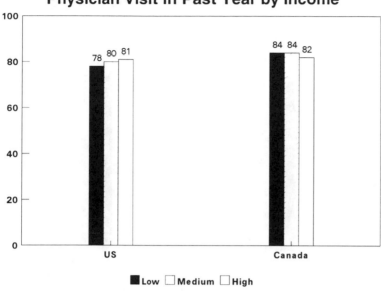

**Fig. 18. Percent of Older People with a Physician Visit in Past Year by Income**

■ Low ☐ Medium ☐ High

* p < .05

Only Medicaid significantly increases access to home based services including nursing and homemaker services. It is perhaps not surprising that private insurance coverage is inversely related to use of these in-home services. Private insurance coverage of these services would be prohibitively expensive. The Medicare program also provides little in the way of in home services. It is interesting that only the very poorest elderly in the U.S. are provided these services. Perhaps these services are seen as possibly effective in preventing even more expensive nursing home care that would have to be born by the Medicaid program, and, therefore, worth the expense.

## CONCLUSIONS

In conclusion, this research has shown that the patterns of use of health care services and the predictors of the use of health care services in the United States, Canada and Great Britain do differ. Contrary to the first hypothesis of this research, older adults in the United States and Canada are more likely to use physicians than are older adults in Great Britain; however, nearly one-third of older adults in Britain have had physician visits in their homes in the past year, a phenomenon that is virtually nonexistent in the U.S. and Canada. While office visits with physicians increase slightly with age in the U.S. and Canada, office visits tend to decline dramatically with age in Britain but home visits with physicians increase with age. Older Americans and

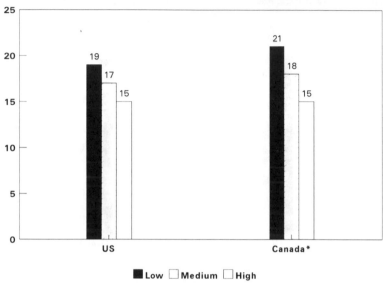

## Fig. 19. Percent of Older People Hospitalized in Past Year by Income

* p < .05

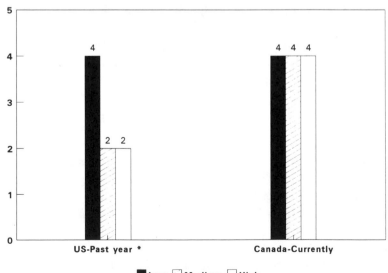

## Fig. 20. Percent of Older People with Nurse Home Visit by Income

* p. < .05

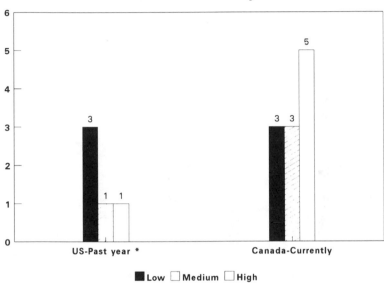

Fig. 21. Percent of Older People
with Homemaker Visit by Income

■ Low □ Medium □ High

\* p < .05

older Canadians are more likely to have been hospitalized in the preceding year, although this difference is decreasing in the U.S. as a result of declining hospitalizations due to the effect of prospective payment in the Medicare and Medicaid programs.

In the U.S., Great Britain, and Canada, use of hospitals increases with age, although older adults are much less likely to use hospital services in Britain than in the other two countries. The differences are due to policy differences in setting priorities for the health care delivery system in Britain, compared to Canada and the United States. In the U.S., people can generally get all the health care they want if they have public or private health insurance or discretionary income to pay for the care. The Canadian system is also biased toward hospital care. In Britain, the priorities are designed to provide the greatest good for the greatest number and access to services is limited for those people who have limited potential to benefit from the services.

Older adults in Britain are much more likely to use nurses and homemaking services than are older adults in the U.S. and Canada, and, in all three countries, use of these services increases with age and they are more likely to be used by older women than by older men. The sex difference may be due to the fact that older women are more likely than older men to be widowed with no spouse in the home to assist them when their health declines.

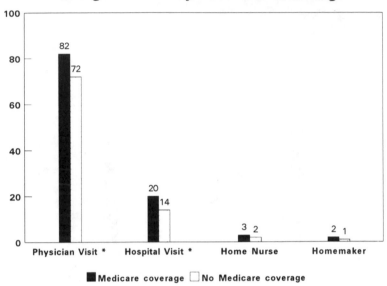

## Fig. 22. Percent of Older People in US Using Services by Medicare Coverage

* p < .05

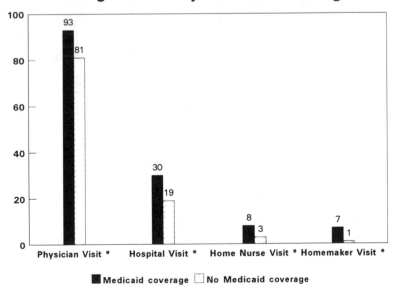

## Fig. 23. Percent of Older People in US Using Services by Medicaid Coverage

* p < .05

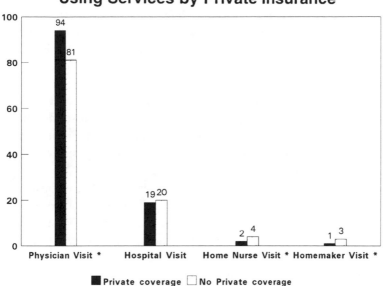

**Fig. 24. Percent of Older People in US Using Services by Private Insurance**

■ Private coverage ☐ No Private coverage

* p < .05

Although the health care delivery systems are very different, both the U.S. and Canadian systems are reasonably accessible by the older adults with low incomes. Those older adults with the lowest incomes also tend to have the poorest health. In fact, coverage by Medicaid of low income older adults renders home based nursing and homemaker services more accessible to this group of elderly than to any other group in the United States. In all three countries, older adults with the poorest health are also the most likely to use all four of the health care services. Thus, older Americans and older Canadians use more physician and hospital services than do older Britons; however, older Britons have greater access to health and social support services in the community and are even able to get physician care in the home if their health warrants it. These differences were greatest for those most in need, those in poor health and the oldest-old.

Examination of these data have indicated that the different systems have different strengths. Clearly, the British system is strongest in the provision of home based services for older adults, including home visits from physicians and the provision of district nurses, homemakers and health visitors. These services appear to be especially heavily used by the oldest-old adults who are in the poorest health. The Canadian and American systems are especially strong in providing access to physicians in their offices and providing access to hospital services.

Based on these findings, there are two specific policy recommendations which can be made. First, it would seem that the American and Canadian policy makers should examine the structure of home service for older people in Great Britain, especially as the 85-year-old and older populations of those two countries are projected to quadruple in the next forty years. This oldest-old population is the most likely to be in the greatest need for health and social support services but is the least likely to have discretionary income with which to buy these services or to pay for insurance for such services. Thus, home based services financed by the government may be the most feasible way of providing these services. Certainly, provision of visiting nurses and homemakers primarily through the private sector in Canada and the U.S. has not been as successful in reaching the older adult population as has the British provision of these services through the public sector.

Second, the British might benefit from examining the U.S. and Canadian methods of financing expensive hospital care for older people. Both countries use forms of national insurance to finance this care. In Canada, the National Insurance system is universally available, while in the U.S. the Medicare system is available only to older adults and must be supplemented by private insurance for the middle class and by Medicaid for the poor elderly. Despite their differences, both the Canadian system and the American system are more effective than the British National Health Service in making high cost hospital care available for the elderly. With the increasing effectiveness of high cost, high technology medicine in improving the quality of life of older adults, it would seem to be desirable to make such care as accessible to older adults as to younger populations.

## References

Abel-Smith, B. 1983. *Value for money in health services*. London: Heinemann Educational Books.

Andersen, R. and Newman, J. 1973. Societal and individual determinants of medical care utilization in the U.S. *Milbank Memorial Fund Quarterly* 51:95–124.

Barker, W. H. 1987. *Adding life to years*. Baltimore, MD: Johns Hopkins.

Bayer, R. Caplan, A. L. and Daniels, N. 1983. *In search of equity: Health needs and the health care systems*: New York: Plenum Press.

Brown, R. G. S. 1979. *Reorganizing the National Health Service: A case study in administrative change*. Oxford: Basil Blackwell and Mott.

Burt, M. and Pittman, K. J. 1985. *Testing the social safety net: Impact of changes in the support program during the Reagan administration*. Washington, DC: The Urban Institute.

Butler, John R. and Vaile, Michael S. B. 1984. *Health and health services: An introduction to health care in Britain*. London: Routledge & Kegan Paul.

Crichton, A. 1981. Health policy making: *Fundamental issues in the United States, Canada, Great Britain and Australia*. Ann Arbor, Michigan: Health Administration Press.

Davis, E. M. and Millman, M. 1983. *Health care for the urban poor: Directions for Policy*. Totowa, NJ: Roman and Allanheld.

Davis, K.; Anderson, G. F.; Rowland, D.; and Steinberg, E. P. 1983. *Health care cost containment*. Baltimore, MD: The Allanheld.

Davis, K. and Rowland, D. 1984. Medicare financing reform: A new Medicare premium. *Milbank Memorial Fund Quarterly* 62:300–316.

Davis, K. and Schoen, C. 1978. *Health and the war on poverty: A ten year appraisal*. Washington, DC: The Brookings Institute.

Estes, C. L.; Gerard, L. E.; Zones, J. S.; and Swan, J. H. 1984. *Political economy, health and aging*. Boston: Little, Brown.

Estes, C. L.; Newcomer, R. J.; and Associates. 1983. *Fiscal austerity and aging: Shifting government responsibility for the elderly*. Beverly Hills: Sage Publications.

Eve, S. B. 1982. Use of Health Maintenance Organizations by older adults. *Research on Aging* 4:179–203.

Eve, S. B. 1984. Age strata differences in health care services utilization among adults in the United States. *Sociological Focus* 17:105–120.

Eve, S. B. 1988. A longitudinal study of use of health care services among older women. *Journal of Gerontology* 43:M31–M39.

Eve, S. B. and Friedsam, H. J. 1979. Ethnic differences in health care among older Texans. *The Journal of Minority Aging* 4:62–75.

Eve, S. B. and Friedsam, H. J. 1980. Multivariate analysis of health care services utilization among older Texans. *Journal of Health and Human Resources Administration* 3:169–191.

Ginsburg, P. B. and Moon, M. 1984. An introduction to the Medicare financing problem. *Milbank Memorial Fund Quarterly* 62:167–182.

Goodman, J. C. 1980. *National Health Care in Great Britain: Lessons for the U.S.A.* USA.

Hadley, J. 1984. How should Medicare pay physicians? *Milbank Memorial Fund Quarterly* 62:279–299.

Hatcher, G. H.; Hatcher, P. R. and Hatcher, E. C. 1986. Canada. In *Comparative Health Care Systems* M.W. Raffell (ed.), pp. 86–132. University Park, PA: Pennsylvania State University Press, 1986.

Hedley, R.; Ebrahim, S. and Sheldon, M. 1986. Opportunities for anticipatory care with the elderly. *Journal of Family Practice* 22:141–145.

Hollingsworth, J. R. 1986. *A political economy of medicine: Great Britain and the United States*. Baltimore MD: Johns Hopkins.

Haiso, W. C. and Kelly, N. L. 1984. Medicare benefits: A reassessment. *Milbank Memorial Fund Quarterly* 62:207–229.

Jeffreys, M. 1983. The over-eighties in Britain: The social construction of panic. *Journal of Public Health Policy* 367–372.

Kane, R. L.; Kasteler, J. M. and Gray, R. M. eds. 1976. *The health gap: Medical services and the poor*. New York: Springer Publishing Co.

Klein, R. 1983. *The politics of the National Health Service*. New York: Longman.

Long, S. H. and Smeeding, T. M. 1984. Alternative Medicare financing sources. *Milbank Memorial Fund Quarterly* 62:325–348.

Luft, H. S. 1984. On the use of vouchers for Medicare. *Milbank Memorial Fund Quarterly* 62:237–250.

Manton, Kenneth G. and Soldo, Beth. 1985. Dynamics of health changes in the oldest old: New perspectives and evidence. *Milbank Memorial Fund Quarterly* 63:206-285.

Martin, C. A. and Eve, S. B. 1984. The changing use of health care services among unmarried older women: 1969 to 1979. *Convergence*, 2:37–55.

Minaker, K. L. and Rowe, J. W. 1985. Health and disease among the oldest old: A clinical perspective. *Milbank Memorial Fund   Quarterly* 63:324–349.

National Center for Health Statistics, P.W. Ries. 1986. Current estimates from the National Health Interview Survey, United States, 1984. *Vital and Health Statistics*. Series 10, No. 156. DHHS Pub. No (PHS) 86–1584. Public Health Service. Washington: U.S. Government Printing Office.

Nusberg, C. 1984. *Innovative aging programs abroad*. Westport, CT: Greenwood Press.

Odam, R. J. 1987. Crossing the great divide—from NHS to private care services to the elderly. *Geriatric Nursing Home Care* 7:23–5.

Office of Population Censuses and Surveys. 1987. *General Household Survey: 1985*. London: Her Majesty's Stationery Office.

Palmer, J. L. and Sawhill, I. 1982. *Reagan experiment: An examination of economic and social policies under the Reagan administration*. Washington, DC: The Urban Institute.

Read, S. 1982. Elderly people at home—Do health and social services reach those most in need? *Health Visitor* 55:600–602.

Roemer, M. I. 1985. *National strategies for health care organization*. Ann Arbor MI: Health Administration Press.

Sapolsky, H. M.; Altman, D.; Greene, R.; and Moore, J. D. 1981. Corporate attitudes toward health care costs. *Milbank Memorial Fund Quarterly*, 59:561–585.

Shanas, E.; Townsend, P., Wedderbum, D., Friis, H., Milhoj, P., and Stenhouwer, J. 1968. *Older People in Three Industrial Societies*. New York: Atherton Press.

Soldo, B. and Manton, K. G. 1985. Changes in the health status and service needs of the oldest old: Current patterns and future trends. *Milbank Memorial Fund Quarterly* 63:286–323.

Statistics Canada. 1987. *General Social Survey:Health and  Social Support*. Catalogue 11-612 E, No. 1, Ottowa, Canada.

Taylor-Gooby, P. 1983. Public belt and private braces. *New Society* 14:51–53.

Townsend, P. and Davidson, N., eds. 1982. *Inequalities in health? The Black report*. London: Penquin.

Vetter, N. J.; Jones, D. A.; and Victor, C. R. 1984. Projected use in two general practices of services by the elderly at home. *British Medical Journal* 289:1193–5.

Vetter, N. J.; Jones, D. A.; and Victor, C. R. 1985. Use of medications on the restricted list by the elderly. *British Medical Journal* 290:1712–4.

Vetter, N. J.; Jones, D. A., and Victor, C. R. 1987. The relationship between the receipt of supplementary pension, disability and use of services by the elderly. *Archives of Gerontology and Geriatrics* 6:33–41.

Victor, C. R. and Vetter, N. V. 1985. Use of community services by the elderly 3 and 12 months after discharge from hospital. *International Rehabilitation Medicine* 7:56–59.

Victor, C. R. and Vetter, N. J. 1986. Poverty, disability, and use of services by the elderly: Analysis of the 1980 General Household Survey. *Social Science and Medicine* 22:1087–1091.

Walter, Vivienne. 1980. *Class inequality and health care*. London: Croom Helm.

Yaggy, Duncan, ed. 1984. *Health care for the poor and elderly: Meeting the challenge*. Durham, NC: Duke University Press.

# Chapter 5

## Health Care and Social Service Utilization and Perceived Need among the Disabled Elderly in Canada

*Tracy L. Dietz*
University of North Texas

The world is experiencing an aging of its population. With this aging, it is expected that the world, and more specifically the Western world, will see a dramatic increase in the proportion of its population which is chronically disabled. This could prove to be quite costly for everyone concerned, the elderly and their families as well as the government and service providers in the many nations that are on the verge of an aging explosion. Thus, it becomes important to understand who the elderly service utilizers and nonutilizers are so that better services can be made available to the disabled elderly while at the same time being cost efficient.

### REVIEW OF LITERATURE

By the end of this century, more than 6 percent of the world's population will be 65 years of age or older (Chappell, Strain, and Blandford 1986). With this aging of the population, there has been an increase in the concern over the elderly population in Canada, as well as in the United States. It has been estimated that in the 2020s and 2030s, Canada will witness a peak in the number of retirements when the baby boom cohorts will reach retirement age. Also, the number of elderly residents in Canada will reach more than 7 million by the twenty-first century, approximately 13 percent of the population (McDaniel 1986; Rathbone-McCuan and Havens 1988). A similar trend exists in the United States where the elderly population grew almost 56 percent—by 9.3 million—from 1960 to 1980 and this growth is continuing (Famighetti 1985) with the elderly population growing to 36.3 million by 2000 and nearly 70 million by 2040 (Manton and Soldo 1985). Wolinsky, Mosely, and Coe (1986) point out that even though the elderly population within the United States composes only about 12 percent of the total population, they account for about one-third of all health care expenditures within the nation.

Perhaps of even greater importance is the fact that the number of those elderly over the age of 85 has skyrocketed. Thirty years ago, there were fewer than one million individuals who were 85 or older in the United States. However, by 1980, there were nearly three million and by the year 2000 it is expected that the population of those 85 or older will reach 5.4 million (Wolinsky, Mosely, and Coe 1986).

This increase in the proportion of the population which is elderly is growing primarily because of a decline in the fertility rate; however, advanced medical technology has played an important role as well (McDaniel 1986). In addition, medical technology may also be cited as responsible for increasing the expected longevity of disabled elders as well as prolonging the onset of disability (McDaniel 1986). Therefore, with this increase in the life expectancy and the decline in the fertility rate increasing the proportion of the population which is elderly, Canada and the United States can expect to witness a dramatic increase in the proportion of the population which is disabled as well. Manton (1989) states that in the United States, the number of chronically disabled elderly will increase by about 30 percent with the number of those most severely disabled increasing by about 37 percent by the year 2000. This, in part, is due to the aging of those born during the baby boom who will reach age 85 by the year 2060, thus further increasing the disabled population. About 35 percent of the disabled elderly living within the community report that they need help with activities of daily living (Manton 1989).

## The Canadian Health Care System

Equal access to medical services for all Canadians is the basis for the health care delivery system in Canada. The Canadian government has progressed toward a nationalized health service delivery program with both voluntary and commercial health insurance developing in the 1940s and 1950s. By 1960, all the provinces had introduced universal hospital insurance, subsidized by federal grants that paid about half of the cost for health care within hospitals and by 1971 they had introduced universal medical insurance similar to the hospital insurance. Thus, access to medical care is no longer dependent upon income or age within Canada (Hatcher, Hatcher, and Hatcher 1984).

Provincial governments within Canada determine the standards for the medical professionals and institutions within the nation and are also responsible for providing some of the services while the federal government is responsible for others (Fletcher, Stone, and Tholl 1987). Even though state subsidized medical care is available to all Canadian citizens, about 25 percent of all health care expenditures in Canada still originate from private sources. It would seem that the expense for such a program that provides health care and social services as a benefit of citizenship would be drastic; however, Canada managed to contain the cost of all health care services to a proportion of the Gross National Product—about 8.5 percent—for nearly ten years, until 1983 (Hatcher, Hatcher, and Hatcher 1984; Moon 1987).

The Canadian medical model is based primarily on the premise that illness results from a malfunction within the body that may be treated through medication or surgery; thus, the system has earned itself the name of "health cure system." (McDaniel 1986). By taking this approach, the system treats illnesses rather than preventing them or treating long-term conditions, an approach which McDaniel criticizes (McDaniel 1986). In recent discussions of health care policy within Canada, it is the cost of services that has received an abundance of attention with little focus given toward the changing health needs of the aging community. However, as McDaniel (1986) points out, the cost for caring for a child is typically much greater—one-third to one-fourth higher—than for caring for an elder. She further states that there needs to be "better coordination and integration of social and health services" (84).

Even though the Canadian government has adopted a nationalized health care delivery system, not all citizens use the services they need and are entitled to. In fact, the Canadian Health Care Survey of 1978–79 found that 46 percent of residents 65 years old or older never visited a doctor or made only one visit to a doctor in the year preceding the survey, while 66 percent of those younger did not visit a physician more than once during the year prior to the survey (McDaniel 1986). Although it is often mentioned that the elderly are the greatest users of health care services, it sometimes is not mentioned that a small proportion of the elderly population use a majority of the services, thereby accounting for the increase in the utilization by the group (Roos, et al. 1984). This fact becomes an even more important concern for policy makers when the well-being of the disabled elderly and their utilization of services is considered.

This failure to use services is not related only to the need for such services, although need is a major factor in deciding whether or not to use a service. For instance, the disability-free life expectancy for wealthy Canadians is approximately 7.7 years longer than for the poor. Granted, targeting services toward the poor will not eliminate this difference between social classes in that many illnesses are a result of the quality of life that a person lives, that is whether or not the standard of living is such that a person can live a healthy life, but the use of certain services by the poor might possibly make the difference smaller (McDaniel 1986). Moreover, there are several other factors that play important roles in the determination to use a particular service or not.

Less than 10 percent of those Canadians and Americans aged 65 or older are in long-term institutional care, but is estimated that one-tenth of the elderly living within the community are as ill as those within the institutions. Most of the care given those outside these facilities is performed by a network of family and friends. Only about 20 percent of the care for elderly Canadians comes from the formal care system.

Home health care is yet another important topic for Canada and the United States. Most elderly residents own their own homes even though the upkeep and heating cost are usually immense. But, as McDaniel (1986) states, evidence suggests that the longer an elderly person is kept in the community, the longer the onset of disabilities can be postponed. Assuming then that if a person already had a disability, providing services to help accommodate that person might prolong the onset of more chronic illnesses or the worsening of the present one. Thus, this is a common theme throughout service policy in Canada—to provide services so that the elderly population might be able to remain within the community for as long as possible (Chappell, Strain and Blandford 1986). Additionally, within the United States, there is an estimated 3.4 million noninstitutionalized elderly who need some type of ongoing support and home care (Chappell, Strain, and Blandford 1986). In Canada, the cost of many of these social services are paid for through the medical coverage (Chappell, Strain and Blandford 1986).

**The Disabled Elderly**

One should note that even though the proportion of the population in the United States which is elderly is still only around 11 percent, the elderly represent about one-third of the patients staying overnight in hospitals and about one-fourth of the total expenditures for health care in the United States (Wolinsky, Coe, Miller, Pendergrast, Creel, and Chavez 1983). As stated previously, the need for social and health care services does play a large role in the determination to utilize the services. Chappell and Blandford (1987) show that 80 percent of persons 65 or older report having at least one chronic illness, but this figure drops to about one-half when considering only functional limitations and decreases even further to approximately 20 percent for those with major limitations and as Hamilton (1989) discovered with the Health and Activities Limitation Survey, the proportion of the population having a disability increases with age.

According to Chappell, Strain, and Blandford, the Canadian Health Survey showed that almost half of those 65 or older report having no chronic conditions. However, the number of chronic conditions and the extent of the disability do tend to increase with age and not until age 85 do more than half report not being able to carry on a major activity by themselves (Chappell, Strain, and Blandford 1986). In the United States there are 29 million elderly living within the community. Of these, more than 5 million suffer from functional limitations and more than 1.5 million are severely disabled (Rowland 1989). Nearly three-quarters of these severely impaired elderly rely solely on the informal care given them by friends and family.

However, in terms of disability measurements, many of the measures look at actual assistance with an activity, not at whether or not the individual can perform the activity alone. Thus, many times it would appear that men are more disabled than are women (Chappell, Strain, and Blandford 1986). This is not the case in Canada where women are actually much more disabled than men. Of those 80 years old and older, 45 percent of the men need help while 70 percent of the women do (Stone 1988). Also of significance is that the poor tend to be more ill; thus, they require more medical assistance (Chappell, Strain, and Blandford 1986). Minority groups also fall into a higher category of need, especially within the United States (Wright, Creecy and Berg 1979).

## THREE BASIC APPROACHES TO HEALTH CARE UTILIZATION

There are at least three basic approaches to explaining utilization behavior. One of the oldest is the health belief model which is a psychosocial framework suggesting that utilization or non-utilization is related to personal attitudes and beliefs about health and health care facilities and professionals. According to the idea, good health is a goal of all people, but their perceptions differ (Chappell, Strain, and Blandford 1986).

The social network model contributes the difference in health utilization behavior as a result of various characteristics of the social group which an individual is a member of. This differs from the health belief model in that the characteristics are those of the entire group rather than just of the individual (Chappell, Strain, and Blandford 1986).

A third framework that has become increasingly more popular is that which was proposed by Andersen and Newman (1973). This model suggests that there are three types of independent variables associated with the utilization of health care services.

### The Andersen Model

The first type of independent variables are the illness or need variables which include items such as the number of disabilities and the extent of those disabilities. These, Andersen and Newman say, explain the most variance in the utilization of health care services. A second type of variable are those labelled as enabling, which are said to explain a moderate amount of variance. Family level variables such as income and insurance coverage and community level variables such as region of residence, urban or rural residence and public transportation are examples of enabling variables. Lastly, those variables explaining the least amount of variance are the predisposing variables. Predisposing variables are basic demographic variables such as gender, age, race or ethnicity, education and marital status (Andersen and Newman 1973). Mindel and Wright (1982) state that most of the predisposing variables have no direct effect on the utilization of health care and social services by the elderly, but are important when mediated through the enabling and need variables.

The Andersen model has been used extensively in studying health care utilization behavior. However, as Eve (1988) points out, there is a problem with most utilization models in that they typically do not explain a large amount of variance in the utilization of services. The Andersen model is no exception. Mechanic (1979) writes that these models often do not consider those dynamic processes that an individual experiences when choosing to use a health care service.

Most studies that have been conducted using the Andersen model have very similar results. However, nearly all of the studies done using the Andersen model are American and, as stated before, the Canadian system differs from that in the United States in two very important respects. First, there is universal insurance coverage and second, social services are included within the medical insurance in Manitoba (Chappell and Blandford 1987).

**Previous Research on Service Utilization**

*The Effect of Need*

Most researchers find that in the United States, as is probably the case in Canada too, those who are the most ill or the most needy of the services tend to patronize them more frequently (Freeborn, *et al.* 1990; Mindel and Wright 1982; Scitovsky 1988; Wolinsky, *et al.* 1983; Wright, Creecy and Berg 1979). Wolinsky and Coe (1984) estimated that in the United States almost two-thirds of the variance in the use of physician services and three-fourths of the variance in the use of hospital services may be explained by the need variables. Meanwhile, Wan and Soifer (1974) found that within New York and Pennsylvania the more health problems a person had accompanied with a high propensity to respond to illnesses, the more likely that person was to report to a physician. Wan and Soifer (1974) further state that they found this need of the individual to be the greatest predictor of physician visits.

*The Effect of Income and Insurance Coverage*

Wan and Soifer (1974) closely studied the effect that income and insurance benefits on health care service utilization to find that the cost of a physician visit and insurance coverage had nearly an equivalent, although opposite, effect on the utilization behavior. They did discover, however, that actual income has a almost no direct effect on the utilization of health care services. Additionally, "low income persons do not necessarily take advantage of public assistance by increasing their overall volume of physician visits and the poor do not change their behavior patterns even when financial barriers to health services are removed" (Wan and Soifer 1974, p. 105). Moreover, Wan and Soifer (1974) found that the accessibility of the service, such as travel time, distance, and waiting time, also played an important role in the decision to visit a physician. Patrick, *et al.* (1988) found that those who were poor and those with insurance were also more apt to use health care services. However, Wright, Creecy, and Berg found in 1979 that income and insurance coverage had a very limited effect in the utilization of health care services by the black elderly within the United States.

*The Effect of Age, Race, Gender, Marital Status*

High users of services are more likely to be older than low users (Freeborn, et al 1990; Mindel and Wright 1982; Patrick, *et al*. 1988). Wan and Soifer (1974) found that in New York and Pennsylvania, the older the individuals, the more likely they were to visit a doctor. Wolinsky, Mosely, and Coe (1986) also found that older individuals tend to have a greater number of physician contacts and hospital visits than younger cohorts. In addition, race seems to have an indirect effect on the propensity to utilize social services (Mindel and Wright 1982). Many researchers have also discovered that women tend to utilize health care and social services more frequently than do men (Freeborn, *et al*. 1990; Marcus and Siegel 1982; Mindel and Wright 1982; Patrick, *et al*. 1988). Women in Wan and Soifer's (1974) study were also more likely to visit a physician's office for a health problem. However, as Marshall, Gregorio, and Walsh point out, women more frequently experience illness, but the illnesses are, for the most part, milder than that illness experienced by men (1982).

As Coulton and Frost (1982) point out, marital status, too, has an effect on health care service utilization. "In fact, one study demonstrated that being married was the strongest predictor of under-utilization of medical care for serious health problems in persons over 60." (p. 331).

*Social Service Utilization*

Very few studies using the Andersen-Newman model have been conducted in the area of social service utilization. However, Coulton, and Frost (1982) indicated that in their study, almost half of the elderly respondents used at least one personal care service and almost 15 percent used three or more. They discovered that once need was considered, the effects of the enabling and predisposing variables were relatively small. The relationships between the enabling and predisposing variables and the dependent variables measuring social service utilization were found to be with the Canadian disabled elderly as well. This is not surprising when one considers that those with lower incomes often may be forced to turn to the formal system because they lack the resources that enable them to avoid the formal delivery system. As Arling and McAuley (1981) point out, this reliance upon family, friends and neighbors often results in the complete avoidance of institutionalization—a state that is quite costly.

*Policy Implications*

As Wolinsky, Mosely, and Coe (1986) state there is first an urgent need to obtain more extensive data relating to the elderly in both the United States and Canada. Second, they further state that these findings should have an impact on the planning of health care delivery to the elderly. For this reason, as well as for similar applications within the United States, it is important to understand the utilization behavior of the disabled elderly and know the variables associated with the utilization of health care and social services by the disabled elderly.


METHODOLOGY

The objective of this research was to determine the predictors associated with the utilization of health care and social services by the disabled elderly in Canada. The data for this study was obtained from Statistics Canada's Health and Activity Limitation Survey (H.A.L.S.) for 1986 and 1987. This is the latest available dataset of this kind (Statistics Canada 1990).

Ronald Andersen and his colleagues at the University of Chicago's Health Services Research Center developed the health care utilization framework that served as the theoretical model for this project (Andersen and Newman 1973). The primary dependent variables for this study were the utilization of hospitals, physicians and other health professionals as well as the utilization of both informal and formal social services and perceived need for services. This health care utilization framework incorporates the use of three types of predictor variables. The need variables include self-evaluated health as well as evaluations made by health care professionals. Meanwhile, enabling variables include family level variables such as income and accessibility to transportation and community level variables which measure the availability of health care services using variables such as urban/rural residence. Lastly, the predisposing variables include demographic characteristics and health belief variables.

**The Hypotheses to Be Tested by the Project**

Hypotheses: Using the health care services utilization framework to predict the use of hospitals, physicians and other health care professionals among the disabled elderly in Canada, it is hypothesized that the need variables will be the best predictors of health care utilization. Meanwhile the enabling variables will have secondary explanatory power, and the predisposing variables will have tertiary power.

## Description of the Data

The Health and Activity Limitation Survey which was conducted by Statistics Canada, an agency funded by the Canadian government and located in Ottawa, Ontario, will be used as the dataset for this study. The Health and Activity Limitation Survey (HALS) is a 1986-1987 post-censal survey of disabled adults aged 15 or older who reside in households and institutions in Canada. The HALS microfile data to be used contains 132,337 records. There is included with each file a record layout as well as a description of each of the 553 variables (Statistics Canada 1990).

## The Sample

All persons living in Canada at the time of the 1986 Census who were aged 15 or older and who reported having a physical or psychological disability were included in the sampling frame. Although persons residing in correctional facilities were not included in the survey, residents of the Northwest Territories, the Yukon, most collective dwellings, health care institutions, and persons living on Indian reserves were (Statistics Canada 1990).

HALS is composed of a household survey, which was completed just after the 1986 Census and an institution survey, which was conducted in the spring of 1987. Approximately 73,000 individuals were selected to take part in the interviews. An interview was conducted with each of the selected persons. If a respondent answered positively to one or more of the screening questions, the entire questionnaire was completed. After being asked these questions, 5 percent of those who had previously indicated that they were not disabled were included in the sample as disabled. The respondents were interviewed in their homes and although the intent of the research was that the interviews would be done with the individuals themselves, about 12 percent were conducted with another member of the household due to severe physical or psychological impairments of the respondent. There was a 90 percent response rate to the survey. The validity and consistency of the responses were checked using computer editing which defined missing or erroneous data as "unknown" or imputed a valid response using information found elsewhere in the survey.

The sample that was used for the HALS research included approximately 1 out of every 25 persons in the "Yes" sample and 1 out of every 300 persons in the sample which had been identified as non-disabled in the census. Because the statistics from the HALS dataset are estimates which are based upon this sample of a portion of the Canadian population, the results are subject to two types of error—sampling and non-sampling errors.

## Data Analysis

The statistical analysis of the data was completed through the use of SPSS-X (Norusis 1985). Basic frequencies of the variables utilized in the analyses will be given along with various descriptive statistics such as the mode, median, and mean.

For the purposes of this study, only those respondents considered to be members of the elderly population were kept for the analysis. These respondents were separated into groups according to their age. The groups consist of the following age classifications: 60–64, 65–69, 70–74, 75–79, 80–84, and 85 and older.

Crosstabulations as well as relevant statistics were computed using some of the variables that Andersen states are highly associated with the use of health care as well as social services to determine the relationship between the various dependent variables and the independent variables. In addition, the model was used to determine the predictors of perceived need among the respondents.

The analysis included measures of both health care service utilization and the utilization of social services as well as perceived needs. Hospital use was measured according to the number of times the respondent was hospitalized within the past year, while the number of times the respondent was seen by a physician or other types of health professionals in the previous three months was used to measure other health service utilization. Variables indicating that the respondent was typically helped by someone other than a relative or neighbor in performing daily functions such as the preparation of meals and personal care measure the utilization of social services.

The illness or need variables include indices of functional limitations and activities of daily living and instrumental activities of daily living limitations. The ADL index was composed of the number of limitations that the respondent has according to whether he/she does or does not have trouble dressing and undressing him/herself, getting in and out of bed and eating. Meanwhile, the IADL index was composed of variables indicating the respondent's limitations in the following areas and other areas: grasping and handling objects, cutting toenails and bending to pick up objects. Other indicators have been included as well. Meanwhile, the functional limitations index included the number of limitations that the respondent reports having from the following list: mobility, agility, seeing, hearing, speaking or other limitation.

In addition, the enabling variables at the family level included income and pension variables and at the community level urban or rural residence was used. Lastly, the predisposing variables included various demographic characteristics of the respondent. In conclusion, it should be noted that most of the variables contained within this dataset are dichotomous or are ordinal level variables. For the purposes of this research, 1 will indicate the presence of whatever the variable is measuring, while 0 indicates the absence of it. Thus, the means of the dummy variables will be meaningful in showing the presence of the variable in the sample.


## FINDINGS

The analysis for this research was performed utilizing SPSS-X (Norusis 1985). Frequency distributions as well as crosstabulations utilizing the Andersen Model (Andersen, *et al.* 1973) was computed. The proportion of the dataset that was used included all those disabled elderly aged 60 and older for a total of 50,672 cases.

### The Demographics of the Sample

A little more than 46 percent of the respondents included in the analysis were male. Twenty-four percent of the respondents were 60 to 64 years old, while 23 percent were between 65 and 69. Moreover, 21 percent of the respondents fell into the 70- to 74-year range and slightly more than 15 percent were in the 75- to 79-year-old category while almost 10 percent of the respondents were between the ages of 80 and 84. Meanwhile, 7 percent were 85 or older.

More than half of the respondents were of British origin while slightly fewer than one-fifth of the population was French and 30 percent of the respondents indicated that they affiliated with some other descent. Moreover, nearly 70 percent of the respondents were urban dwellers.

Most of the respondents—86 percent—were not employed at the time the survey was conducted, but 8 percent were employed full-time. In addition, most of the respondents—75 percent—had not received any schooling past high school. Furthermore, most of these had completed less than eleven years of school. Moreover, almost 60 percent reported a yearly income of less than $20,000 and 25 percent reportedly had an income for the previous year of less than $15,000. Meanwhile, less than 10 percent of the respondents indicated that they received supplemental benefits from one of the pension plans noted previously (Table 1).

### Their Disabilities and Limitations

Of those respondents who were 60 years of age or older at the time of the survey almost two-thirds—31,239 total—reported having a mobility problem while nearly one-fifth reported a problem with their vision and 4.5 percent reported having trouble speaking clearly. In addition, 30 percent reported that they have a hearing problem that has not been corrected, while more than half—52 percent—claimed that they are no longer agile. Approximately 20 percent reported that they had some other problem as well.

A scale to measure the number of functional limitations was derived using the data above. A score from 0 to 6 was utilized to indicate the number of functional limitations with 0 representing no limitations and 6 representing limitations in all of the areas. Almost one-third of the respondents had no limitations, while 15.2 had one limitation and 27.5 percent had two limitations. This is important to note in that if a person had one limitation, he/she probably had another. Slightly more than ten percent of the population had three limitations, while almost 10 percent had four limitations. Meanwhile, only 5.8 percent had five.

Two scales were constructed to indicate if and how many limitations the respondents had in their activities of daily living and instrumental activities of daily living. The scales were constructed using the aforementioned variables with the scores ranging from 0, representing no limitations, to 3 representing three limitations of activities of daily living on the ADL scale and 15 representing fifteen limitations of instrumental activities of daily living.

Slightly more than 25 percent of the respondents said that they had no limitations on their instrumental activities of daily living. Meanwhile, a few more than one-third of the respondents stated that they experienced between one and four limitations of instrumental activities. Yet another third reported to have between five and nine limitations of instrumental activities. About 10 percent had more than nine limitations of instrumental activities. More than 80 percent of the respondents indicated that they experienced no limitations of their activities of daily living while 10 percent reported having two or three limitations (Table 2).

## Health Care Service Utilization

In consideration of the frequency of utilization of health care services, the findings were not unlike the findings of previous researchers. An overwhelming majority of the elderly disabled visited hospitals and physicians as well as nurses minimally, while a minute proportion made several visits.

Of those with valid responses, about 47 percent of the population had not been hospitalized at all in the twelve months prior to the survey with more than 11 percent reporting to have been hospitalized 2 or more times during the previous year (Figure 1). In addition, more than 15 percent of the respondents had not visited a physician at any time during the three months prior to the survey. However, almost 15 percent had made four or more visits to the doctor in that three month period (Figure 2). Most of the respondents had not received medical care from a nurse during the three months

## Table 1: The Demographics of the Sample

| Characteristic | Frequency | Percent |
|---|---|---|
| Gender | | |
|     Male | 23,677 | 46.7 |
|     Female | 26,995 | 53.3 |
| Age Group | | |
|     60-64 | 12,184 | 24.0 |
|     65-69 | 11,626 | 22.9 |
|     70-74 | 10,636 | 21.0 |
|     75-79 | 7,782 | 15.4 |
|     80-84 | 4,944 | 9.8 |
|     85+ | 3,530 | 7.0 |
| Origin | | |
|     British | 26,092 | 51.5 |
|     French | 9,405 | 18.6 |
|     Other | 15,175 | 29.9 |
| Residence | | |
|     Urban | 33,628 | 66.4 |
|     Rural | 17,044 | 33.6 |
| Employment Status | | |
|     Not employed | 43,726 | 86.3 |
|     Part-time | 2,880 | 5.7 |
|     Full-time | 4,066 | 8.0 |
| Education | | |
|     No formal schooling | 3,058 | 6.0 |
|     Grades 1-4 | 5,598 | 11.0 |
|     Grades 5-8 | 18,212 | 35.9 |
|     Grades 9-10 | 7,367 | 14.5 |
|     Grades 11-13 | 3,863 | 7.6 |
|     Trade School | 11,359 | 22.4 |
|     Bachelor's degree | 930 | 1.8 |
|     Master's degree | 222 | 0.4 |
|     Doctoral degree | 63 | 0.1 |
| Family Income | | |
|     0 or less than 0 | 361 | 0.7 |
|     $1 - 4,999 | 1,332 | 2.6 |
|     $5,000 - 9,999 | 9,680 | 19.1 |
|     $10,000 - 14,999 | 9,987 | 19.7 |
|     $15,000 - 19,999 | 5,022 | 9.9 |
|     $20,000 - 24,999 | 3,665 | 7.2 |
|     $25,000 - 29,999 | 2,784 | 5.5 |
|     $30,000 - 39,999 | 2,134 | 4.2 |
|     $40,000 - 49,999 | 2,816 | 5.6 |
|     $50,000+ | 4,138 | 8.2 |
| Pension Benefits | | |
|     Yes | 3,736 | 7.4 |

N = 50,672

preceding the survey; however, 2,373 respondents had seen a nurse four or more times (Figure 3).

## Social Service Utilization and Need

Researchers have not given as much attention to the utilization of social services among the elderly until recently. However, the Andersen model has been used by some researchers to determine social service utilization as well (Coulton and Frost, 1982; Mindel and Wright, 1982). This research revealed that Canadian elderly who are disabled rely upon various individuals and organizations to help them with their needs. The significant and substantive predictors of this utilization are discussed in the sections which follow.

## Predictors of Utilization

According to this research, the relationships between the dependent variables and the independent variables as indicated by the Anderson Model varies drastically. The following text discusses the variables that were predictive of both health care and social service utilization by the sample.

## The Similarities and Differences between Previous Research in the United States and this Research

### *Health Care Service Utilization*
As formerly stated, most of the studies conducted in the past have been performed in the United States. Thus, this research is beneficial in comparing those findings from the United States to these from Canada. Previous research conducted in the United States using the Andersen-Newman model exhibits similar results as those found in this study. Generally speaking, most studies have failed to achieve substantively significant results when using the Andersen and Newman or any other utilization model for that matter (Eve 1988; Wolinsky *et al.*, 1983). Like these previous studies, there were relatively few substantively significant relationships between the dependent and independent variables. However, those relationships discovered to be significant in Canada were, for the most part, similar to those found in the United States and predicted by the Andersen-Newman Model (1973).

### *Variables Associated with Hospitalization*
Crosstabulations indicate that with reference to hospital utilization, the ADL, IADL and functional limitations indices were positively associated with increased

## Table 2: The Limitations of the Respondents

| Characteristic | Frequency | Percentage |
| --- | --- | --- |
| Limitations | | |
|     Mobility | 31,239 | 61.6 |
|     Vision | 9,436 | 18.6 |
|     Speaking | 2,302 | 4.5 |
|     Hearing | 15,095 | 29.8 |
|     Agility | 26,130 | 51.6 |
|     Other | 10,853 | 21.4 |
| Number of Functional limitations | | |
|     None | 14,849 | 29.3 |
|     One | 7,709 | 15.2 |
|     Two | 13,919 | 27.5 |
|     Three | 5,694 | 11.2 |
|     Four | 4,941 | 9.8 |
|     Five | 2,940 | 5.8 |
| Limitations of Activities of Daily Living | | |
|     None | 40,280 | 81.1 |
|     One | 5,313 | 10.7 |
|     Two | 2,577 | 5.2 |
|     Three | 1,498 | 3.0 |
| Limitations of Instrumental Activities of Daily Living | | |
|     None | 13,011 | 26.7 |
|     One | 3,416 | 7.0 |
|     Two | 4,754 | 9.7 |
|     Three | 4,474 | 9.2 |
|     Four | 4,538 | 9.3 |
|     Five | 4,125 | 8.5 |
|     Six | 3,786 | 7.8 |
|     Seven | 3,335 | 6.8 |
|     Eight | 2,602 | 5.3 |
|     Nine | 1,972 | 4.0 |
|     Ten | 1,308 | 2.7 |
|     Eleven | 746 | 1.5 |
|     Twelve | 388 | 0.8 |
|     Thirteen | 212 | 0.4 |
|     Fourteen | 82 | 0.2 |
|     Fifteen | 12 | <0.0 |

N = 50,672

**Figure 1: Hospitalization Service Utilization**

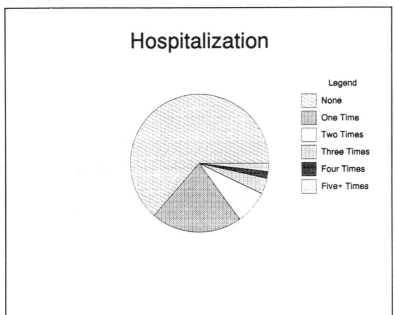

hospitalization over the 12 months prior to the survey. In analyzing the relationship between the enabling variables and hospitalization as well as the relationships between the predisposing variables and hospitalization, it was discovered that there were no substantively significant relationships (Table 3).

*Variables Associated with Physician Visitation*
The crosstabulations reveal that, again, increased limitations (ADL, IADL, Functional Limitations) are associated with an increased utilization of available services. Moreover, like the analysis of the relationships between the enabling and predisposing variables, there were no substantial relationships (Table 3).

*Variables Associated with Nurse Visits*
Again, the crosstabulation revealed that the number of limitations (ADL, IADL, Functional) a respondent had was positively associated with the frequency of nurse visits. Individuals who had not been employed and those who were not receiving a pension had more nurse visits. In addition, older respondents and those who were not married as well as those who lived in Alberta, Ontario and Quebec visiting nurses more frequently (Table 3).

**Figure 2: Physician Services Utilization**

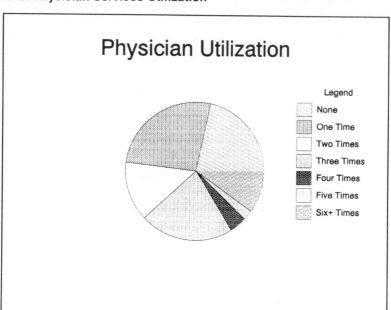

**Figure 3: Nursing Services Utilization**

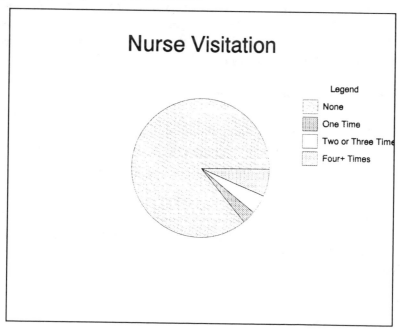

*Social Service Utilization*

Just as with the utilization of health care services, social service utilization varied among the respondents. In terms of formal social service utilization, the percentage of the respondents who relied upon formal agencies to provide services varied from between 20 percent for grocery shopping to almost 40 percent for everyday housework. However, nearly three-fourths of the sample called upon formal agencies for help with heavy household chores. In addition, most of those who received help from informal support systems, did so from family members, with less than 15 percent relying upon friends for these activities. Furthermore, the respondents indicated that the area in which they needed the most help was with heavy household chores with more than half indicating this as a need. This was followed by need for help with everyday household chores (32.0%) and grocery shopping (28.2%) (Figure 4).

*Variables Associated with Formal Social Service Utilization*

In observing the relationship between the need variables and the utilization of formal social services, it was determined that while there was an increase in utilization rates with an increased IADL score. It was observed, however, that a substantial number of respondents, including those who expressed a significant number of limitations did not receive any formal services at all. In addition, it appears that those individuals who had not worked during the past year received a greater number of formal social services. Respondents who were in the middle of the social class continuum utilized more formal social services than either the very poor of the very wealth, representing a curvilinear relationship. Moreover, those who were not married received more formal services as did those who lived in Quebec and Ontario. Those who spoke neither French nor English and younger respondents used fewer formal social services (Table 4).

*Variables Associated with Informal Social Service Utilization*

While there was no significant relationship between the number of reported ADLs and IADLs and informal social service utilization, it was indicated that there was a positive relationship between the number of reported functional limitations and the utilization of informal social services with most of the respondents relying on friend, relatives and family members for five or six services. The survey results indicated there to be a curvilinear relationship between income and informal social service utilization, with the middle class disabled, elderly relying more heavily upon informal supports. Those who had not worked during the previous year also indicated more informal social supports. In addition, married respondents looked to informal support systems for service delivery more often (Table 4).

### Table 3: Summary of Cramer's V Values of Predictor Variables on Health Care Service Utilization

| Variable | Cramer's V Values | | |
|---|---|---|---|
|  | Hospitalization | Physician | Nurse |
| ADL | .08 | .07 | .11 |
| IADL | .09 | .08 | .13 |
| Functional | .07 | .06 | .10 |
| Work Activity | .03 | .04 | .04 |
| Pension | .01 | .04 | .04 |
| Income | .02 | .02 | .04 |
| Province | .04 | .05 | .08 |
| Gender | .02 | .05 | .07 |
| Marital Status | .01 | .03 | .09 |
| Age group | .03 | .03 | .08 |
| Language | .01 | .03 | .07 |

*Variables Associated with the Perceived Need for Additional Services*

The crosstabulations revealed there to be a positive relationship between the perceived need for services and the number of ADLs a person reported. However, the survey revealed the relationship between the number of functional limitations and the number of IADLs and the perceived need for additional services to be curvilinear. Moreover, unmarried respondents and men reported a need for additional social services (Table 4).

### Discussion

The crosstabulations analyzing the relationships between the dependent variables and the independent variables do not, generally speaking, represent any surprises. It was discovered that limitation indices were significantly associated with the utilization of health care services and social services as well as the perceived need for additional social services.

In reviewing the relationships between the dependent variables and the enabling variables, it was discovered that income was a significant factor. While, the Canadian health care service delivery system, with its universal coverage attempts to ensure

**Figure 4: Social Service Utilization and Need**

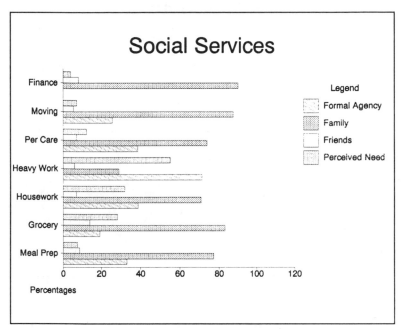

adequate health care delivery, it is evident that income remains an important factor. This may be explained by a variety of factors, including the financial capability to remain at home for care or that particular groups of people are more likely to be aware of particular services. Moreover, those who were able to work during this time, it may be assumed, may need fewer services.

In terms of the predisposing variables and their relationships with the dependent variables, it was discovered that with the exception of informal social service utilization and hospitalization women utilized more services than men. This is reflected in other literature as well. Again, this is not surprising when considering that those taking care of men are often their wives, while women live longer and must turn to formal support systems. Also, when considering that women visit their physician more often, one might assume that women often receive the help they need before hospitalization is needed, thereby, possibly, explaining the lower utilization of hospital services by women. It was discovered that it many cases, those respondents who did not speak English or French used services less often. This is probably the result of these individuals not feeling comfortable with the delivery sights that do not accommodate

**Table 4: Summary of Cramer's V Values of Predictor Variables
on Social Service Utilization**

| Variable | Cramer's V Values | | |
|---|---|---|---|
|  | Formal | Informal | Need |
| ADL | .10 | .11 | .25 |
| IADL | .13 | .14 | .18 |
| Functional | .08 | .16 | .13 |
| Work Activity | .13 | .16 | .07 |
| Pension | .11 | .12 | .03 |
| Income | .16 | .17 | .06 |
| Province | .13 | .15 | .05 |
| Gender | .11 | .11 | .12 |
| Marital Status | .24 | .26 | .10 |
| Age group | .12 | .13 | .09 |
| Language | .15 | .14 | .05 |

their language as well as due to a lack of knowledge of the available services. One surprise was the decline in utilization of those respondents were 85 years of age or older. However, perhaps those individuals merely represent a group of individuals who have been quite healthy and have lived much longer than other disabled individuals.

## CONCLUSION

In light of the current debates regarding the state of the United States and its health delivery system, this research should prove to be beneficial for U.S. policy-makers as well as academicians. This research indicates that Canada's elderly population is quite similar to that found in the United States in that a minority are frequent users of services while a majority use only a few of the services. In addition, it is evident that the predictors of such services appear to be the same for both nations. Thus, one could conclude that perhaps the system of universal coverage found in Canada does not provide adequate accessibility for the citizens.

However, based upon the results of this research, the United States should not disregard the Canadian system as a whole. In fact, as Mechanic (1979) notes, cross-sectional data cannot take into consideration the various dynamic processes that encourage or discourage a person from seeking services. However, both nations should note the variables that are associated with utilization or nonutilization in order that existing and developing services and service delivery may be modified to make such services more accessible to those who need them.

From this analysis, it may be concluded that the Andersen-Newman Model (1973) does define the importance of various levels of variables in predicting utilization behavior. However, it may be concluded that while the model has been utilized to explain health care service utilization behavior, it appears to be a much better predictor of social service utilization and perceived need for additional services.

## REFERENCES

American Association of Retired Persons. 1988. *National survey of caregivers: Summary of findings.* Hartford: Travelers Companies Foundation.

Andersen, R. and Newman, J. F. 1973. Societal and individual determinants of medical care utilization in the United States. *Milbank Memorial Fund Quarterly* 51:95–124.

Arling, G. and McAuley, W. J. 1981. The feasibility of public payments for family caregiving: Policy and impact. Paper read at the annual conference of the Gerontological Society of America at Toronto, Canada.

Chappell, N. L. and Blandford, A. A. 1987. Health service utilization by elderly persons. *Canadian Journal of Sociology* 12:195–215.

Chappell, N. L.; Strain, L. A. and Blandford, A. A. 1986. *Aging and health care: A social perspective.* Toronto, Ontario: Holt, Rinehart and Winston.

Coulton, C. and Frost, A. K. 1982. Use of social services by the elderly. *Journal of Health and Social Behavior* 23:330–339.

Eve, S. B. 1988. A longitudinal study of use of health care services among older women. *Journal of Gerontology*: 43.

Famighetti, R. 1985 Meeting an emergent need in curriculum development: Aging and developmental disabilities. *Gerontology and Geriatrics Education*:6.

Fletcher, S.; Stone, L. and Tholl, W. 1987. Cost and financing of long term care in Canada. In *Proceedings of the U.S./Canadian Expert Group Meeting on Policies for Midlife and Older Women*, ed. M. J. Gibson, pp. 31–48. Washington, D.C.: American Association of Retired Persons.

Freeborn, D. K.; Pope, C. R.; Mullooly, J. P. and McFarland, B. H. 1990. Consistently high users of medical care among the elderly. *Medical Care* 28:527-540.

Hamilton, M. K. 1989. The health and activities limitation survey. *Health Reports* 1:175–187.

Hatcher, G. H.; Hatcher, P. R. and Hatcher, E. C. 1984. Health services in Canada. In *Comparative Health Systems*, ed. M. W. Raffel, pp. 86–132. University Park: The Penn State University Press.

Manton, K. J. 1989. Epidemiological, demographic,and societal correlates of disability among the elderly. *Milbank Memorial Fund Quarterly* 67:11–57.

Manton, K. J. and Soldo, B. J. 1985. Dynamics of health changes in the oldest old: New perspectives and evidence. *Milbank Memorial Fund Quarterly* 63:206–285.

Marcus, A. C. and Siegel, J. M. 1982. Sex differences in the use of physician services: A preliminary test of the fixed role hypothesis. *Journal of Health and Social Behavior* 23:186–197.

Marshall, J. R.; Gregorio, D. I. and Walsh, D. 1982. Sex differences in illness behavior: Care seeking among cancer patients. *Journal of Health and Social Behavior* 23:197–204.

McDaniel, S. A. 1986. *Canada's Aging Population*. Toronto: Butterworths.

Mechanic, D. 1979. Correlates of physician utilization. *Journal of Health and Social Behavior* 20:387–396.

Mindel, C. H. and Wright, R. 1982. The use of social services by black and white elderly: The role of social support systems. *Journal of Gerontological Social Work* 4:107–125.

Moon, M. 1987. Cost and financing of long term care in Canada: A U.S. response. In *Proceedings of the U.S./Canadian Expert Group Meeting on Policies for Midlife and Older Women*, ed, M. J. Gibson, pp.49–51. Washington, D.C.: American Association of Retired Persons.

Norusis, M. J. 1985. *SPSS-X Advanced Statistics Guide*. New York: McGraw-Hill.

Patrick, D. L.; Stein, J.; Porta, M.; Porter, C. and Ricketts, T. C. 1988. Poverty, health services, and health status in rural America. The Milbank Memorial Fund Quarterly 66: 105–136.

Roos, N. P.; Shapiro, E. and Roos, L. L. 1984. Aging and the demand for health services: Which aged and whose demand? *The Gerontologist* 24:31–36.

Rowland, D. 1989. *Help at home: Long-term care assistance for impaired elderly people*. Baltimore, MD: Commonwealth Fund. Scitovsky, A. A. 1988. Medical care in the last twelve months of life: The relation between age, functional status and medical care expenditures. *The Milbank Memorial Fund Quarterly* 66:640–659.

Shanas, E. 1979. The family as a social support system in old age. *The Gerontologist* 19:169–174.

Statistics Canada. 1988. *The Health and Activity Limitation Survey: User's Guide*. Ottawa: Statistics Canada.

Statistics Canada. 1990. *The Health and Activity Limitation Survey Highlights: Disabled Persons in Canada*. Ottawa: Statistics Canada.

Stone, L. O. 1988. *Family and friendship ties among Canada's seniors: An introductory report from the General Social Survey*. Ottawa: Statistics Canada.

Stone, L. O. and Fletcher, S. 1988. Demographic variations in North America. In *North American elders: United States and Canadian perspectives*, ed, E. Rathbone-McCuan and B. Havens. Westport, CT: Greenwood Press.

Wan, T. and Soifer, S. 1974. Determinants of physician utilization: A causal analysis. *Journal of Health and Social Behavior* 15:100–108.

Wolinsky, F. D.; Coe, R. M.; Miller, D. K.; Pendergrast, J. M.; Creel, M. J. and Chavez, N. M. 1983. Health services utilization among the non-institutionalized elderly. *Journal of Health and Social Behavior* 24:325–337.

Wolinsky, F. D.; Mosely, R. R. and Coe, R. M. 1986. A cohort of the use of health services by elderly Americans. *Journal of Health and Social Behavior* 27:209–219.

Wright, R.; Creecy, R. F. and Berg, W. E. 1979. The black elderly and their use of health care services: A causal analysis. *Journal of the Gerontological Social Work* 2:11–28.

# Chapter 6

## Older Canadians with Developmental Disabilities Access to Health Care and Social Services[1]

*Calvin Henry Easterling, Ph.D.*
Department of Behavioral Science
Oral Roberts University

*Susan Brown Eve, Ph.D.*
Department of Sociology and Social Work
University of North Texas

### INTRODUCTION

The accessibility, predictors, and use of health care and social services among developmentally disabled elderly adults in Canada were examined using data from the Canadian Health and Activities Limitation Survey. Data were obtained from 640 developmentally disabled adults interviewed in a nationally representative household survey of 184,500 persons. Dependent variables included measures of respondents' use of physicians, hospitals, nurses, chiropractors, occupational therapists/physical therapists/speech therapists, and prescription medicines; use of aids for hearing, vision and mobility impairment; and use of non family helpers and special transportation. Predictors of use of these services included illness or need variables (self-assessed health status, activity limitations, activities of daily living, and functional limitations); enabling variables (employment or retirement status, family income, receipt of income supplements for low-income developmentally disabled elderly, and urban/rural residence); and predisposing variables (age, gender, marital status, and race/ethnicity).

### The Developmentally Disabled Elderly

A society's commitment to health care reflects its fundamental attitudes about what it is to be a human being. Society has a moral burden to assure impartial access to health care for all its citizens.

[1]This research was funded in part by Faculty Research Grants at the University of North Texas and Oral Roberts University.

A particularly fascinating aspect of investigating the health care delivery system of a particular nation is the insight such a probe provides into the nature of that society. As Donald Light (1986) has pointed out, medical care and health services are functions of political philosophy; therefore, social and political values underlie the options chosen, the institutions developed, and the quantity of funding given. A nation's approach to health care is based upon its historical background, culture and religion, monetary resources, political ideology, social structure, level of education, standard of living, and perspectives of welfare and the role of government.

It is necessary to address some of the issues faced by the increasing population of elderly developmentally disabled individuals in Canada and the need for the various helping professions, educational disciplines, and public policy agencies to understand this special population.

Research data and findings associated with aging among the developmentally disabled must be reviewed and some of the program and policy implications discussed, keeping in mind that those who influence policy decisions in the United States can be informed by studies of the Canadian health care system.

By definition, a developmental disability is an administrative designation used by the federal government to refer to certain individuals. According to Public Law 98-527 of the Developmental Disabilities Act of 1984, a developmental disability is a severe chronic disability of a person which:

1.   is attributable to a physical or mental impairment (or combination of impairments);
2.   is manifest before age 22;
3.   is likely to continue indefinitely;
4.   results in substantial functional limitations in three or more of the following areas: self care, receptive and expressive language, learning, mobility, self direction, capacity for independent living or economic self-sufficiency; and
5.   reflects the need for a combination and sequence of special, interdisciplinary, or generic care, treatment, or other services which are (a) of lifelong or extended duration and are (b) individually planned and coordinated (Walz, Harper, & Wilson, 1986:623).

This means that a developmentally disabled person is one with mental retardation, cerebral palsy, Down's Syndrome, epilepsy, autism, or dyslexia manifested prior to age 22. The most prevalent developmental disability is mental retardation. Mental retardation is defined as: "subaverage intellectual functioning along with deficits in adaptive behavior that occur first in childhood and are carried over into adulthood" (Rose & Janicki, 1986:1).

The literature reveals that the life expectancy for all developmentally disabled groups has increased. Walz, *et al.* (1986) compared documents showing mortality of the developmentally disabled over a widely separated interval of time. In 1932, 28% of persons with mental retardation (studied at age 10) survived to age 60. In a 1976 study, however, 46% survived to age 60. This figure is still lower than that of the general population (Carter & Jancar, 1983). Within the developmentally disabled population, women, ambulatory persons, non-Down's Syndrome, the less severely mentally retarded, and those who have remained in their home communities have the greatest life expectancies (Jacobson, Sutton, & Janicki, 1985).

According to the Association of Retarded Citizens, approximately 3% of the United States population, or 6 million persons, have mental retardation. The United Cerebral Palsy Association estimates the number of persons with cerebral palsy at 750,000, and the Epilepsy Foundation of America claims close to one million epileptics, while the National Society for Children and Adults with Autism estimates approximately 80,000 autistic Americans (Lippman & Loberg, 1985).

In a major research study of Ohio, Indiana, Illinois, Michigan, Wisconsin, and Minnesota, Sweeney (1980) found that over 10% of the developmentally disabled population for this region were over the age of 65. Based on current estimates from a number of sources, Walz, *et al.* (1986) state that there are a quarter of a million elderly developmentally disabled in the United States aged 65 and over. If age 55 were used for the estimation, the number would be 1,380,000 (Seltzer & Seltzer, 1984). It is obvious that with extended life expectancy the subpopulation of developmentally disabled elderly will continue to increase in the coming years. Demographers have estimated that the elderly population in the United States will double in the next thirty years (Rose and Ansello, 1987; Rose & Janicki, 1986). It is safe to assume that there will be a comparable increase in the number of adults with developmental disabilities.

## Issues

### *Drug Interactions*
There are several problem areas at issue for those who deal with the developmentally disabled elderly. For one thing, when they are prescribed medications for geriatric illnesses, they may experience drug interactions with medicines previously prescribed to help control seizures, depression, or other effects of their primary disability.

*Communication Problems*

Secondly, a common result of a developmental disability is impairment of the ability to communicate. This tends to interfere with the identification, diagnosis, and treatment of chronic illnesses, since physicians rely heavily upon patients' verbal descriptions of their ailments. For this reason, researchers have found that chronic conditions often persist or recur over prolonged periods of time among the developmentally disabled (Nelson & Crocker, 1979).

*Competition for Resources*

A third issue is competition for limited health and welfare resources. The disability agencies are already heavily weighted toward the needs of children and young adults and the aging network is heavily oriented toward the needs of the general aging population. "In any intergenerational 'battle,' aging MR/DD people are unlikely to do very well. This subgroup is . . . without an organized advocacy group" (Walz, *et al.*, 1986:627). The charge has jointly been blatantly made by the Director of Planning at the New York State Office of Mental Retardation and Developmental Disabilities and the Co-director of the Aging and Developmental Disabilities Research and Planning Project at the Center for Aging at the University of Maryland at College Park:

> There have been many instances where disabled individuals have been denied services by local aging agencies even though they were entitled to such services due to their eligibility under the Older Americans Act. The barriers that have been set in place are often times insurmountable without extraordinary interventions. (Rose & Janicki, 1986:14)

Many times such barriers are financial in nature. Limited funds are allocated to area agencies on aging and priorities are set to help the greatest number of people. The needs of the developmentally disabled, whose conditions often require more constant and expensive assistance, are therefore not considered. Sometimes the barriers may be due to "handicapism" on the part of those officials who simply do not wish to deal with the "distasteful" aspects of developmentally disabled behavior.

Changes in characterizing mental retardation from a medical problem to a social problem have served to shift the focus of professional attention from the medical practitioner to the professional educator and social worker (Kelly, Larson, & Groeneweg, 1988). Consequently, in some cases, either important health care needs have gone undetected by these professionals because of their lack of specialized training in health care (Weinberg, 1977), or the health care technologists who have been called in to deal with these individuals have been reluctant or unable to provide adequate service because of their unfamiliarity with developmental disability (Kelly *et al.*, 1988).

*Caregiving and Residence*

Improvements in caregiving and residential setting can increase the longevity and life satisfaction of the developmentally disabled. Long term care, particularly in relation to the dimensions of its quality and accessibility, is probably the most important issue currently affecting the developmentally disabled elderly.

The historical pattern for developmentally disabled adults has been institutionalization in long-term care residential units. Approximately 55% of the developmentally disabled elderly reside in institutional settings, as opposed to only 5% (9% in Canada [Wasylenki, 1982]) of the non-developmentally disabled elderly. In a recent study by the International Social Security Association, the institutionalization rate of seniors in Canada was one of the highest among eighteen industrialized nations (Statistics Canada, 1989). There has been, nevertheless, an emphasis on deinstitutionalization and community-based services. In general, there is agreement that institutional care is rarely the most appropriate setting for developmentally disabled persons and that residential services should be provided in the least restrictive environment (Hauber, Rotegard, & Bruininks, 1985).

Deinstitutionalization often takes the form of small "family-sized" group housing. Many times, the older developmentally disabled person resides with parents, relatives, or foster parents (Rose & Janicki, 1986). This can result in "two-generation senior citizen families." The parents or foster care providers are often in their seventies or eighties and are becoming progressively less able to care for their aging developmentally disabled child (Rose & Janicki, 1986). In such instances, both the parents and the developmentally disabled child are in need of assistance. The family may have had their standard of living dramatically reduced due to financial obligations relating to the developmental disability. The parents should not be seen as simply resources of support for their developmentally disabled child who need to be supported and eventually replaced when they die, but they should be seen as ". . . individuals, facing life's last great crisis, but with the additional and tragic task of making arrangements for children who are adults, yet still dependent" (Dobrof, 1985:414).

Though remaining at home with the parents may have some drawbacks, especially where there exists a "reclusive" kind of environment, this living arrangement is nevertheless superior to some archaic mental institution or non-therapeutic nursing home. At least the developmentally disabled person at home retains communication with those with whom he has established primary relationships. Additionally, much of the deterioration and early deaths of the developmentally disabled was a direct result of poor institutional care and lack of rehabilitation (Cotton, Sison, & Starr, 1981).

*Access to Health Care*

Another issue regards health care. As a group, the developmentally disabled elderly tend to need and use health services more than other elderly persons. The movement of the developmentally disabled from institutions to community settings has shifted their dependence for health care from the segregated medical services of institutions to the health care structures of communities (Janicki *et al.*, 1985). They tend to experience, with increasing age, increases in mobility impairments, medication usage, need for special diets, and decreases in self-care skills. They must be carefully observed for adverse reactions to drugs, particularly those persons with communication disablements, who cannot readily report symptoms.

Persons with developmental disabilities tend to die of a pattern of disease somewhat different from that of the general population. Respiratory infections attributed to cerebral palsy, epilepsy, and reduced efficiency in coughing, feeding, and breathing are factors in the excess mortality among the more severely retarded individuals. The mildly mentally retarded, on the other hand, are more likely to die from a cerebrovascular or cardiovascular disease. Persons with developmental disabilities are 50% more likely to die from carcinoma or cardiac failure than is the general population (Carter & Jancar, 1983).

Secondary health problems of the developmentally disabled adult include obesity, chronic skin problems, hygiene related problems, and early aging in the forty to sixty age group (including Alzheimer's Disease). In fact, one researcher performed actual autopsies on a group of former Down's Syndrome patients who had reached at least the age of forty. He found that 100% had suffered from Alzheimer's Disease (Miniszek, 1983). Buehler, Smith, and Fifield (1985) blame many of these secondary health problems on lack of access to adequate health care due to a lack of availability, expertise, and interest in the medical community.

*Day Services*

Daytime program services for the developmentally disabled elderly are still in the embryonic stage. The programs that do exist share as their primary goals:

(a) prevention of regression due to inactivity;
(b) minimization of mental and physical debilitation;
(c) enhancement of the quality of life for participants; and
(d) prolongation of community placement (Catapano, Levy, & Levy, 1985:315).

More service approaches need to be created, especially for those who are unable to travel to day programs due to medical restrictions.

*The Need For Understanding*

In most areas of the United States both an aging network to help meet the needs of the elderly and a network of agencies to serve the developmentally disabled are already in place. Why, then, have many of the developmentally disabled elderly "fallen through the cracks" of the system? Some insist that a lack of understanding on the part of both helping networks is the problem. The developmental disabilities service providers generally do not have a familiarity with the Older Americans Act, nor do many in the aging network have much knowledge concerning developmental disabilities (Rose & Janicki, 1986). Because of this situation, both the American Association on Mental Deficiency and the Gerontological Society of America now have special membership sections to address the special needs of this sub-group of older Americans (Rose & Janicki, 1986).

A clear need exists for a greater number of gerontologists, mental health professionals, physicians, policymakers, and educators to be more properly educated and trained to more adequately service the specific needs of the elderly developmentally disabled. Many persons, including some in positions of influence, carry with them myths, stereotypes, and prejudices that hinder the advancement of the developmentally disabled elderly.

Unfortunately, the business community and society in general often embrace stereotypical beliefs that the developmentally disabled person is "senile" and may be a threat to other workers or to the general population (Robinson, 1987). Obviously, this view is distorted. A small percentage of the developmentally disabled eventually get married. Some can drive their own automobiles. Many are gainfully employed, and sometimes the employer receives tax credits for hiring them. It is to be hoped that with better education and sensitization, the general public will accept the developmentally disabled elderly with respect and understanding.

Employers often use persons' disabilities as excuses for not hiring them. In most cases, only minor adjustments or provisions are necessary for the developmentally disabled to be successful on the job. Sometimes over-protective family members prevent developmentally disabled persons from working in a competitive employment situation because they do not want them to be hurt or embarrassed. Developmentally disabled persons should be given trust and some latitude in order to develop the concept that other people have confidence in and can rely upon them, rather than their always being dependent on others (Robinson, 1987).

The developmentally disabled elderly person faces the prejudices and discriminations of society as both elderly and developmentally disabled. The person is thus the victim of both ageism and handicapism. Dobrof (1985:412) states that these persons have ". . . been subjected to 'systematic stereotyping and discrimination,' and are often seen as different and not identified as human beings."

Helping professionals are not immune to a reluctance to work with this group of people. In the first place, both the elderly and the developmentally disabled generally have low social status in our society. Staff persons of service providers may fear being stigmatized by their association with the clients. Secondly, in the process of dealing with this subpopulation, they are forced to come to grips with their own mortality as well as vague feelings of inadequacy because they have not achieved more even though they are not handicapped. A third conflict is the crude question of whether the scarce time and expertise spent in working with a person who may soon be dead is really worth it (Kastenbaum, 1964).

Elderly persons have the right to continue to be educated, to enhance or reduce their involvement in work, retire, relax, volunteer their time, engage in religious activities, and participate in social and recreational activities. The developmentally disabled elderly have the same rights. Service providers should therefore act as advocates for this group who cannot promote their own needs.

### Andersen's Conceptual Framework of Health Care Utilization

The most widely adopted and empirically assessed model of health services utilization is Andersen's (1968) behavioral model. This model has been expanded, modified, and used extensively by Andersen and other health services researchers in the 1970s and 1980s; it is likely to be the dominant model in the 1990s (Wolinsky, 1988). This model aims to be a simplified representation of empirical reality portraying the causal process of health services utilization. Andersen and Anderson (1979:384) suggest that this model of health services utilization may serve any one or more of the following purposes:

1.  to illustrate the interrelationships among the determinants of health services utilization;
2.  to facilitate the prediction of future health services needs;
3.  to determine whether or not the distribution of health services is equitable;
4.  to suggest ways to manipulate policy relevant variables in order to bring about desired changes;
5.  to evaluate the impact of new health care delivery programs or projects.

The original model developed by Andersen (1968) and expanded by Andersen and Newman (1973) has been empirically assessed in a number of regional and national studies with considerable success. (Andersen, 1968; Andersen & Newman, 1973; Wan & Soifer, 1974; Andersen, Kravits, & Anderson, 1975, 1976; Berki & Kobashigawa,

1976; Wolinsky, 1976, 1978; Eve & Friedsam, 1980; Eve, Watson, & Reis, 1980; Aday, Andersen, & Fleming, 1980; Eve, 1982; Wolinsky, Coe, Miller, Prendergrast, Creel, & Chavez, 1983; Eve, 1984; Wolinsky & Coe, 1984; Aday, Fleming, & Andersen, 1984; Wolinsky, Moseley, & Coe, 1986; Chappell & Blandford, 1987; Eve, 1988). "This health systems model is very useful because it provides both a conceptual and a methodological framework for the study of health services utilization. Indeed, it has become the standard framework used in health policy studies" (Wolinsky, 1988:133). A summary of Andersen and Newman's (1973) model for explaining the utilization of health care services by the elderly appears in Figure 1. What Andersen and Newman conceived as predisposing variables are characteristics which exist prior to one's illness and which may affect the need for services but may not necessarily be the cause of utilization. Predisposing factors include, for example, demographic factors such as age and sex, social structure factors such as ethnicity and education, and attitudinal factors such as attitudes and beliefs. Enabling factors may be thought of as characteristics or circumstances which can either hinder or facilitate the use of appropriate services once the need has been recognized. Examples of enabling factors include family income, health insurance, region of country, and whether residence is rural or urban. The third category, illness (need) factors, includes both the respondent's own perception of her/his health status and evaluation of the respondent's health by a health care professional.

Despite variations in measurement, there has been some consistency in concluding that illness (need) is the most predictive determinant of use of physician and hospital services (Eve & Friedsam, 1980; Eve *et al.*, 1980; Eve, 1982; Eve, 1984; Wolinsky, Moseley, & Coe, 1986; Chappell & Blandford, 1987; Eve, 1988). When applied to the use of health services, Aday and Andersen (1981) argue that an equitable situation is one in which only medical need determines health services utilization (in addition to some vestiges of a relationship with age and sex, as proxies of biological need). Inequity is said to exist when health services are distributed on the basis of race, income, or place of residence.

Andersen and Newman's (1973) model, conceptualizes utilization as the end product of a complex pattern of interrelationships between predisposing, enabling, and need factors. It suggests that some individuals have a higher propensity to use social services than do others, and that this propensity can be viewed as the outcome of certain background characteristics of the individual (Starrett, Wright, Mindel, & Tran, 1989). This propensity is associated with such variables as ethnicity or race, age, sex, education, marital status, and attitudes. Starrett, *et al.* (1989), working with the Andersen-Newman theoretical framework, found that a high of 44% of the variance in utilization was explained for Cuban elderly, 41% for Puerto Rican elderly, and a low of 35% was explained for Mexican American elderly.

**Figure 1.**
**Summary of Variables in the Andersen-Newman (1973) Model.**

    I.    Utilization of Health Care Services
          A.    Contact
          B.    Volume of use
          C.    Frequency of Use
    II.    Illness (Need) Variables
          A.    Perceived health by respondent
          B.    Evaluated health by health care professional
    III.    Enabling Variables
          A.    Family level variables
             1.    Income
             2.    Insurance
             3.    Access to transportation
          B.    Community level variables
             1.    Region of residence
             2.    Urban/rural residence
    IV.    Predisposing Variables
          A.    Demographic variables
             1.    Age
             2.    Sex
          B.    Social structure variables
             1.    Education
             2.    Occupational status
             3.    Marital status
             4.    Race/ethnicity
          C.    Beliefs
             1.    Health values
             2.    Attitudes toward services
             3.    Knowledge about disease

## Canadian Studies

With the notable exceptions of Snider's (1980) study of noninstitutionalized Canadians and Chappell and Blandford's (1987) study of the Manitoba system, all of these studies are American. None specifically relates to the developmentally disabled elderly.

A few surveys have been conducted to attempt to determine the health care and/ or social service needs of the developmentally disabled elderly in Canada. Badry, Vrbancic, Groeneweg, McDonald, and Hornick (1986), in a survey of the developmentally disabled elderly in Alberta, concluded that leisure activities represented the greatest need for this group. Similarly, Berg and Dalton (1980) and Delaney (1984) studied the needs of the developmentally disabled elderly in Ontario, as did Anglin (1981) in the metro Toronto area. None of these is national in scope and none resembles the Andersen-Newman theoretical framework.

The area of aging and developmental disabilities remains relatively unexplored in Canada. One reason for this is that this is a relatively "new" population. This is the case due to two major factors. Prior to the 1950s, the developmentally disabled were primarily institutionalized in Canada (Canada has the highest percentage of institutionalized elderly among the industrialized nations, at 9% [Wasylenki, 1982]). The other factor is that the developmentally disabled did not live long lives. Neither of these is any longer the case. The developmentally disabled are aging along with the remainder of society and there are a number of issues regarding this population which must be addressed. Some of these issues (discussed in the Introduction) include drug interactions, communication problems, competition for resources, caregiving, institutionalization vs. community residence, access to health care, day services, and legal concerns. This research deals with the issues of access to health care and social services for those in community residences.

The health care needs of developmentally disabled adults who are now participating in community living are poorly understood. This project was developed to survey the current health care situation for this population living in Canada. Kelly *et al.* (1988), have concluded from their qualitative survey in Alberta that health care needs are not being adequately addressed; a lack of professional services was identified by both administrators of health care agencies and health care service providers.

Over the last two decades there has been an overall increase in the number of individuals in Canada with developmental handicaps who have maintained residency in community versus institutional environments (Kelly *et al.*, 1988). Correspondingly, there has been an increase in the number and variety of health care services required to meet their individual needs. On the surface, this seems to be an optimal situation; however, the needs are poorly understood and the level of service and expertise required to meet them may be considerably lacking within existing health care systems (Kelly *et al.*, 1988).

Researchers in Toronto (Wasylenki *et al.*, 1985) have added a valuable dimension to previous studies by looking at estimated and met needs in five separate dimensions as well as outcomes. They examined perceived and met needs in the five dimensions of medical therapeutic, social recreational, vocational educational, housing, and financial needs. Only the medical therapeutic needs were fairly well met. The other needs were dealt with poorly, particularly the social recreational component. Similar concerns with regard to the "disabled" were raised in the comprehensive report of the Mental Health Planning Survey in British Columbia (1979).

## Policy Implications

The Canadian health care delivery system differs from that of the United States in at least one fundamental respect: there is universal insurance coverage in Canada. The Canadian federal government pays one third and each province pays two thirds of the costs of health care in Canada. Health care is thus almost entirely funded publicly and is available to Canadians of any age (Kane & Kane, 1990). The health care delivery system in the United States is a direct-fee system, in which patients pay directly for services provided by physicians and hospitals.

It could be argued that universal access in Canada should result in the lesser importance of enabling factors such as family income, access to services, ratios of health personnel and facilities to the population, region of the country, etc. It is not known whether this is actually the case.

The proposed research project is not a cross-cultural comparison between the United States and Canada. It will, however, undoubtedly be of interest to U.S. policymakers who desire the best system possible for their population.

## METHODOLOGY

The objective of this research is to examine the accessibility of, and the predictors of, use of health care and social services among noninstitutionalized developmentally disabled elderly adults in Canada. Data for older developmentally disabled adults in Canada was obtained from Statistics Canada's Health and Activity Limitation Survey (H.A.L.S.) for 1986 and 1987 (the latest available).

For the current research certain characteristics have been selected for the purpose of analyzing the developmentally disabled elderly rather than the entire sample of disabled persons in Canadian households. These characteristics are:

> Aged 55 or older, and
> Mental retardation,
> Down's Syndrome or similar chromosomal anomaly,
> Cerebral palsy,
> Epilepsy, and/or
> Other cerebral degenerations.

## Data Analysis

The data analysis was done using SPSS-X (Norusis, 1985). Descriptive statistics, including mean, median, mode, standard deviation, and measures of skewness and kurtosis, were used to describe the data in the H.A.L.S. dataset. Step-wise multiple regression analysis was used to compare the strength of the predictors of use of specific health care and social services.

## Figure 2.
## Summarized Adaptation of Andersen-Newman model.

Utilization of Health Care Services
    No. of doctor visits past 3 months
    No. of hospital days past 12 months
    No. of nurse visits in past 3 months
    No. of physio/occupational/speech therapist visits
    Aids for hearing impaired used
    Aids for visually impaired used
    Aids for mobility impaired used
    No. of prescription drugs used daily
Utilization of Social Services
    How often use special bus/van
    Receive outside help with daily activities
Illness (Need) Variables
    Trouble dressing or getting out of bed
    Learning disability
    Activities limited due to learning disability
    Difficulty using public transportation
    Condition caused difficulty riding in car
Enabling Variables (Family Level)
    Total income from pensions or welfare
    Total income
    Low-income status
Enabling Variables (Community Level)
    Rural/urban
    Province of residence
Predisposing Variables
    Ethnic origin
    Marital status
    Sex
    Age group
    Educational level

RESULTS

**Descriptives**

After selecting respondents according to the characteristics listed above, a total of 640 developmentally disabled over age 55 remain as valid cases for the current research. Of the 640 in the sample, nearly half (47.5 percent) are ages 55 to 64, one third (32 percent) are ages 65 to 74, less than one fifth (17.5 percent) are ages 75 to 84, and only 3 percent are aged 85 or over. The median age is 62.

In terms of disabling conditions, over a third (35.1 percent) have been diagnosed as being developmentally delayed. Nearly equal in number to each other are those who are either mentally retarded (21.2 percent) or suffer from cerebral palsy or similar cerebral degeneration (21.4 percent). Epilepsy accounts for 15 percent, Down's Syndrome 1 percent, and other related conditions 6.3 percent of the cases.

The sample is divided almost evenly on the category of sex. One half (50.2 percent) are female and one half (49.8 percent) of the 640 respondents are male.

Over half the respondents are either married (36.6 percent) or widowed (15.8 percent). Less than one tenth are either divorced (3.1 percent) or separated (4.1 percent). A large percentage (40.5 percent) have remained single throughout their lifetimes, and 58 percent are currently living completely apart from any family members. Interestingly, 2.5 percent are female single parents and 1.1 percent are male single parents. Only 3.1 percent are adult children living with their parents.

About one quarter (27 percent) have attained more than eight years of formal education. One fifth (19.5 percent) have no formal education or kindergarten only. Very few (1.9 percent) are college graduates. One respondent has an earned doctorate.

About two-thirds (65.6 percent) speak English as their first language. Only a fifth (21.2 percent) speak French as their first language, although nearly a third (30.3 percent) claim French ethnicity, and a tenth (10.2 percent) are bilingual. A small number (2.5 percent) are proficient in neither English nor French.

Fully 64.4 percent of the respondents live in urban areas. About half reside in the provinces of Quebec (28 percent) and Ontario (19.8 percent). The next most prevalent home provinces of respondents are Saskatchewan (12 percent) and British Columbia (11.7 percent).

The median total annual income for all respondents is $8,499. Over one-third (36.6 percent) fall below the poverty line. Three-quarters of the respondents receive less than $500 per year in pensions and welfare payments.

One-fourth to one-half of the older developmentally disabled older adults report functional difficulties with hearing (26.9 percent); eyesight (32.2 percent); speaking (34.0 percent); walking (52.6 percent); carrying, moving or standing (53.4 percent);

bending or stooping (36.6 percent); dressing or getting in or out of bed (28.5 percent); using their fingers or hands to grasp (51.6 percent); and reaching readily in any direction (34.0 percent). These data are presented in Figures 3A and 3B. Overall, 79.8 percent of the older developmentally disabled adults report limitation in activity. As one would expect, more than half of the older adults surveyed report a learning disability or a learning problem . Seventy percent report that their activities are limited by their conditions. Refer to Figures 4A and 4B. As a result of their learning disability, significant proportions of the older adults report difficulty using public transportation (11.9 percent), one-third cannot take long trips, nearly half cannot drive, 6.7 percent have difficulty even being a passenger in a car, and 15 percent have difficulty using a train, plane or bus on long trips. One-third report that their condition completely prevents them from working.

Data on use of health care services are presented in Figure 5. Over two-thirds (69 percent) of the older adults report having seen a physician in the past three months. Exactly one-third (33.3 percent) report having been hospitalized in the past year. One-seventh (14.1 percent) of the respondents have seen a nurse in the same period, while only three percent have visited a chiropractor. Fewer still are the cases of respondents who have seen a physical, occupational, or speech therapist (1.8 percent). However, 69 percent report currently using prescription medicines. Of these, 45.6 percent take three or more different prescription drugs daily. As shown in Figures 6 and 7, over a quarter (27 percent) of the cases indicate using aids for the hearing impaired, but 7.7 percent indicate an unfulfilled need for such aids. Aids for the visually impaired are used by one-tenth (10.9 percent) of the respondents, while 33.2 percent need visual aids but are not utilizing them. Fully 17 percent make use of aids for the mobility impaired, with only 2.2 percent indicating that they have such a need but do not have the aids.

With regard to social services utilization (Figure 8), less than half of the sample (42.5 percent) report receiving outside help with the activities of daily living. By "outside help" is meant a non-child, non-parent, non-spouse, non-relative, or non-neighbor. In other words, the helper is either hired or has volunteered to perform social service work. The services provided include meal preparation, shopping for groceries, housework, heavy household chores, looking after personal finances, personal care, and help moving around within the residence. In addition, 4.2 percent report using a special bus or van for transportation. In spite of the help available, substantial proportions of these older adults report needing assistance that they cannot get. As shown in Figures 9A-C, one-fourth to one-third of the older adults need assistance with meal preparation, shopping, housework, heavy chore, personal finances, personal care, and taking short or long trips. Approximately ten percent or fewer report needing help with signing,  moving about in their residence, special transportation, and special residential adaptation.

Multiple regression was used to examine the predictors of use of health services, use of aids for impairments, and use of social services. The simple correlation coefficients and the betas for the predictors of the use of physicians, hospitals, nurses and prescription medicines are reported in Table 1. If health care services are equitably available to all, the Andersen and Newman model would predict that indicators of health would be most predictive of use of these services. For use of hospitals, nurses and prescription medicines, need variables are significant predictors of use of these services, although not for use of physicians. The strongest predictor of use of these services in general is a predisposing variable—being of French ethnic origin. Being French is significantly negatively correlated with use of physicians (Beta=-.20), and with having seen a nurse (Beta=-.30), but positively related to having been hospitalized (Beta=.14), and strongly positively related to use of prescription medicines (Beta=.39). Gender is also a significant predictor, with men being more likely to have been hospitalized (Beta=.17) and to use prescription medicines (Beta=.19), and women being more likely to have seen a physician (Beta=-.16) and a nurse (Beta=-.22). Enabling variables— low income status and rural residence—were also significantly related to use of physicians and nurses. Older developmentally disabled adults who had low incomes were more likely to have used both these services (Beta=.13 and .14 respectively). Those who lived in rural areas were less likely to have seen a physician (Betas=-.11) or a nurse (Betas= -.19). Thus, National Health Insurance appears to be working in that those in the greatest need with the lowest incomes are most able to use

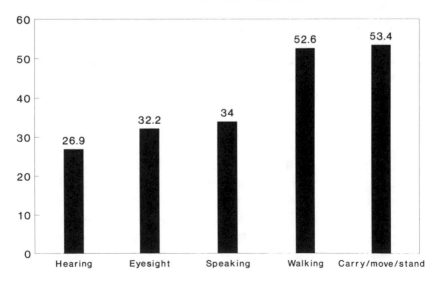

**Figure 3A: Percent of Older DD
with Functional Difficulties**

N=640

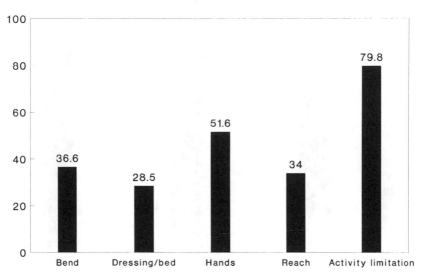

Figure 3B: Percent of Older DD
with Functional Difficulties

N=640

these services, but physicians and nurses continue to be less readily available in rural areas. Overall, 30 percent of the variance in use of nurses services was explained, 20 percent of use of prescription medicines, 14 percent of use of hospital services and 13 percent of use of physician services.

Predictors of use of aids for hearing, mobility and vision impairments are presented in Table 2. The strongest predictors of use of these aids are the variables that are indicators of functional impairment, especially having difficulty dressing or getting out of bed, which is positively related to all three variables (Beta=.18 for hearing aids, .23 for mobility aids and .15 for vision aids). It is interesting that having activities limited by learning disabilities is strongly inversely related to using aids for mobility impairment (Beta=-.30). Perhaps those older adults with activity limitations due to learning disabilities do not tend to have mobility impairments. The predisposing variables are also significantly related to use of impairment aids. Age is positively related to use of hearing aids (Beta=.13). Males are more likely to use hearing aids (Beta=.16), but women are more likely to use mobility aids (Beta=-.15). French ethnics are more likely to use hearing aids (Beta=.15), but less likely to use mobility aids (Beta=-.12). The better educated are less likely to use vision aids (Beta=-.14), and those older adults who are married are less likely to use mobility aids. Finally, older adults who are rural residents are less likely to use mobility aids or vision aids. Overall, the

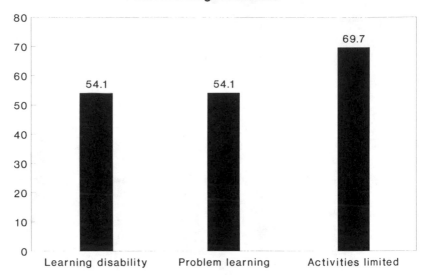

**Figure 4A: Percent of Older DD
with Learning Disabilities**

N=640

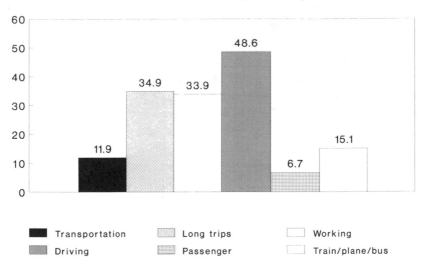

**Figure 4B: Percent of Older DD with
Limitation due to Learning Disability**

N=640

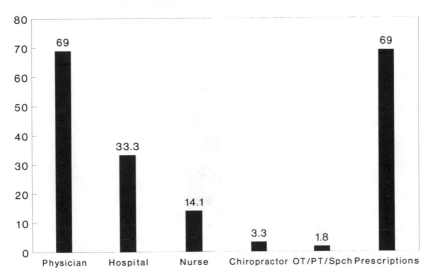

**Figure 5: Percent of Older DD Using Health Services in Past Three Months**

N=640

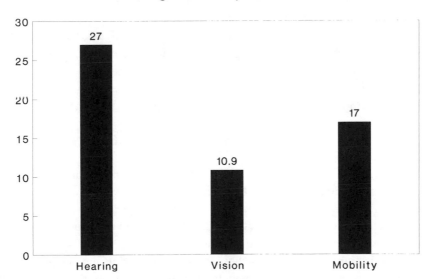

**Figure 6: Percent of Older DD Currently Using Aids for Impairment**

N=640

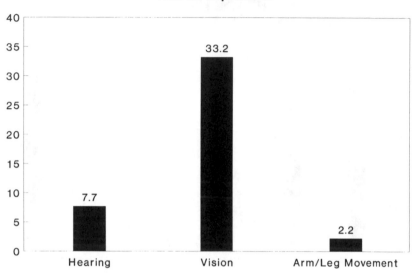

**Figure 7: Percent of Older DD Needing Aids for Impairment**

N=640

analysis explained 21 percent of the variance in use of mobility aids, 12 percent in use of hearing aids, and seven percent in use of vision aids.

Use of a non-family member to help with daily activities was most strongly predicted by having trouble dressing and getting into and out of bed (Beta=.18), and having activities limited due to learning disabilities (Beta=.19). Use of non-family helpers also increased with age (Beta=.18). Overall, 13 percent of the variance in the use of non-family helpers was explained by these predictors as shown in Table 3.

## CONCLUSIONS AND IMPLICATIONS

In summary, older developmentally disabled Canadians report significant difficulties with functional abilities that are necessary for daily living. Their activities are also significantly limited by their learning disabilities, especially in their abilities to get outside their homes. Thus, these older adults have a great need for health and social services. As one would predict, their use of physicians, hospitals and prescription medicines is high. Aids for use by those impaired in hearing and mobility appears to be readily available to the developmentally disabled, but more than one-third report needing vision aids that they do not have. As for non-family assistants, more than 40

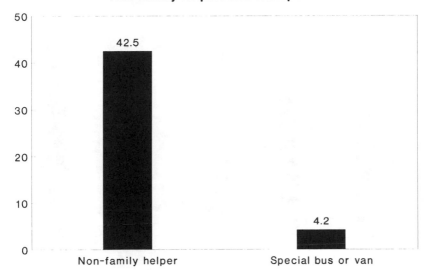

**Figure 8: Percent of Older DD Using
Non-Family Helpers and Transportation**

N=640

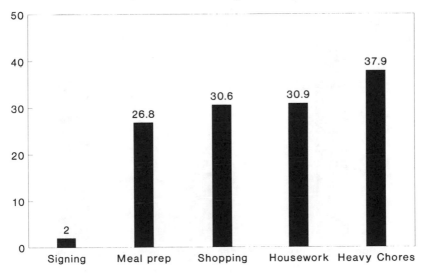

**Figure 9A: Percent of Older DD Needing
Social Services They Do Not Have**

N=640

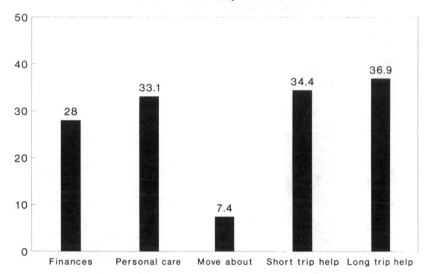

Figure 9B: Percent of Older DD Needing
Social Services They Do Not Have

N=640

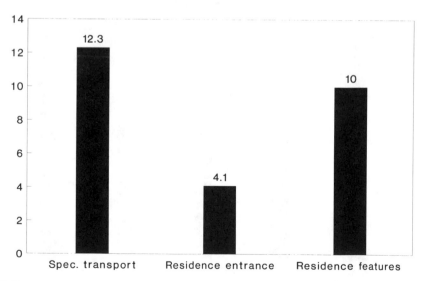

Figure 9C: Percent of Older DD Needing
Social Services They Do Not Have

N=640

percent of these older adults report having such assistance, but one-fourth to one-third report needing assistance with basic activities of daily living.

In an ideal health and social service delivery system, all the variance in the use of health and social services would be explained by the need for those services. In the Canadian system, need tends be a strong, if not the strongest predictor of the use of health and social services examined in this research. However, the continued influence of factors such as minority ethnic status and rural residence remains cause for concern. It was heartening to find that in only two instances—utilization of physician services and having seen a nurse—was the enabling category of income significantly correlated

**Table 1. Regression of Predictor Variables on Use of Health Care Services among Older Developmentally Disabled Adults in Canada**

|  | Physician | | Hospital | | Nurse | | Prescription | |
|---|---|---|---|---|---|---|---|---|
|  | r | Beta | r | Beta | r | Beta | r | Beta |
| **Need Level** | | | | | | | | |
| Trouble dressing/ getting out of bed | | | .28 | .18 | | | | |
| Diagnosed with Learning disabilities | | | | .25 | .17 | -.15 | -.12 | |
| Activities limited/ learning disability | | | .18 | .11 | -.30 | -.12 | | |
| Trouble using public transportation | | | | | -.15 | -.10 | | |
| **Predisposing** | | | | | | | | |
| Age | | | | | .00 | .11 | | |
| Sex | -.16 | -.11 | .24 | .17 | -.31 | -.22 | .20 | .19 |
| French origin | -.20 | -.20 | .14 | .13 | -.31 | -.30 | .41 | .39 |
| Years of education | .17 | .13 | .16 | .12 | | | | |
| Marital status | .06 | .10 | | | | | | |
| **Enabling—family level** | | | | | | | | |
| Low income status | .15 | .13 | | | .30 | .14 | | |
| **Enabling—community level** | | | | | | | | |
| Rural residence | -.15 | -.11 | | | -.24 | -.19 | | |
| Adjusted R-squared | | .13 | | .14 | | .30 | | .20 |

with use of services. In both instances, persons with incomes below the poverty line had greatest access to services, as they should given their poorer health. This undoubtedly reflects Canada's health care delivery system, which is a mixture of private enterprise and nationalized medicine.

This research has important policy implications that should be informative for policymakers in both the United States and Canada. The implications will be particularly relevant to those persons in both the private and public sectors who are in positions from which to influence policies concerning the developmentally disabled elderly. The Andersen-Newman theoretical framework was conceived and has been replicated in the United States. The findings of this research indicate that enabling factors such as income, which are so important to health care and social services access in the United States, are not as significant in Canada. The fact that need emerges as being correlated with the use of services and income does not suggest that health care and social services are provided equitably for Canadian developmentally disabled elderly. This is not to say that the services offered in Canada are necessarily superior or particularly appropriate, but only that they are accessible to those most in need.

The findings of this study, when combined with other facts about the Canadian and United States health care delivery systems, suggest that the United States would do well to emulate at least some aspects of the Canadian system. Free access to physicians' offices, hospitals, nurses, and other health care practitioners and services tends to provide more care for those who need it most. Following the introduction of cost-free medical care in Canada (Hatcher *et al.*, 1984), physicians reported seeing fewer patients for frivolous reasons and more persons with serious complaints. Canada provides equal service for rich and poor alike. It is not a two-class health care system.

The quality of health care in Canada is similar to that of the United States. The major emphasis is upon general practitioners rather than specialists, and there are twice as many general practitioners per capita in Canada than in the United States (Hatcher *et al.*, 1984). Cockerham (1989:295) states, "The health profile of Canadians with respect to infant mortality and life expectancy is somewhat better than for Americans." The infant mortality rate (per 1,000 live births) in Canada is the third lowest in the world at 7.2 (Hatcher *et al.*, 1984). This is substantially lower than that of the United States, at 10.5 (Schaefer, 1989).

The outcome of deinstitutionalization has been less unfavorable in Canada than in the United States. The mental health services in Canada have been evaluated as superior to those throughout most of the United States (Smith & Herman, 1988).

Despite the equality and generosity of its health care program, Canada is one of the few countries that has held the cost of all health care to a constant proportion of the Gross National Product (Hatcher *et al.*, 1984). Per capita health care costs in Canada are only half those in the United States, even though most hospitals are privately owned

**Table 2. Regression of Predictor Variables on Use of Aids for Impairment among Older Developmentally Disabled Adults in Canada**

|  | Hearing | | Mobility | | Vision | |
|---|---|---|---|---|---|---|
|  | r | Beta | r | Beta | r | Beta |
| **Need level** | | | | | | |
| Trouble dressing/ getting out of bed | .26 | .18 | .12 | .23 | .14 | .15 |
| Activities limited/ learning disability | | | -.32 | -.30 | .17 | .12 |
| **Predisposing** | | | | | | |
| Age | .22 | .13 | | | | |
| Sex | .13 | .16 | -.24 | -.15 | | |
| French origin | .21 | .15 | -.10 | -.12 | | |
| Years of education | | | | | -.12 | -.14 |
| Marital status | | | -.12 | -.10 | | |
| **Enabling—community level** | | | | | | |
| Rural residence | | | -.25 | -.18 | -.16 | -.14 |
| Adjusted R-squared | | .12 | | .21 | | .07 |

and most physicians are in independent private practice. Only 1.5 percent is spent on administrative costs, making the Canadian system possibly the most efficient in the world (Hatcher *et al.*, 1984). In Canada, malpractice insurance is not a factor in medical costs. In addition, there is not a large insurance industry to contribute to spiraling health care costs, as in the U.S. (Kane & Kane, 1990).

For Canadian policymakers there is much to gain from a study of the Canadian health care delivery system as it applies to the developmentally disabled elderly. Having empirical information on variables that differentiate and characterize (and are potentially modifiable via social policy) those elderly respondents prone to use services will enable policymakers and program developers to structure or restructure the service delivery system in ways that will effectively meet the needs of the developmentally disabled.

As with health care utilization, need factors emerged in this research as the most significant determinants of social services utilization. For both the United States and Canada, it will be beneficial for policymakers and social services practitioners who work with elderly developmentally disabled persons to have an understanding of the

Table 3. Regression of Predictor Variables on Use of Social Services
among Older Developmentally Disabled Adults in Canada

|  | Non-Family Helper | | |
|  | r | Beta | |
| --- | --- | --- | --- |
| **Need level** | | | |
| Trouble dressing/ getting out of bed | .26 | .18 | |
| Activities limited/ learning disability | .24 | .19 | |
| **Predisposing** | | | |
| Age | .24 | .18 | |
| **Enabling—family level** | | | |
| Low income status | | | |
| **Enabling—community level** | | | |
| Rural Residence | | | |
| Adjusted R-squared | | .13 | |

different variables that predict the utilization of services. This kind of information is mandatory for effective service programs to be developed and implemented, particularly in an environment in which resources are limited.

An important concept concerning social services is that they have historically been equated with welfare, usually in a negative sense, and recipients have been stigmatized (Tenhoor, 1982). In times of financial exigency, they are often targeted for elimination. In actuality, however, social services such as the ones investigated in this research (receiving help with the activities of daily living and the use of a bus or van) ". . . are frequently preventive in nature, and . . . prevention is generally accepted as less costly than diagnosis and treatment" (Chappell, 1988:83).

A few final comments about the limitations of this research are in order. A relatively small portion of the variance was explained for some of the dependent variables by the application of multivariate analysis. Similar results have been obtained in other studies (Eve *et al.*, 1980; Wolinsky & Coe, 1984) dealing with different categories of respondents. In particular, the enabling variables account for a disappointingly small proportion of the variance in the model. The variables in this study, though taken from a scientifically designed questionnaire, did not provide as much insight as might have been desirable. For example, the study would have been enhanced had it been possible to distinguish among physician visits which were initiated by the patient, visits initiated at the physician's request, and by some third party, such as a social service worker or a relative. Future research should attempt to obtain information which can be more conducive to such considerations.

Future studies should also attempt to incorporate variables, unavailable in this research, that indicate the respondents' knowledge of health care and social services and how and when to use them. Such knowledge could be operationalized as an enabling variable and would logically have some predictive power in the utilization model.

## References

Aday, L. and Andersen, R. 1981. Equity of access to medical care: A conceptual and empirical overview. *Medical Care* 19(December Supplement):4-27.

Aday, L.; Andersen, R. and Fleming, G. 1980. *Health care in the U.S.: Equitable for whom?* Beverly Hills, California: Sage Publications.

Aday, L.l Fleming, G. and Andersen, R. 1984. *Access to medical care in the U.S.: Who has it, who doesn't.* Chicago: Pluribus Press.

Andersen, R. 1968. *A behavioral model of families' use of health services.* Chicago: Center for Health Administration Studies.

Andersen, R. and Newman, J. 1973. Societal and individual determinants of medical care utilization in the United States. *Milbank Memorial fund Quarterly* 51:95–124.

Andersen, R. and Anderson, O. 1979. Trends in the use of health services. In Freeman, H., Levine, S. & Reeder, L., eds. *Handbook of medical sociology.* 371-91. Englewood Cliffs, NJ: Prentice-Hall.

Andersen, R.; Kravits, J. and Anderson, O. 1975. *Equity in health services.* Cambridge, MA: Ballinger.

Andersen, R.; Kravits, J. and Anderson, O. 1976. *Two decades of health services.* Cambridge, MA: Ballinger.

Anglin, B. 1981. *They never asked for help: A study on the needs of the elderly retarded people in metro Toronto.* Maple, Ontario: Belsten.

Badry, D.; Vrbancic, M.; Groeneweg, G.; McDonald, L. and Hornick, J. 1986. *An examination of the service needs of older developmentally disabled persons in the province of Alberta, Canada.* Calgary, Alberta: The Vocational and Rehabilitation Research Institute.

Berg, J. and Dalton, A. 1980. *The mentally retarded in middle age.* Toronto, Ontario: Ontario Ministry of Community and Social Services.

Berki, S. and Kobashigawa, B. 1976. Socioeconomic and need determinants of ambulatory care use: Path analysis of the 1970 health interview survey. *Medical Care* 14:405–17.

Buehler, B.; Smith, B. and Fifield, M. 1985. *Medical issues in serving adults with developmental disabilities.* Technical Report #4. Logan, UT: Utah State University Developmental Center for Handicapped Persons.

Carter, G. and Jancar, J. 1983. Mortality in the mentally handicapped: A 50 year survey at the stoke park group of hospitals. *American Journal of Mental Deficiency Research* 27:143–56.

Catapano, P.; Levy, J. and Levy, P. 1985. Day activity and vocational program services. In Janicki, M. & Wisniewski, H., eds. *Aging and developmental disabilities: Issues and approaches.* 305–23. Baltimore: Paul H. Brookes.

Chappell, N. 1988. Long term care in Canada. In Rathbone-McGuan, E. & Havens, B., eds. *North American elders: United States and Canadian perspectives.* 73–88. New York: Greenwood Press.

Chappell, N. and Blandford, A. 1987. Health service utilization by elderly persons. *Canadian Journal of Sociology* 12:195–214.

Cockerham, W. 1989. *Medical sociology.* Englewood Cliffs, NJ: Prentice Hall.

Cotton, P.; Sison, G. and Starr, S. 1981. Comparing elderly mentally retarded and non-mentally retarded individuals: Who are they? What are their needs? *The Gerontologist.* 21:359–60.

Dobrof, R. 1985. Some observations from the field of aging. In Janicki, M. & Wisniewski, H., eds. *Aging and developmental disabilities: Issues and approaches.* 403–15. Baltimore: Paul H. Brookes.

Eve, S. 1982. Use of health maintenance organizations by older adults. *Research on Aging* 4:179–203.

Eve, S. 1984. Age strata differences in health care services utilization among adults in the United States. *Sociological Focus* 17:105–20.

Eve, S. 1988. A longitudinal study of use of health care services among older women. *Journal of Gerontology* 43.

Eve, S. and Friedsam, H. 1980. Multivariate analysis of health care services utilization among older Texans. *Journal of Health and Human Resources Administration* 3:169–91.

Eve, S.; Watson, J. and Reiss, E. 1980. *Use of health care services among older adults.* Paper presented at the annual meeting of the Gerontological Society of America, San Diego, California.

Hatcher, G. H.; Hatcher, P. R. and Hatcher, E. C. 1984. Health services in Canada. In Raffel, M. W., ed. *Comparative health systems: Descriptive analyses of fourteen national health systems.* 86–132. University Park, PA: The Pennsylvania State University Press.

Hauber, F.; Rotegard, L. and Bruininks, R. 1985. Characteristics of residential services for older/elderly mentally retarded persons. In Janicki, M. & Wisniewski, H., eds. *Aging and developmental disabilities: Issues and approaches.* 327–50. Baltimore, Maryland: Paul H. Brookes.

Jacobson, J.; Sutton, M. and Janicki, M. 1985. Demography and characteristics of aging and aged mentally retarded persons. In Janicki, M. & Wisniewski, H., eds. *Aging and developmental disabilities: Issues and approaches.* 115–41. Baltimore: Paul H. Brookes.

Kane, R. and Kane, R. 1990. Health care for older people: organizational and policy issues. In Binstock, R. & George, L., eds. *Handbook of aging and the social sciences.* 415–37. San Diego: Academic Press.

Kastenbaum, R. 1964. The reluctant therapist. In Kastenbaum, R., ed. *New thoughts on old age.* 139–45. New York: Springer Publishing.

Kelly, S.; Larsen, P. and Groeneweg, G. 1988. *A survey of the health care needs and the accessibility of the appropriate generic health services for adults with developmental disabilities.* Calgary, Alberta: The Vocational and Rehabilitation Research Institute.

Light, D. 1986. Comparing health care systems: Lessons from East and West Germany. In Conrad, P. & Kern, R., eds. *The sociology of health and illness.* 429–43. New York: St. Martin's Press.

Lippman, L. and Loberg, D. 1985. An overview of developmental disabilities. In Janicki, M. & Wisniewski, H., eds. *Aging and developmental disabilities: Issues and approaches.* 41–58. Baltimore: Paul H. Brookes.

*Mental health planning survey.* 1979. Report of the Mental Health Planning Survey of British Columbia. British Columbia.

Miniszek, N. 1983. Development of Alzheimer's disease in Down's syndrome individuals. *American Journal of Mental Deficiency Research* 87:377–85.

Nelson, R. and Crocker, A. 1979. The medical care of mentally retarded persons in public residential facilities. *New England Journal of Medicine* 299:1039–44.

Norusis, M. 1988. *SPSS-X advanced statistics guide.* New York, New York: McGraw-Hill.

Robinson, D. 1987. *The mentally retarded elderly: Their problems, options, and the future.* Unpublished manuscript, University of North Texas.

Rose, T. and Ansello, E. 1987. *Aging and developmental disabilities: Research and planning.* College Park, MD: Center on Aging, University of Maryland.

Rose, T. and Janicki, M. 1986. Older developmentally disabled adults: A forgotten population. *Aging Network News* III(5):1.

Schaefer, R. T. 1989. *Sociology.* New York: McGraw-Hill.

Seltzer, M. and Seltzer, G. 1985. The elderly mentally retarded: A group in need of service. *Journal of Gerontological Social Work* 8:99–119.

Smith, C. and Herman, N. 1988. The chronic mentally ill in Canada. In Rathbone-McGuan, E. & Havens, B., eds. *North American Elders: United States and Canadian Perspectives.* 111–21. New York: Greenwood Press.

Snider, E. 1980. Factors influencing health service knowledge among the elderly. *Journal of Health and Social Behavior* 21:371–7.

Starrett, R. A.; Wright, R.; Mindel, C. H. and Tran, T. V. 1989. The use of social services by Hispanic elderly: A comparison of Mexican American, Puerto Rican, and Cuban elderly. *Journal of Social Service Research* 13(1):1–25.

Statistics Canada. 1989. *Disabled persons have higher institutionalization rate: Focus on seniors.* Ottawa, Ontario: Statistics Canada.

Statistics Canada. 1988. *Health and activity limitation survey: User's guide.* Ottawa, Ontario: Statistics Canada.

Sweeney, D. 1980. Denied, ignored, or forgotten? An assessment of community services for older developmentally disabled persons. In Sweeney, D. & Wilson, T., eds. *Double jeopardy: The plight of aging and aged developmentally disabled Americans.* Ann Arbor: University of Michigan Institute for the Study of Mental Retardation and Related Disabilities.

Tenhoor, W. 1982. United States: Health and personal social services. In Hokenstad, M. & Ritvo, R., eds. *Linking health care and social services.* 25–59. Beverly Hills, California: Sage Publications.

Walz, T.; Harper, D. and Wilson, J. 1986. The aging developmentally disabled person. *The Gerontologist* 26(6):622–9.

Wan, T. and Soifer, S. 1974. Determinants of physician utilization: A causal analysis. *Journal of Health and Social Behavior* 15:100–8.

Wasylenki, D. 1982. The psychogeriatric problem. *Canada's Mental Health* 30(3):16–19.

Wasylenki, D.; Doering, P.; Lancee, W. and Freedman, S. 1985. Psychiatric aftercare in a metropolitan setting. *Canadian Journal of Psychiatry* 30:329–36.

Weinberg, M. 1977. Penwern Hall: Lifetime care for the mentally handicapped. *Social Work Today* 8(44):7–9.

Wolinsky, F. 1976. Health service utilization and attitudes toward health maintenance organizations: A theoretical and methodological discussion. *Journal of Health and Social Behavior* 17:221–36.

Wolinsky, F. 1978. Assessing the effects of predisposing, enabling, and illness-morbidity characteristics on health service utilization. *Journal of Health and Social Behavior* 19:384–96.

Wolinsky, F., 1988. *The sociology of health: principles, practitioners, and issues.* Belmont, CA: Wadsworth.

Wolinsky, F.; Coe, R.; Miller, D.; Prendergrast, J.; Creel, M. and Chavez, M. 1983. Health services utilization among the noninstitutionalized elderly. *Journal of Health and Social Behavior* 24:325–36.

Wolinsky, F. and Coe, R. 1984. Physician and hospital utilization among elderly adults: An analysis of the health interview survey. *Journal of Gerontology* 39:334–41.

Wolinsky, F.; Moseley, R. and Coe, R. 1986. A cohort analysis of the use of health services by elderly Americans. *Journal of Health and Social Behavior* 27:209–19.

# Section 2

# Critical
# Perspectives

# Critical Perspectives

In the second section of this edited volume, six papers are presented that take a critical look at the Canadian health care system.

The first chapter is by Michael Rachlis, a Canadian physician who is currently an independent consultant specializing in policy analysis, epidemiology and program analysis, and the author of the acclaimed book, *The Canadian Health Care System: A Second Opinion*. Dr. Rachlis compares the Canadian and the U.S. health care systems and draws a number of comparisons of the two systems, including costs of the system (the U.S. system costs more); eligibility and access to care (all Canadians are eligible for health insurance as a right of citizenship while in the U.S. one-third of the population is uninsured or underinsured); access to high technology specialized services (poor Canadians have greater access than poor Americans but rich Americans have greater access than rich Canadians); access to non-high technology services (Canadians use more hospital and physicians services than do Americans); medical practice (most Canadian physicians are in private practice on a fee for service basis and multispecialty group practice is very uncommon); and health status (Canadians are healthier than Americans on most indicators). Rachlis identified the three major problems with the Canadian system as (1) too much emphasis on curative medicine rather than health promotion and disease prevention; inefficient organization and financing (including too much use of institutional care and use of the fee for service payment mechanism); and too little assurance of quality of care including too little monitoring of physicians. Rachlis concludes by emphasizing that these three problems are not a necessary consequence of a single payer system but are related primarily to methods os organization and financing.

Mark Rosenberg, Ph.D., is a geographer at Queen's University in Ontario. In his chapter, "Aging and Public Policy for Canada in the Year 200," Dr. Rosenberg examines Canada's increasing characteristics as a post-industrial ˙nation and the increasing percentage of the population that is over the age of 65. He examines the question "What kind of health care systems can Canada and the United States produce as they become increasingly post-industrial societies where a growing percentage of the population is elderly?" He predicts that future policy debates in Canada will include discussions of targeting those elderly people most in need; rationalization, or consolidation and/or closure of services and facilities; privatization of services; encouraging families to provide more services for the elderly, and re-allocation of public spending to different sectors and/or to different groups.

Chapter 9 is co-authored by Joseph R. Oppong, Ph.D., of the Department of Geography at the University of North Texas, and Joseph Mensah of the Department of

Humanities and Social Sciences in Medicine Hat College in Alberta. The chapter, "The Canadian Health System: Lessons from Alberta for the United States," argues that the province of Ontario, the site of the majority of research on the Canadian health care system, is very different from most of the other eleven provinces and territories and that these other areas need to be studied to provide a fuller picture of the advantages and disadvantages of the Canadian health care system. Alberta has only one-fifth the population of Ontario and a lower percentage of its population is over the age of 65. Older adults use a disproportionate share of the health care services and this trend is expected to continue with the aging of the population. Alberta is one of only two provinces that charge residents a monthly premium for their health insurance coverage. The province raises one-third of the cost of the plan annually and the goal is to have premiums cover one-half of the annual costs. However, the fee is waived for basic care for senior citizens, widows and their dependents. Health and support services are provided to help older people remain in their homes as long as possible, and the Alberta Aids to Daily Living Program provided medical equipment and supplies to older adults living at home with a chronic or terminal illness or a disability. Major problems that the province faces include limiting the number of physicians and the number of physician initiated visits. Recommendations for the U.S. include making primary care coverage universal, encouraging alternative primary care providers, limiting the increase in number of physicians, developing physician benefit schemes to limit malpractice insurance, and developing cost effective care for the elderly.

Ralph Anderson, M.D., Professor and Chairman of the Department of Obstetrics and Gynecology at John Peter Smith Hospital in Fort Worth, is a Canadian physician who is currently practicing in the United States. In the chapter "Health Care Reform in the United States: The Canadian Health Care System: What Should We Adopt?" he discusses ten principals that he believes the U.S. should focus on in developing health care reform. These principals are: (1) comprehensive services, (2) reasonable access to services, (3) universal coverage, (4) portable services, (5) patient's right to choose, (6) high quality treatment with state of the art technology, (7) comprehensible, efficient and easily managed bureaucracy, (8) affordability and fair financing, (9) medical liability insurance reform, and (10) support from patients, providers, and financial supporters. In his conclusion, Dr. Anderson argues that an ideal health care system can be created which combines the American values of freedom and market forces with the Canadian values of fairness and equity.

Ralph A. H. Kinch, M.D., is a British physician who practiced for many years in Quebec before coming to the United States to practice in John Peter Smith Hospital in Fort Worth, Texas. In his chapter, "The Rocky Trail of Acceptance of Medicare by

Canadian Physicians: A Short History," Dr. Kinch outlines the history of physician reaction to the Canadian Medicare plan. He focuses on the influence of Norman Bethune, a physician at the Royal Victoria Hospital in Quebec who advocated adopting a system of socialized medicine for Canada in the 1930s, and Tommy Douglas, who headed the Socialist Cooperation Commonwealth Foundation government in Saskatchewan in 1994, and who introduced a proposal for comprehensive health care benefits for the elderly, mothers and wards of the state. When the Federal Government passed the Hospital Insurance and Diagnostic Services in 1957, he had the money to expand these services to the entire population of the province. Physicians resisted that plan and responded with a strike in 1962. When the National Medicare Plan was adopted in 1966, physicians in Quebec staged a second strike, which coincided with a nation emergency in which a Canadian cabinet minister was murdered. Physicians returned to work, disheartened by the bloodshed. A final crisis occurred when a bill was introduced in 1984 to prohibit extra billing over and above the rates Medicare paid. The pressure of public opinion led to liberals, socialists and conservatives unanimously passing the bill.

# Chapter 7

## The Canadian Experience with Public Health Insurance

*Michael M. Rachlis, MD, MSc, FRCPC*
*Epidemiology, Program Evaluation, Policy Analysis*
*Toronto, Ontario*

### INTRODUCTION

Recently, representatives of the American Medical Association and the health insurance industry have launched a well-funded attack on the Canadian health care system. Typically, the stories tell of long lines for high technology services. In 1992, President Bush claimed that Canadians had to wait six months for heart surgery and couldn't choose their own doctors. Newt Gingrich, Republican whip in the House of Representatives claimed that it was illegal for Canadians over 65 to get many operations. None of these assertions are true. However, the Canadian system does have its problems and a careful study of the Canadian system is essential for Americans to make wise choices about the future of their system.

This paper compares the two systems, identifies the problems which the Canadian system faces, and then outlines some lessons Americans might draw from the Canadian example.

**The costs of the two systems**

There are many different methods of comparing the costs of two countries' health care systems (Scheiber and Poullier, 1989). However, if one is interested in relative cost-control for health care amongst different countries the best method of comparison is the proportion of the economy devoted to health care (e. g., gross domestic product or GDP). The proportion of GDP also allows comparisons to be made both at a point in time and over time (Scheiber, Poullier and Greenwald, 1992). It is important to remember that this statistic is a ratio and an increased proportion of GDP devoted to health care could reflect either increasing health care costs or poor GDP growth or both.

In 1971, when Canada had fully implemented national health insurance both the US and Canada spent approximately 7% of their GDPs on health care. By 1991, Canada spent 9.9% of GDP on health care while the US spent 13.2% (Scheiber, Poullier and Greenwald, 1992).

Most of this difference is due to lower costs of administration, lower payments to physicians, and lower hospital costs. In 1985, these three items were responsible for 0.59%, 4.18%, and 2.07% of the US Gross National Product[1] respectively compared to 0.11%, 3.48%, and 1.35% of the Canadian GNP (Evans, Lomas, Barer, *et al.*, 1989).

Administrative savings are mainly due to the efficiencies from the economies of scale of Canada's large provincial health insurance plans (Woolhandler and Himmelstein, 1991). Hospital expenditures are higher in the US primarily because of the higher intensity of servicing of hospitalized patients (Redelmeier and Fuchs, 1993). However, there may be little, if any, benefits from this increased servicing (Rouleau, Moye, Pfeffer, *et al.*, 1993).

**Eligibility and Access to Care**

All Canadians are eligible for health insurance as a right of citizenship. In fact, landed immigrants, established refugees, and foreigners claiming refugee status are also eligible for health insurance. Two provinces (Alberta and British Columbia) and one territory (The Yukon) charge their residents health insurance premiums although payment of premiums is not required to be eligible for insurance coverage. There have been anecdotal reports of persons being denied care in these provinces if they have not paid their premiums (Hall, 1980 and NCW, 1982).

The Canada Health Act passed by the Canadian parliament in 1984 outlines the criteria which must be met by provincial health insurance plans to be eligible for federal government assistance. One of the criteria, comprehensiveness, requires the provinces to insure all 'medically necessary' care provided by dentists within hospitals and physicians in hospitals and ambulatory care settings. There is considerable variation in the other services provided but most provinces provide some coverage for prescription drugs and long-term care (both institutional and community).

Almost all Canadians live within 30 miles of a hospital. There are large numbers of physicians in urban areas and the south of the country within 100 miles of the American border. Physicians do locate their practices within poor urban neighbourhoods, contrary to the US situation. There are problems attracting physicians to northern and rural areas of the country (Borsellino, 1991 and Johnston, 1992). There is some evidence that rural residents in southern Canada consume the same number of physicians services although they may have to travel to receive them (Horne, 1986). Canadians in rural and remote settings also have less accessibility to non-medical services such as psychology and rehabilitation. Primary care nursing services are available in almost all remote communities.

Canadians may visit any doctor they wish at any time when they can arrange an appointment. Provincial health insurance plans only pay specialists at general practitioner rates if there is no GP referral. However, specialists will often extract the name of a GP from the patient and add that doctor's health insurance billing number to the insurance claim to ensure payment at the higher rate. In some communities doctors focus care through family physicians but in others internists, gynecologists, and pediatricians provide significant amounts of primary care.

**Access and Utilization of high-technology specialized services**

The most serious American criticisms of the Canadian health care system focus on access to high technology care. Typically, provincial governments must provide specific approvals for expensive high-technology services such as open-heart surgery, transplantation, and magnetic resonance imaging (MRI). There are limitations to the data in making these comparisons. However, the overall conclusions of the existing data are:

> 1. Canadians do have lower utilization of high capital, high-technology services, especially open-heart surgery, CAT scanners, and MRI scanners.
> 2. Low income Canadians have better access to high technology services than uninsured or poorly insured Americans.
> 3. Canadians, on average, have similar access to high-technology services for emergent and urgent conditions as well-insured Americans.
> 4. Canadians, on average, have less access to high-technology services for elective and non-urgent conditions than well-insured Americans.

The United States has over 2000 MRI scanners while, as of October, 1992, Canada had only 22 (Morgan, 1993). However, when there are many scanners with most operating at below peak capacity, the price per unit of service is increased. Also, uninsured and poorly insured Americans, representing perhaps 25% of the population, have little or no access to MRI (Morgan, 1993).

In 1987, the overall US rate for coronary artery bypass surgery (CABS) was 95 per 100,000 (Killip, 1988), while the Canadian rate for 1988-89 fiscal was approximately 55 (Higginson, Cairns, Keon and Smith, 1992). The US rate for those under 65 is only about 30% higher than in Canada while the rate is 50 to 75% higher for the elderly. In the US there is a strong positive association between insurance status and rates of CABS while in Canada there is not (Wenneker, Weissman and Epstein, 1990; Goldberg, *et al.*, 1992; Anderson, Grumbach, Luft, *et al.*, 1993).

There has been particular concern raised in the US about lack of access to CABS in Canada. However, US opponents of public health insurance have played on the general ignorance about the urgent nature of this procedure. The public tends to believe that once CABS is recommended it is necessary immediately or the patient is at great vital risk. In fact, only patients with left main coronary artery obstruction or multi-vessel disease with very unstable angina have more than a 0.33% death rate per month on a waiting list (Rachlis, Olak, and Naylor, 1991). Many patients face no vital risk while waiting although they may suffer physically, psychologically, and economically (Mulgan and Logan, 1990; Dupuis, Kennedy, Perrault, Lambany and David, 1990). High risk patients are typically only 15 to 20% of any centre's total patients (Christakis, Ivanov, Weisel, *et al.*, and Naylor, 1993).

One study has noted that Canadian doctors have implicitly used clinical criteria to priorize patients waiting for CABS (Naylor). Starting with Ontario in 1989, the Canadian provinces have been developing explicit priorization processes for CABS. Various investigations of heart surgery waiting lists have revealed that some surgeons (and institutions) have long waiting lists while others have much shorter lists (Vancouver General Hospital, 1990; Katz, Mizgala and Welch, 1991; Naylor, 1991). Unfortunately, these investigations have revealed little sharing of patients between surgeons and hospitals to optimize waiting times. In Ontario, waiting times for CABS have been reduced through a provincial triage and registry program and only a 10% increase in overall surgical capacity.

One Canadian investigator of waiting lists, Dr. C. David Naylor of Toronto has called for, "explicit queue-forming criteria, audits for institution-specific referral biases, and mechanisms to redistribute patients . . . to optimize queue-based allocating of scarce hospital services."

**Access and Utilization of non-high technology services**

Canadians consume more hospital and physicians services than do Americans. In 1989, Americans used 814 hospital days per 1000 (National Center for Health Statistics, 1992) while the comparable figure was 1164 days per 1000 in Ontario, Canada's largest province (Ontario Ministry of Health, 1988/89). In 1987, Canadians used 50% more physicians' services than Americans (Fuchs and Hahn, 1990). In 1987, residents of Ontario had a rate of major surgery[2] 35% higher than California and 15% higher than New York State (Anderson, 1993).

Canadians have much better access to primary care services. In 1988, 52.5% of Canadian physicians were general or family practitioners whereas in the US only 13.3% of physicians were in these categories (U.S. General Accounting Office, 1991). One study across ten countries found that Canada had a much higher rating than the US on five characteristics of primary care (Starfield, 1991).

Most hospitals are non-profit private corporations. Some boards are elected by general suffrage from local government area but most hospital corporations have limited membership with self-replicating boards. The provincial ministries of health make almost no decisions about which services are offered by hospitals. There is little government oversight of a hospital operations. In fact, the hospital branch of the Ontario ministry of health has only 80 non-clerical staff to manage a budget of over $8 billion (CAN). In 1991, the Toronto General Hospital told the Ontario provincial auditor that it could not look at the records of a $3.2 million expenditure. Hospital administration claimed that these expenditures were made with non-government money. It is true that about 25% of the hospital's $300 million budget is from non-Ontario government sources (fees for private rooms, televisions, parking, etc.) but as the auditor commented,

> Because the hospital operates with one main bank account, we could not verify that these items had been purchased with non-ministry funds. (Ontario Provincial Auditor, 1991)

The unaudited expenditures had included $1.2 million for a controversial and dysfunctional computer system. Two years later, the details of that expenditure remain unexamined by a public authority.

Provinces fund their hospitals with global budgets. Some provinces are now using a modification of the DRG system to calculate a portion of the budget but, by and large, the budgets have been increased over time across the board with little adjustment for volume or case mix. The result is a situation where some communities are relatively richly endowed with resources compared to others. However, there is little hard data of the scope of the problem and the same situation pertains in other countries with as widely disparate funding mechanisms as the U.S. (Wennberg, Freeman and Culp, 1987) and the United Kingdom (Rodwin, 1984).

The decisions about resource allocation within hospitals are determined mainly by the physician group. For example, the chief of surgery is typically responsible for the allocation of operating room time. On closer examination many complaints about lack of funding for certain specialty services are really a cry for public assistance when the specialist has lost the internal .hospital debate. Recently, with increased budgetary pressures, hospital administrators have been playing a more active role. With the development of better systems for determining actual patient costs, administrators have targeted high cost services such as orthopedics and neurosurgery for cuts.

Certain especially high-cost services such as transplantation, cardiac surgery, and diagnostic imaging require specific ministry of health approval. However, doctors and administrators have some discretion in these areas as well. In 1988 doctors and hospitals put political pressure on the Ontario Ministry of Health to increase funding for cardiac surgery. However, a later government inquiry found that at the height of the perceived crisis, the Toronto General Hospital department of surgery had re-allocated one and one-half days of operating room time from cardiac surgery to general surgery (Kaminski, Sibbald and Davis, 1989).[3]

## Medical practice

Most Canadian physicians are in private practice and are paid on a fee-for-service basis. Most provinces have instituted electronic billing and most doctors are paid within 2 to 4 weeks of claim submission. In Ontario in fiscal 1992–93, 96.5 percent of claims were paid within four weeks of submission (Fitzpatrick, 1993). In Ontario from 1982 to 1992, an average of 0.2% of doctors per year were asked to repay moneys which had been paid by the province's health insurance plan (Peachey, 1993). There are no user charges allowed for basic medical and hospital care. Doctors do submit bills to workers' compensation agencies and, are allowed to bill patients directly for services not covered by the plan (e. g., insurance forms, cosmetic plastic surgery).

Multi-specialty group practice is very uncommon. There are about 250 community health centres (CHCs) where doctors are paid salaries and there are other primary care professionals (nurses, social workers). 170 of these are in Quebec where they are called CLSCs (Centre Local Services Communitaire. Quebec has given CLSCs a clear mandate to provide general primary care as well as home care and children's mental health. CLSCs have community boards are given discretion to identify three priority areas to meet their own local community needs. Quebec now devotes over 5% of its overall health budget to the CLSCs.

Ontario has almost 50 CHCs and the province is committed to expanding the program by 3 centres per year. Ontario's CHCs are largely designed to alleviate non-financial barriers to access for specific groups (e.g., the poor, frail elderly, immigrant communities, francophone minorities).

Ontario has also established 90 health service organizations (HSOs) which receive capitation payments for ambulatory care. There are three community governed HSOs and two with University affiliation while the balance are owned by family doctors. Most are small (3000 to 6000 patients) but the Sault Ste Marie Group Health Association clinic is governed by a community board and has over 30,000 patients. The program was frozen three years ago because of provincial concerns about lack of accountability. The ministry is currently negotiating program changes with the Ontario Medical Association (for the private HSOs) and individual non-profit HSOs.

Ontario has also initiated the comprehensive health organization (CHO) program. The CHO will receive provincial capitation payments for ambulatory and acute hospital care. It might potentially incorporate funding for long-term care and prescription drugs. CHOs will be governed by non-profit community boards. On paper the funding looks remarkably similar to a US health maintenance organization (HMO).

However, the ministry has only funded two CHOs so far they will not open until the fall of 1994, at the earliest.[4] They are located in remote communities (Fort Francis and Wawa) and will likely function as quasi-governmental regional health authorities.

**Health status**

General social and economic conditions have much more impact than health care on conventional measures of health status such as life expectancy and infant mortality. However, if Canada's health care system was as inadequate as some American critics have suggested, these should be reflected in poorer health status for Canadians. In fact, Canadians enjoy better health status than Americans. (see table one)

In recent years the US record for low birthweight has actually been getting worse while Canada's has continued to improve. Low birthweight is the major predictor of infant mortality and is effected in minor fashion by traditional pre-natal care. One recent study has suggested that 60% of the difference in infant mortality rates between Canada and the US is due to the higher rate of low birthweight in the United States (Liu, Moon, Sulvetta, and Chawla, 1992).

However, there are numerous examples of where US patients' health status has been adversely affected by financial barriers to care. Recent studies have documented decreased access and poorer outcomes according to financial situation and/or insurance status for newborns (Braveman, Oliva, Miller, *et al.*, 1989), glaucoma (Javitt, McBean, Nicholson, *et al.*, 1991 and Sommer, Tielsch, Katz, *et al.*, 1991), childhood immunization (Zylke, 1991), and mammography and pap smears (Calle, Flanders, Thun, *et al.*, 1993). One study showed that the uninsured were more likely to die after hospital admission (Hadley, Steinberg and Feder, 1991).

**Problems with Canada's health care system**

Canada's health care system faces a similar set of problems as do the health care systems of other industrialized countries including the US. However, the US has, by far, the most serious problems with costs and access. The major problems identified with Canada's system by a series of recent government reports include:

1. Too much focus on curative medicine as opposed to health promotion and disease prevention.
2. Inefficiencies due to the organization and financing of the system. For example, Canadians overuse institutional services compared with community services. Also, the predominant method of physician payment is fee-for-service.

3. Inadequate quality assurance leading to the provision of inappropriate care. There are few explicit written standards. There is little monitoring
of physicians, even by other doctors.

It is important for Americans to realize that these problems are specific to the
model of single-payer plan implemented by Canada. None of these problems are
related to public health insurance. Rather, they are related to relatively unaccountable
private management of the system by doctors and hospitals.

**Other effects of public health insurance**

In Canada, management and labour do not negotiate basic health benefits. They do
negotiate for so-called extended health benefits such as dental care and prescription
drugs. However, in the United States, negotiations about basic health benefits have
become increasingly acrimonious. In 1990, health care was the major issue in 83% of
negotiations and 55% of strikes and lockouts (AFL-CIO, 1991).

Also, the US system of health insurance increases costs to business. Chrysler has
estimated that it cost $700 (1988 US dollars) in health benefits for each car it produced
in the US but only $233 for the cars it produced in Canada. This evidence led Ontario
Premier Bob Rae to comment,

> The cost advantage for us in manufacturing in terms of the health care issue
> is enormous and it's growing. The longer the Americans take to resolve this,
> the happier I'll be. (Rae, 1993)

A consistent theme of various government health reports of the past two decades
has been that health care is not nearly as important for the population's health as social
and economic factors. Other countries spend less of their economy on health care than
the US but spend more on other areas of social policy (Health Care Financing Review,
1993 and Smeeding, 1992). This is reflected in the high rates of officially designated
poverty in the US compared to other industrialized nations. There is little discussion
within the United States of the opportunity costs of the world's most expensive health
care system. However, the massive resources allocated to the treatment of illness
clearly preclude investments in other social programs which would more efficiently
promote health.

**Lessons for Americans from Canadian Public Health Insurance**

The main lessons for Americans from Canada's health care system are as follows:

1. The cost savings from a single-payer plan are real. Canada's system is approximately 3% of Gross Domestic Product less expensive that the US. The savings are due to factors associated with a single-payer plan, including lower administrative costs and reduced hospital and physicians costs.

2. Canadians have better access to almost all health services than do Americans. Canadians use more physicians' services and hospital services than do Americans.

3. Canadians, on average, have less access to high-technology services than do well-insured Americans. However, it appears the health impact of this decreased access is minimal, and so far, anecdotal. This is in contrast to the documented adverse impact on the uninsured and poorly insured in the US.

4. The major problems of Canada's health care system have little or nothing to do with single-payer financing. The problems relate to the method of organization and financing of the largely private delivery system. The US could implement its own national health program and avoid Canada's difficulties.

**Table one: Recent health status indicators in Canada and the United States**

|  | Canada | United States |
|---|---|---|
| Infant Mortality | 0.068%<br>1990 | 0.091%<br>1990 |
| Low birthweight<br>(< 2500 grams) | 5.1%<br>1989 | 7.05%<br>1989 |
| Very low birthweight<br>(< 1500 grams) | 0.84%<br>1989 | 1.28%<br>1989 |
| Life expectancy<br>Male | 73.4 years<br>1988 | 71.5 years<br>1988 |
| Female | 80.3 years | 78.3 years |
| Expectancy at 65 years<br>Male | 15.0 years<br>1988 | 14.9 years<br>1988 |
| Female | 19.6 years<br>1988 | 18.6 years<br>1988 |

Sources:
National Center for Health Statistics, 1991.
Scheiber, Poullier, and Greenwald, 1992.
Statistics Canada, 1991.

## Notes

[1]GNP is the same as GDP except it includes profits of national corporations which are repatriated. The difference is less than 5%.

[2]Defined as a procedure which was not performed on a not-for-admission basis in 1987.

[3]This could have increased the number of open-heart procedures in Metropolitan Toronto at the time by almost 10%.

[4]The CHO is to be located in Fort Francis which is a pulp and paper town of 9,000 near the Minnesota border.

## References

AFL-CIO Department of Employee Benefits. 1991. *The permanent replacement of workers striking over health care benefits in 1990*, June.

Anderson, G. 1993. Institute for Clinical Evaluative Sciences. Toronto, Ontario. June 22.

Anderson, G.; Grumbach, K.; Luft, H., *et al*. 1993. The use of coronary artery bypass surgery in the United States and Canada: The influence of age and income.*Journal of the American Medical Association* 269:1661–69.

Borsellino, M. 1991. Jobs still go begging in the 'rural' city of Prince George. *Medical Post*, September 10.

Braveman, P.; Oliva, G.; Miller, M. G., *et al*. 1989. Adverse outcomes and lack of health insurance among newborns in an eight county area of California, 1982–1986. *New England Journal of Medicine* 321:508–13.

Calle, E. E.; Flanders, D.; Thun, M. J.,*et al*. 1993. Demographic predictors of mammography and pap smear screening in US women. *American Journal of Public Health*, 83:53–60.

Christakis G. T.; Ivanov J.; Weisel R. D., *et al*. The changing pattern of coronary artery bypass surgery.

Dupuis, G.; Kennedy, E.; Perrault, J.; Lambany, M. C. and David, P. 1990. The hidden costs of delayed bypass surgery. *Clinical Investigational Medicine* 13(suppl):C35(1).

Evans, R. G.; Lomas, J.; Barer, M. L.; *et al*. 1989. Controlling health expenditures—the Canadian reality. *New England Journal of Medicine* 320:571–7.

Fitzpatrick, S. Personal communication. Ontario Health Insurance Plan. October 13, 1993.

Fuchs, V. R. and Hahn, J. S. 1990. How does Canada do it? A comparison of expenditures for physicians' services in the United States and Canada. *New England Journal of Medicine* 323:884–90.

General Accounting Office. 1991. *Canadian health insurance: lessons for the United States*. June. 38.

Goldberg, K. C.,*et al*. 1992. Racial and community factors influencing coronary artery bypass graft surgery rates for all 1986 medicare patients. *Journal of the American Medical Association* 267:1473–7.

Hadley, J.; Steinberg, E. P. and Feder, J. 1991. *Journal of the American Medical Association* 265:374–9.

Hall, M. 1980. *Canada's national-provincial health program for the 1980s.* Health and Welfare Canada.

Higginson, L. A. J.; Cairns, J. A.; Keon, W. I. and Smith, E. R. 1992. Rates of cardiac catheterization, coronary angioplasty, and open-heart surgery in adults. *Canadian Medical Association Journal* 146:921–5. This article gives the rate for open-heart procedures as 63 per 100,000 population. CABS is typically performed in 85% of open-heart procedures.

Horne, J. M., ed. 1986. Searching for shortage: A population-based analysis of medical care utilization in "underdoctored" and "undoctored" communities in rural Manitoba. *Proceedings of the Third Canadian Conference on Health Economics.* Department of Social and Preventive Medicine. Winnipeg: The University of Manitoba.

Javitt, J. C.; McBean, A. M.; Nicholson, G. A., *et al.* 1991. *New England Journal of Medicine* 325:1418–22.

Johnston 1992. Shortage of psychiatrists plaguing Northern Ontario. *Canadian Medical Association Journal* 146:1625–6.

Kaminski, V. L.; Sibbald, W. J. and Davis, E. M. 1989. Investigation of Cardiac surgery at St. Michael's Hospital. Final Report. Toronto, Ontario. February.

Katz, S. J.; Mizgala, H. F. and Welch, H. G. 1991. British Columbia sends patients to Seattle for Coronary Artery Surgery. *Journal of the American Medical Association* 266:1108–11.

Killip, T. 1988. Twenty years of coronary bypass surgery. *New England Journal of Medicine* 319:366–8.

Liu, K.; Moon, M.; Sulvetta, M. and Chawla, J. 1992. International infant mortality rankings: A look behind the numbers. *Health Care Financing Review* 13(4):105–18.

Morgan, B.G. 1993. Patient access to magnetic resonance imaging centers in Orange County, California. *New England Journal of Medicine* 328:884–5.

Mulgan, R. and Logan, R. L. 1990. The coronary bypass waiting list: A social evaluation. *New Zealand Medical Journal* 103:371–2.

National Center for Health Statistics. 1991. Hyattsville, Maryland: Public Health Service, 1992. The figures used are for care of civilians in non-Federal short stay hospitals.

National Council of Welfare. 1982. *Medicare: The public good and private practice.* Health and Welfare Canada.

Naylor, C. D. 1991. A different view of queues in Ontario. *Health Affairs* 10(3):110–28.

Naylor, C. D. 1993. Queueing for coronary surgery during a severe supply-demand mismatch in a Canadian referral centre: A case study of implicit rationing. *Institute for Clinical Evaluative Sciences.* Working paper #1. Toronto: Sunnybrook Hospital.

Ontario Ministry of Health. 1988. Hospital Statistics 1988/89. This statistic was calculated for Ontario using the population of 9,426,200 from the Vital statistics fo the province for 1988 and the days of care in acute care hospitals.

Ontario Provincial Auditor. 1991. Annual Report.

Peachey, D. K. 1993. The Medical Review Committee in Ontario: A guide for physicians. *Ontario Medical Review* June:15–26.

Rachlis, M. M.; Olak, J. and Naylor, C. D. 1991. The vital risk of delayed coronary surgery: Lessons from the randomized trials. *Iatrogenics* 1:103–11.

Rae, B. 1993. Ontario Premier to the Ontario Home Builders' Association. January 12.

Redelmeier, D. A. and Fuchs, V. R. 1993. Hospital expenditures in the United States and Canada. *New England Journal of Medicine* 328:772–8.

Rodwin, V. 1984. *The Health Planning Predicament*. UK report of the Regional Allocation Working Party (RAWP), Berkeley: The University of California Press.

Rouleau, J. L.; Moye, L. A.; Pfeffer, M. A., *et al.* 1993. A comparison of management patterns after acute myocardial infarction in Canada and the United States. *New England Journal of Medicine* 328:779–84.

Scheiber, G. J. and Poullier, J. P. 1989. Overview of international comparisons of health care expenditures. *Health Care Financing Review*, Annual Supplement:1–7.

Scheiber, G. J.; Poullier, J. P. and Greenwald, L. M. 1992. U.S. health expenditure performance: An international comparison and data update. *Health Care Financing Review* 13(4):1–17.

Smeeding, T. M. 1992. Why the U.S. antipoverty system doesn't work very well. *Chanleenge* January-February, 30–35.

Sommer, A.; Tielsch, J. M.; Katz, J., *et al.* 1991. *New England Journal of Medicine* 325:1412–7.

Starfield, B. 1991. Primary care and health: A cross-national comparison. *Journal of American Medical Association* 266:2268–71.

Statistics Canada. 1991.

Vancouver General Hospital. 1990. Heart surgery waiting list data. February to April.

Wennberg, J. E.; Freeman, J. L. and Culp J. 1987. Are hospital services rationed in New Haven or over-utilized in Boston? *Lancet* i:1185–88.

Wenneker, M. B.; Weissman, J. S. and Epstein, A. M. 1990. The assocation of payer with utilization of cardiac procedures in Massachusetts. *Journal of the American Medical Association* 264:1255–60.

Woolhandler, S. and Himmelstein, D. U. 1991. The deteriorating administrative efficiency of the U.S. health-care system. *New England Journal of Medicine* 324:1253–8.

Zylke, J. W. 1991. Declining childhood immunization rates becoming cause for concern. *Journal of the American Medical Association* 266:1321.

# Chapter 8

## Aging and Public Policy for Canada in the Year 2000

*Mark W. Rosenberg, Ph.D.*
*Department of Geography*
*Queen's University*

### INTRODUCTION

One of the most common themes of the current discussions of the provision of health care is the view put forward by some that the root cause of the funding crisis of health care systems is the growing size of the elderly population (see for example, Denton and Spencer, 1983, Foot, 1982). Although this argument has been convincingly challenged on its own terms (see for example Evans, 1987; McDaniel, 1987), there is a need to examine the funding of health care systems and the growth of the elderly population in a broader policy context. In essence the question I wish to pose is what kind of health care systems can Canada and the United States produce as they become increasingly post-industrial societies where a growing percentage of the population is elderly?

To answer this question, this paper is divided into four parts. First, the major themes of Daniel Bell's concept of the post-industrial society are reviewed. It is argued that Bell's proscriptions for a post-industrial society were essentially positive, ones which spoke directly to the new business élites of our societies (i.e., mainly the investment bankers, the advertising and media executives) and indeed to the intellectual élites (i.e., mainly in the universities). Second, it is argued that indeed Canada has become a post-industrial society, but through a different route than the one Bell hypothesized, and therefore the implications for the Canadian population have been different than those that Bell suggested. The route has been through de-industrialization and the concomitant growth of what will be called *low-end services*. The implications are a society that now seems trapped with relatively high structural unemployment rates and growing public sector deficits. In the third part of the paper, the focus is on Canada's elderly population. Links are made between the growing size of the elderly population and the growth in the provision of services which are part of the core of post-industrial society, and at the same time part of its crisis. Finally, the implications for aging and public policy are examined for the elderly population living in post-industrial Canadian society and lessons are drawn for the United States.

### Daniel Bell's Post-Industrial Society

The idea of reviving Daniel Bell's thesis of the post-industrial society at a time when Western Europe is on the brink of uniting, and Eastern Europe and the Commonwealth of Independent States have entered an era of unprecedented uncertainty might seem irrelevant to some, and oddly out of touch to others given the current debates on such topics as *post-modernism* and *eco-feminism* which are now sweeping the social sciences. It is suggested, however, that it is a useful exercise to reflect upon a set of ideas which today has become a reality to the way many live their lives in the most developed countries.

Who would argue that the service sector does not dominate the economies of more and more of the developed countries? What government, be it the government of Canada or the United States, at least in theory, does not actively promote *high technology* and what will be called *high-end services* as the basis for the future prosperity of their people? In making a distinction between *production* and *assembly*, who would argue against the trend, at least in a North American context, towards more and more production moving to Third World countries leaving an industrial sector which is increasingly assembly activities?

If we are going to use post-industrial society as a theme for what follows, then it is useful to begin by reviewing the key elements of Bell's conceptualization of post-industrial society. Bell (1976, p. 12) divides society into three parts: *the social structure, the polity,* and *culture.* These parts of society are further subdivided and each is "ruled by a different axial principle." The social structure consists of the economy, technology and the occupational system and its axial principle is "*economizing*—a way of allocating resources according to principles of least cost, substitutability, optimization, maximization, . . ." The polity is the legislative and judicial institutions of society whose axial principle is "*participation*," mobilized, controlled or demanded by members of society. Culture is the "realm of expressive symbols and meanings" where the axial principle "is the desire for *fulfillment and enhancement of the self.*"

Without dwelling on the adequacy of the division of society or the axial principles, it is important to recognize that the foundation on which Bell builds his forecasts is a debatable one. For instance, take one of the key aspects of post-industrial society, the merging of domestic life and the economy. By this, it is meant that there are now a whole range of service sector industries whose raison d'être is to substitute for various activities associated with domestic life. For example, the fast food industry is a substitute for preparing and eating a meal at home. This aspect of post-industrial society sits ambiguously within Bell's schema. Is it part of the social structure (i.e., based on individuals or families economizing), part of our culture, the realm of expressive symbols and meanings (i.e., the golden arches of MacDonald's, the icon of a material and global world, an expression of ourselves), is it partly both or neither?

A second key aspect of Bell's schema are the *dimensions* of post-industrial society. In the foreword to the 1976 edition, the original 5 dimensions of post-industrial society are expanded to 11. They are only briefly reviewed here. First, there is "*the centrality of theoretical knowledge*" where the departure from industrial society is the merger of abstract ideas and applied science to create new "science-based industries" such as microelectronics, fibre optics and biotechnology. Second is "*the creation of a new intellectual technology*" based on computer programming and high level mathematics which has allowed the development of modelling, simulation, artificial intelligence, etc. Third is "*the spread of a knowledge class*" which is nothing more than the forecast of the growth of a technical and professional class, in a sense the group who are the creators and controllers of theoretical knowledge and intellectual technology. It is the importance that Bell gives to these three dimensions of post-industrial society which is at least part of the reason why the academic community found Bell's arguments so seductive.

The fourth dimension of Bell's post-industrial society is "*the change from goods to services.*" An aspect of Bell's argument is often lost in discussing this dimension of his forecast. For Bell (1976, p. xvi), post-industrial society does not displace industrial society but overlays it "erasing some features and thickening the texture of society as a whole." It follows from this, for Bell, in every society there has been a service sector, but its basis has changed with the evolution of society from pre-industrial to post-industrial. In pre-industrial society, the service sector is associated with the household and domestic service. Bell (1976, p. xvi) writes:

> In an industrial society, the services are transportation utilities, and finance, which are auxiliary to the production of goods and personal services. ... But in a post-industrial society, the new services are primarily human services (principally in health, education and social services) and professional and technical services (e.g., research, evaluation, computers and systems analysis).

The fifth dimension of post-industrial society is "*a change in the character of work.*" By this, Bell means that if in pre-industrial society humankind was essentially in competition with nature, and in industrial society the competition was with machines, then in post-industrial society the "experience of work" is between persons. This follows logically from the notion that if post-industrial society is an essentially service sector society, then the competition among service deliverers is in essence competition among people. Bell's sixth dimension is the *increasing participation of women in the labour force.* It is a reality that virtually every developed country has been experiencing since the end of World War Two.

The seventh dimension, Bell calls *"science as the imago."* In post-industrial society, the institutions of science cannot be separated from the polity and therefore the character of the institutions of science in relation to other societal institutions is crucial for the questions which are investigated and how knowledge is used. The eighth dimension is a vertical political ordering of society, Bell calls *"situses as political units"* and the ninth dimension is post-industrial society as a particular form of *"meritocracy."* These three dimensions represent an expansion of Bell's earlier description of post-industrial society where he reflects upon various possible political outcomes of a post-industrial society organized around dimensions one to six.

Bell rejects *"the end of scarcity"* as his tenth dimension. The critical scarcity in post-industrial society, however, is not the scarcity of resources which will continue to exist, but the scarcity of information and time. The scarcity of information and time is then linked to the final dimension of post-industrial society, *"the economics of information."* Who and how is information controlled?

The remainder of the paper could be spent discussing the difficulties of the arguments that led Bell to identify these dimensions as the keys to a post-industrial society. Instead, Canada is now introduced as a case study. It is argued that Canada has become a post-industrial society, and indeed some of the key dimensions that Bell forecasted are part of Canada as a post-industrial society. The question which must also be kept in mind, however, is whether the lack of some key dimensions is because of conditions particular to Canada or is it because of conceptual problems which exist in Bell's schema.

## Canada as a Post-Industrial Society

Canada's population has grown from about 2.4 million in 1851 to 27,296,855 in 1991. During roughly the same period, fertility rates have gone from slightly over 7.0 infants per female to about 1.7 infants per female, well below the replacement rate of 2.1. In terms of its post World War Two development, Canada's "baby boom" lasted from about 1946 to 1966. In other words, Canada is a very large country where the population has grown at comparable rates to those in Western Europe since the middle of the last century with similar declining fertility rates, but a much smaller total population than many of the European Community countries (Beaujot, 1991).

Three key dimensions of post-industrial society as defined by Bell can be used to decide whether Canada has become a post-industrial society. They are: 1) the spread of a knowledge class, measured by the growth in the size of the labour force in technical and professional areas of the economy; 2) the shift from a goods producing to a service producing society, measured by the relative growth in high end services (health, education social, professional and technical services) and the decline in goods producing activities; and 3) the growing participation of women in the labour force.

Canada's labour force as defined by the population aged 15 and over has been growing steadily during this century (Figure 1). In 1989, the population aged 15 and over stood at 20,141,000. Of this group, 13,503,000 were counted in the labour force, 12,486,000 were employed and 1,018,000 were unemployed for an unemployment rate of about 7.5 percent. Canada slid steadily deeper into a recession with unemployment over 11 percent in the late 1980s and early 1990s.

## Figure 1: Growth in the Canadian Labour Force, 1926 to 1989

Source: CANSIM

Disaggregating the labour force into agricultural and non-agricultural employment, the overarching trend of this century has been the disappearance of an agricultural class of workers in Canada (Figure 2). Only about 423,000 Canadians were employed in agriculture in 1989 compared to slightly over 12 million who were employed in non-agricultural activities.

Further disaggregation of the labour force statistics, shows Canada's transition from an industrial to post-industrial society since World War Two. For this purpose, the labour force is divided into: agriculture; primary industries other than agriculture (mainly fishing, forestry and mining); manufacturing; construction (the goods producing sectors); and transportation and public utilities (mainly electrical power); trade;

## Figure 2: Percent of the Labour Force
## Employed in Agriculture and Non-agriculture

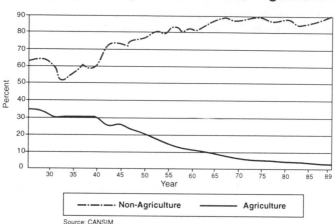

Source: CANSIM

finance, insurance and real estate; community, business and personal services, and public administration (the service producing sectors). Even for the much more attenuated time period of 1970 to 1989, the decline in the percentage of the labour force employed in the manufacturing sector, down to about 17 percent from about 23 percent, and the growth of those employed in community, business and personal services from just over 25 percent of the labour force to about 34 percent of the labour force can be observed (Figures 3 and 4).

Community, business and personal services are also those where the low-end service sector dominates. Low-end services are those services where a low level of education or minimum skill levels are required and wages are low in contrast to the high-end service sector where a higher level of education and/or skill is required and wages are commensurately higher. Notice also over this same period, that there has been little growth in any of the areas of the high end service sector. The percentage of people employed in finance, insurance and real estate has grown only modestly from just under 5 percent of the labour force to just over 5 percent of the labour force and the percentage of the labour force employed in public administration has stayed virtually constant at between 6 and 7 percent. Re-aggregated, the high end service sector has represented only about 11 percent of the Canadian labour force since 1970, and has not increased with respect to the low end service sector. Looked at another way, about 70 percent of the Canadian labour force is now employed in service industries compared to 30 percent who are employed in goods producing industries (Figure 5).

When looked at from a fiscal perspective, the evidence is not quite so overwhelming, but certainly supports the notion that the goods producing sectors are declining compared to the service producing sectors of the economy. In Figure 6, comparing

## Figure 3: Percent of Labour Force Employed by Sector, 1970 to 1989

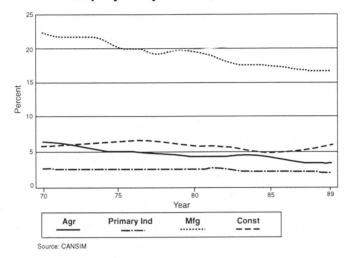

Source: CANSIM

## Figure 4: Percent of Labour Force Employed by Sector, 1970 to 1989

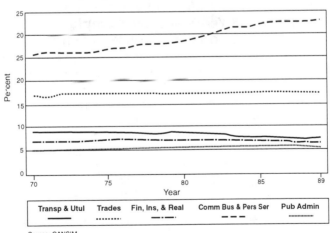

Source: CANSIM

sectors as a percentage of gross domestic product at factor cost by industry, it is clear that the goods producing sectors are all contributing less to the economy and the service producing sectors are contributing more. Note when measured this way, it is finance, insurance and real estate services followed by transportation, communications and utilities which show growth compared to trade, community, business and personal services and public administration.

The third set of measures of post-industrial society relate to the increased participation rates of women in the labour force. Figure 7 illustrates the truly remarkable rate of increase in female participation rates in the labour force. In 1966, about 35 percent of women aged 15 and over participated in the labour force. By 1989, female labour force participation rates were approaching 60 percent, and the female participation rate is converging with the overall participation rate. As well as being evidence for Canada as a post-industrial society, the growing participation rate has implications for the elderly population (See below).

There are, however, some disturbing aspects to women's participation in the labour force. Historically, unemployment rates for women have been higher than for men (Figure 8). Except for a brief period during the early 1980s recession in Canada, female unemployment rates have been higher than the overall rate. The convergence of rates during periods of recession is likely due, at least in part, to the concentration of men in those industries such as resource extraction and construction which are

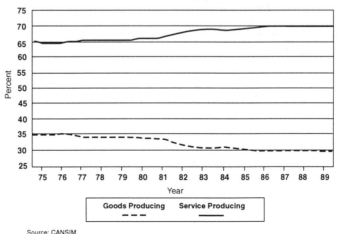

**Figure 5: Percent of the Population
15 Years and Over Employed
in Goods vs. Service Industries**

Source: CANSIM

## Figure 6: Sectors Compared as a Percent of Gross Domestic Product

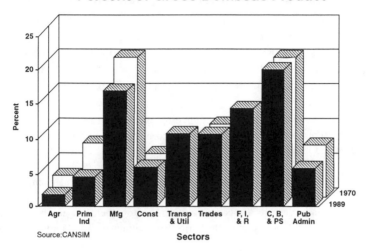

Source:CANSIM

## Figure 7: Labour Force Participation Rates Compared

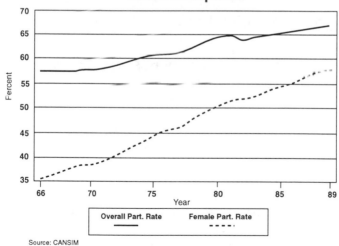

Source: CANSIM

highly cyclical giving the impression that women are "better protected" than men against the impact of recession when in fact they are not. What is also disturbing is that as the economy improves, the gap between female and overall unemployment rates begins to widen again.

Yet another contradictory aspect of the increase in participation of women in the labour force, is there dominance in the low-end service sector and part-time positions. To quote a recent report from Statistics Canada (1990, p. 74), *Women in Canada*:

> Although the number of women employed has increased substantially, they themselves are mostly concentrated in non-unionized service industries and in lower-paying occupations.
>
> Women formed the overwhelming majority in clerical occupations (approximately 80% in 1988) and were significantly represented in service (57%) and sales (46%) occupations. Taken together as a group clerical, sales and services employed the majority of women in 1988 (approximately 58%), . . .

In the same study, Statistics Canada (1990, p. 83) also reports that 25.2 percent of women worked part-time compared to 7.7 percent of men in 1988, and that this was part of a trend where the percentage of women working part-time has been increasing since 1975. As Boyd *et al.* (1991, p. 428) point out the increase in participation rates of women in the post-industrial Canadian labour force, "not only represents the continuation of female subordination, but also represents it consolidation."

## Figure 8: Unemployment Rates Compared

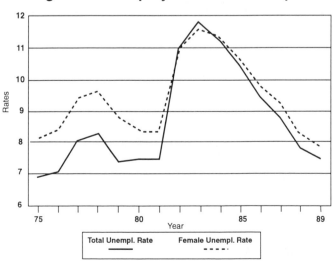

Source: CANSIM

So, has Canada become a post-industrial society? The answer is "yes," but not in the way that Bell forecast nor in its composition. The change to a low-end service sector society is undeniable, as is the growing participation of women in the labour force. While it would be difficult to argue that new technologies have not played a role in the growth of Canada as a post-industrial society, what is argued here is that the *deindustrialization* of Canada has been even more important in creating a post-industrial society.

While there is much debate over which processes are dominant in explaining the deindustrialization phenomenon, space precludes an in-depth discussion of the various points of view (see for example, Bluestone and Harrison, 1981; Drache and Gertler, 1991; Piore and Sabel, 1984). The scenario which has occurred in Canada's development into a post-industrial society and the various factors which have played a role in this process can be briefly sketched. After World War Two, Canada's manufacturing sector grew very rapidly in response to the consumer demand generated by the baby boom. Much of the secondary manufacturing which began in Canada was located in the Windsor to Quebec corridor and were branch plants of mainly United States based multinational corporations. No industrial sector better illustrates this process than the automobile industry. General Motors, Ford and Chrysler all invested heavily in locations throughout the Windsor-Quebec corridor, and as the result of the Auto Pact, automobiles and auto parts moved duty free between the two countries. Holmes (1991) has documented how the 1980s have wreaked havoc on the automobile industry in Canada as part of this process of deindustrialization.

Among the factors that one can point to in the deindustrialization of Canada which began in the 1970s are the globalisation of production, the substitution of capital for labour (e.g., the development of industrial robotics), high interest rates and consequently an over-valued currency, the North American Free Trade Agreement (NAFTA) and the recessions of the early 1980s and the late 1980s and early 1990s. While some might argue for the pre-eminence of one explanation over another, deindustrialization of Canada can be seen as the cumulative result of *all* these factors making Canada less attractive to foreign investors and making other places and other sectors more attractive to domestic entrepreneurs.

What Canada is fast becoming is what John Myles (1991) has called "a dualization—high-employment" post-industrial society. He describes this as a country where there has been success "in creating a large number of new jobs but mainly at the bottom of the labour market" and where the government provides various support mechanisms to maintain the working poor (Myles, 1991, pp. 362-363). While the forces that are at work towards deindustrialization, larger trading blocs or free trade zones are not likely to diminish in the foreseeable future, what is critical is how one structures the labour force in becoming a post-industrial society. In contrast to the dualization—high-employment society that Canada has become, the alternatives are what Myles (1991, p. 362) calls the "high-wage—low-employment" strategy or the "high-wage—high-employment" strategy. The former can be described as state where productivity gains are translated into less employment, and the role of the government is to implement labour market "exit" strategies (i.e., the social welfare system is used to absorb surplus labour). The latter strategy is dependent on a high degree of cooperation between government and the private sector to allow the government to act as "employer and manager of labour market transitions as employees shift from declining to expanding industries." (Myles, 1991, p. 362).

Either the high-wage—low-employment or the high-wage—high-employment strategy would appear to have greater potential to support an elderly population and the type of health care system Canadians have come to expect because they are based on people contributing to the public purse at higher wage levels over longer periods of time. What is not so obvious is how Canada would create the types of jobs, labour force and institutions required to achieve these alternative strategies.

In a more recent paper, Myles *et al.* (1993, p. 20) have also argued that while post-industrialism may not be creating a "new class structure," it is creating a "new economic life course" for young workers in post-industrial societies. They start from a lower relative economic position in the labour market and because of slow economic growth will not achieve the living standards achieved by their parents during the 1950s and 1960s.

### Canada's Elderly Population

The changing nature of the economy and the labour force is the point of departure then for examining Canada's elderly population and the implications for them of living in a post-industrial society. In 1991, 3,169,970 people were aged 65 and over. For most administrative purposes in Canada, being aged 65 and over means that you are part of the elderly population whether you feel "young at heart," are working, married, divorced, have recently had a child or whatever. In the "eyes" of the government you are elderly! These slightly over 3 million Canadians also represented about 11.6 percent of the total population in 1991.

By international standards, Canada still has a young population compared to most other developed countries, but has an obviously older population than is found in developing countries (Demographic Review, 1989, p. 21). As the baby boomer cohorts, begin to reach age 65, the growth in the size of the elderly population will begin to increase rapidly. In 2001, about 13.7 percent of the total population will be elderly. By 2036, it will almost have doubled to about 25.7 percent of the total population (Demographic Review, 1989, p. 22). The ratio favouring elderly women to men is part of a much longer demographic process which will become even more exaggerated in the next century (Demographic Review, 1989, p. 23).

The growth in the elderly population also has implications for the dependency ratio (Demographic Review, 1989, p. 25). From 1851 to 1951, the overall dependency ratio declined with the contributions of the young and the elderly to it remaining fairly constant. With the baby boom, the dependency ratio shot up as the percentage of the young increased dramatically in the 1950s and 1960s. By the 1970s, the baby boomers had entered the labour force and the dependency ratio began to even out overall, but the ratio of the elderly to the young began to change. After 2001, this trend will increase in velocity as baby boomers become the elderly; not only dominating the young component of the dependency ratio, but also generating increases in the overall dependency ratio.

The geography of Canada's elderly population is also quite specific. By the 1980s, three demographic processes were at work creating the geographic distribution of the elderly population. In the Prairie Region of Canada and in the Atlantic Provinces, the movement of young working age people from rural areas to larger urban centres combined with aging-in-place created high percentages of elderly persons in these regions. The lower mainland of British Columbia in particular and to a lesser extent, the central counties of Ontario attracted persons looking for amenity areas in which to retire. The third demographic process which is beginning is the aging-in-place of the baby boom population in Canada's largest urban areas. These changes are presented in detail in a set of *Atlases of the Elderly Population of Canada* (Moore, *et al.*, 1989).

Rosenberg and Moore (1991) have examined in detail the implications of the changing geographic distribution of the elderly population for financing and providing services for the elderly population of the province of Ontario. They show that the concentration of the elderly population relative to the working age population was greater than 26 percent in some parts of Ontario in 1986. Where the elderly population was relatively large, transfer payments from the provincial and federal governments made up over 13 percent of employment income in some cases. These trends will become increasingly important in the next century when the baby boomers become the elderly. In many parts of southern and northern Ontario, the elderly populations will make up almost 30 percent of the total population. This will mean as a ratio to the working age population, the percentage increases and income from transfer payments will approach 20 percent of employment income in some areas.

## Implications for Aging and Public Policy

These demographic trends, when combined with the type of post-industrial society already described, have wide-ranging implications for the elderly population and the delivery of health care. The issue that needs to be confronted first is whether Canada can continue along the path of a dualization—high employment post-industrial society. It is unlikely because a low wage—high employment strategy cannot be sustained at the nation-state level in a world where goods producing and indeed service producing activities are increasingly globalized. It is no longer a question of Canadians competing among themselves for low or high wage jobs, but competing with labour in other countries (mainly in the United States or developing countries of the world) for jobs where by definition wages are lower, regardless of whether employment is in a goods or service producing sector. Ironically, this threat to the low wage—high employment strategy is only possible because of another aspect of post-industrial society, global telecommunications, another feature of Bell's post-industrial society.

In Canada, what may be a better characterization of post-industrial society is low wage—higher unemployment where greater numbers of people are unemployed for longer periods of time, permanently unemployed, are working part-time or taking more than one job to maintain a minimum standard of living. The implications of these trends is that when these people become elderly they will have had less opportunity to accumulate assets during their working years, they are less likely to have pension income and more likely to be dependent on transfer income. It is also useful to consider whether persons whose employment history is marked by long periods of partial or permanent unemployment, or who have had to work at more than one job for long periods of time will have higher morbidity and disability rates as elderly persons. There is already evidence to indicate lower income Canadians have higher rates of tobacco and alcohol consumption and poorer diets, but the long term connections to health outcomes are not so clear.

The problem of less financial support in retirement will be more acute for women than men. Although women are participating more in the labour force which will improve their financial position in retirement, the fact that they continue to be concentrated in low wage, service sector positions means that many women will continue to be dependent on transfer income to maintain themselves in their elderly years.

A second reason, Canada is not likely to continue along a dualization—high employment path stems directly from the problem that a low wage labour force, especially one where a growing percentage are partially or permanently unemployed, do not generate taxable income. The result is that governments at every level in Canada find that their deficits are increasing and their ability to fund services is decreasing. Although some have suggested that the most obvious implication for the elderly population is that the federal government will no longer be able to afford transfer payments and the principles of the health care system will be altered, these scenario are most unlikely. A more likely scenario is to see the continuation of trends where to paraphrase Lightman et al. (1990, p. 108), since the mid 1970s, the federal government has left the form of the welfare state, but slowly starved the content. "The provinces for their part have responded to the federal financing squeeze in a variety of ways—off-loading of responsibilities to voluntary non-profit agencies; inaction in the face of new and emerging needs; the use of competitive bidding; contracts; purchase of service, etc." Under these conditions, the outcome will be growing policy debates about *targeting, rationalisation, privatization, familism* and *re-allocation.*

Targeting is the identification of those elderly persons most in need and providing them with transfer payments. At the present time, Old Age Security payments in Canada are made to every person age 65 and over regardless of their income. There are already some who would argue that Old Age Security payments should not go to individuals above a certain income level and that payments to those who would be eligible could then be increased or the amount that would have to be spent on Old Age Security payments could be reduced. In the health care system, it is likely to lead to even more debate about whether certain procedures should be denied to the elderly population because the costs are high and the impact on life expectancy marginal.

Rationalisation is the consolidation and/or closure of services and facilities. In a country like Canada where there are three levels of government, the potential for overlap and duplication of services is great. In this respect, rationalisation superficially appears to be a sensible policy option. An example of why it might not be as sensible as it first appears given the changing demographics of the Canadian population is the issue of deinstitutionalisation. In the 1970s, governments in Canada decided to end the institutionalisation of the majority of the mentally disabled in favour of community-based treatment. What had not been recognized and is still not recognized is that with a much larger elderly population in the next century, the number of elderly people who will be mentally disabled as the result of various dementias, Alzheimer's and other diseases of aging will grow dramatically. The ability to care for these people in community-based settings when there will be fewer family care givers and a relatively smaller working age population is questionable. Many will need communal settings which no longer exist because of the deinstitutionalisation process of the 1970s.

Privatization is allowing the private sector to offer services which have previously been offered in the public sector. In Canada the debate is not about whether there should be privatization any more, but how far privatization should go. Two examples illustrate this issue in the context of Canada's elderly population. For many years, there has been parallel public and private operation of nursing homes. "Does Canada need a parallel service?" is the question some are asking. The second example is the health care system. As the result of provincial and federal legislation since the 1950s, Canada's health care system has become almost completely public and access is universal. The combination of lack of government resources to increase funding beyond present levels (about 30 percent of most provincial government budgets now goes to health care) and NAFTA is creating pressure to allow private operators to enter the health care system in various guises.

In the context of post-industrial society, the familism debate is about what role family members play in care giving for the elderly population. As Gee (1990, pp. 195-198) has pointed out, children are obligated by law to provide support for their elderly parents and indeed as virtually all of the research shows children and especially daughters or daughter-in-laws do so. The issues therefore are how to increase independent living for the elderly population, how to provide more support for care-givers and how to change gender attitudes towards care-giving especially as labour force participation rates of women continue to increase. There is, however, an inherent tension in this debate as the federal and provincial governments look to reduce their overall spending on health care and social services by off-loading more care-giving to the private sphere and in particular to the family.

Re-allocation is the transfer of public spending from one sector to another or from one group to another. In light of the deficit problems that the federal and provincial governments face, the creation of new health care and social services for the elderly population is only likely to occur through re-allocation of existing funds. This may eventually turn out to be the most socially divisive debate of all in Canada because it will pit the elderly population against the young in conflicts about the re-allocation of public spending from services for youth (particularly spending on education) to services for the elderly population (particularly spending on health care).

By the next century in specific parts of Canada, the elderly population is likely to be well-over 30 percent of the total population. Since actual service delivery is often at the community level, the outcomes of many of these policy debates will be most visible locally and is likely to depend on the relative size of the elderly population and their ability to promote their own agenda in light of broader social, economic and political trends.

## CONCLUSIONS

In contrast to the generally optimistic picture that Daniel Bell painted of post-industrial society, for many young, working-age people in Canada and the United States, post-industrial society is seen as a new economic life course where earnings will not match those of their parents. For those who will retire in the coming decades, the future seems fraught with uncertainty. In Canada, those who will retire wonder whether they will continue to be guaranteed access to a health care system based on public administration, comprehensiveness, universality, accessibility and portability. In the United States, in the absence of radical reform, the elderly population can only continue to fear the costs of long-term illness and its financial repercussions.

In both countries, change is likely to occur in health care and social service delivery to the elderly populations as they continue to grow in size, and more importantly as the labour forces and the economies of both countries re-define themselves as particular types of post-industrial society.

Given the nature of Canada's current health care and social policy framework, the most likely policy implications are debates over targeting, rationalisation, privatization, familism and re-allocation. The outcomes of these debates are, however, likely to differ spatially depending on the relative size of the local elderly population and their ability to promote their own agendas in the light of broader social, economic and political trends.

For Canada, the challenge is how to transform itself from a dualization—high employment post-industrial society to another type of post-industrial society without sacrificing the welfare of its elderly population and its health care system in the transition. For the United States, the economic challenge is similar but there is the additional task of creating a health care system which is inclusive and supportable in a post-industrial society.

## References

Beaujot, R. 1991. *Population change in Canada: The challenges of policy adaptation.* Toronto: McClelland and Stewart.

Bell, D. 1976. *The coming of post-industrial society: A venture in social forecasting.* New York: Basic Books, Second Edition.

Bluestone, B. and Harrison, B. 1981. *The deindustrialization of America.* New York: Basic Books.

Boyd, M.; Mulvihill, M. A. and Myles, J. 1991. Gender, power and postindustrialism. *Canadian Review of Sociology and Anthropology* 28:407–36.

Demographic Review 1989. *Charting Canada's future: A report of the demographic review.* Ottawa: Health and Welfare Canada.

Denton, F. T. and Spencer, B. G. 1983. Population aging and future health care costs in Canada. *Canadian Public Policy* 9:155–63.

Drache, D. and Gertler, M. S., eds. 1991. *The new era of global competition: state policy and market power.* Montreal: McGill-Queen's University Press.

Evans, R. G. Hang together, or hang separately: the viability of a universal health care system in an aging society. *Canadian Public Policy* 13:165–80.

Foot, D. K. 1982. *Canada's population outlook: demographic futures and economic challenges.* Ottawa: Canadian Institute for Economic Policy.

Holmes, J. 1991. The globalization of production and the future of Canada's mature industries: the case of the automotive industry. in Drache, D. and Gertler, M. S., eds., *The new era of global competition. state policy and market power.* 153–80. Montreal: McGill-Queen's University Press.

Lightman, E.; Freiler, C. and Gandy, J. 1990. A transatlantic view: privatization Canadian-style. in Parry, R., ed., *Privatisation research highlights in social work 18.* 105–16. London: Jessica Kingsley Publishers.

McDaniel, S. A. 1987. Demographic aging as a guiding paradigm in Canada's welfare state. *Canadian Public Policy* 13:330–6.

Moore, E. G.; Rosenberg, M. W. and Bekkering, M. H. 1989. *Atlases of the elderly population of Canada.* Kingston, Canada: Department of Geography, Queen's University.

Myles, J. 1991. Post-industrialism and the service economy. in Drache, D. and Gertler, M.S., eds., *The new era of global competition: state policy and market power.* 350–66. Montreal: McGill-Queen's University Press.

Myles, J.; Picot, G. and Wannell, T. 1993. Does postindustrialism matter? Evidence from the Canadian experience. Mimeograph Copy. Forthcoming in *Changing Classes.* Esping-Andersen, G., ed. London: Sage.

Piore, M. and Sabel, C. 1984. *The second industrial divide.* New York: Basic Books.

Rosenberg, M. W. and Moore, E. G. 1990. The elderly, economic dependency, and local government revenues and expenditures. *Environment and Planning C: Government and Policy* 8:149–65.

Statistics Canada 1990. *Women in Canada: A statistical report.* Ottawa: Supply and Services, Second Edition.

# Chapter 9

## The Canadian Health System: Lessons from Alberta for the United States

*Dr. Joseph R. Oppong*
*Department of Geography*
*University of North Texas*

*Dr. Joseph Mensah*
*Department of Geography*
*Malaspina University College, Nanaimo, B.C.*

### INTRODUCTION

American interest in the Canadian Health Care system has been growing very rapidly in the last few years. Surprisingly, however, many studies have focused primarily on the Ontario Provincial Health Insurance System (General Accounting Office, 1991; Linton and Naylor, 1990; Newhouse *et al.*, 1988). From the frequency of such studies, it would appear that Ontario is synonymous with Canada. Yet, Canada's publicly funded health care system consists of 12 separate provincial and territorial plans sharing basic features, but with considerable differences between programs. For example, while Alberta and British Columbia charge premiums, other provinces do not. This makes it inappropriate to use Ontario's experience alone as representative of the Canadian Health Care system.

Moreover, substantial differences exist between Ontario and other provinces in terms of size, population, age structure and urbanization, that make it unrealistic to assume that Ontario is statistically representative of Canadian provinces. The fact that "Ontario accounts for 37% of the Canadian population, 38% of national health expenditures and 38% of Canadian physicians" (General Accounting Office, 1991) makes it imperative that other, perhaps smaller, provinces be examined as well. This is the general purpose of this paper. To provide a balanced view, it examines the health care system in the province of Alberta and emphasizes those elements that may serve as important lessons for the United States. Health services for the elderly and cost containment measures in the Alberta Health Care Insurance Plan (AHCIP) are highlighted.

**Geographical and other Differences Between Ontario and Other Provinces**

Of the Canadian provinces, Ontario has the largest population (9.4 million in 1988), followed by Quebec with 6.6 million. Each of the remaining 8 provinces and 2 territories has less than 3 million people. The spatial distribution of Ontario's urban population differs considerably from the other provinces. According to Wood (1984), Metro Toronto Census Metropolitan Area (CMA) alone contained almost three million people by 1981. This figure is larger than the entire population of each of the remaining eight provinces and two territories (excluding Quebec). Not surprisingly, Ontario has continued to have the largest urban proportion of the provincial populations. As Wood put it, relentless urbanization is the most spectacular trend in Ontario's population history. This highly urban character motivated Yeates' (1977) term "Main Street." Hardly any corner of southern Ontario is far off Main Street, and thus hardly any corner escapes the urban culture and its pressures. In contrast, Northern Ontario is sparsely populated and isolated from core Ontario.

The health care delivery requirements for such a population configuration should be expected to differ somewhat from provinces with dissimilar configurations. This explains why Ontario's Northern Health Travel Grant is necessary. It provides financial assistance for patients who must travel a minimum of 250 kilometers one way in Northern Ontario or Manitoba or 300 kilometers one way in the rest of Ontario to receive hospital or medical specialist services (Health and Welfare Canada, 1991).

Not only is Ontario's population more urbane, it has a relatively higher proportion of elderly population compared to Alberta. As Table 1 shows, there is considerable spatial variation in the distribution of the elderly population in Canada. Prince Edward Island and Saskatchewan have the highest proportion of older people in their total populations—12.7% for each. In the Northwest Territories and Yukon, the elderly constitute a small percentage of the total population. In absolute numbers, however, the three provinces of Ontario, Quebec and British Columbia carry the bulk of the older people.

Given these statistics, it is unlikely that the level of demand for services in Ontario and attendant "waiting lines" represent the rest of Canada. Certainly, the health care system in other smaller provinces must be examined to obtain a more representative view of the Canadian health care system. Moreover, such a study is more relevant to the several American States with population and urbanization levels considerably different from Ontario's experience.

### Table 1
### Distribution Canadian Elderly by Provinces (1986)

| Province | Number of Persons over 65 years | Percentage |
|---|---|---|
| Prince Edward Island | 16,085 | 12.7 |
| Saskatchewan1 | 28,600 | 12.7 |
| Manitoba1 | 33,885 | 12.6 |
| British Columbia | 349,480 | 12.1 |
| Nova Scotia | 103,835 | 11.9 |
| New Brunswick | 78,740 | 11.1 |
| Ontario | 992,700 | 10.9 |
| Quebec | 650,635 | 10.0 |
| New Foundland | 49,950 | 8.8 |
| Alberta | 191,325 | 8.1 |
| Yukon | 860 | 3.7 |
| Northwest Territories | 1,475 | 2.8 |
| Canada | 2,697,580 | 10.7 |

Source: Statistics Canada, Age, Sex and Marital Status (Cat. 93-101-1986) (Ottawa: Minister of Supply and Services, 1986).

Furthermore, a more basic description of the outworking of the health system is necessary. What programs are available, and how do people interact with the system? What does it mean for the average person? These questions guide this examination of the Alberta Health Care System. The purpose is to assess what lessons, if any, can be drawn for the United States.

### Overview of Canadian Health Care Programs

Constitutionally, health care services come under provincial or territorial jurisdiction; therefore, the specifics of health insurance vary slightly from province to province. The federal government tries to ensure uniformity between provinces and territories by instituting some cost-sharing arrangements (Dickinson and Hay, 1988). The purpose is to tie the receipt of federal funding to the meeting of some standards regarding the major underlying principles of the program.

The Canada Health Act establishes conditions that must be met before full payment may be made by the Federal government in respect of insured health services and extended health care services provided under provincial law. These criteria, conditions and provisions are set out in sections 7 through 12 and sections 13, 18 and

19 of the Act. The *insured* health services defined by the Canada Health Act include all medically necessary hospital services and medically required physician services, as well as medically or dentally required surgical-dental services that demand hospital facilities.

Each provincial health insurance plan must meet the criteria and conditions listed below to receive full federal cash contributions in each fiscal year.

1. Public Administration—The health care insurance plan must be administered and operated on a non-profit basis by a public authority, responsible to the provincial government and subject to audit of its accounts and financial transactions. This is unlike the American system where coverage is provided by an employer or through public programs serving the poor and the needy. In Canada, a person does not lose coverage by changing employers.

In contrast, fear of losing health insurance is a pervasive problem for Americans (Bodenheimer, 1992). Thirty percent of Americans surveyed in a 1991 New York Times - CBS poll said that someone in their household remained in an unwanted job to avoid losing health benefits (Eckholm, 1991).

2. Comprehensiveness—All Canadians should be offered all necessary medical services without a dollar limit, and solely on the basis of medical need (Grant, 1991, p. 203). Thus, there are no upper limits to the provision of care, as long as it is considered medically necessary (Iglehart, 1990). Pre-existing conditions are also covered under this provision.

In the United States in 1990, more than 60% of group health insurance plans contained exclusions of coverage for pre-existing conditions, signifying denial of benefits for any illness at the time the insurance is obtained (Sullivan and Rice, 1991). An estimated 81 million Americans under 65 years of age have medical problems (such as hypertension, diabetes, asthma, and chronic back pain) that insurance companies may consider pre-existing conditions (Citizen's Fund, 1991). Patients sometimes ask physicians not to specify their true diagnosis on insurance claim forms because they fear the invocation of pre-existing illness clauses or cancellations of insurance (Bodenheimer, 1992).

3. Universality—All Canadians should be eligible for coverage on uniform terms and conditions (Northcott, 1988). In contrast, millions are without insurance in the American system. On any given day, an estimated 35 million Americans are without health insurance (Friedman, 1991). In addition, at least 20 million people have insurance that could prove inadequate in the event of serious illness (Pepper Commission, 1990).

4. Portability—Residents moving to another province must continue to be covered by the home province during any minimum waiting period imposed by the new province of residence. Usually, this waiting time does not exceed three months. Furthermore, insured health services must be made available while they are temporarily absent from their own provinces. Health services received out-of-province, but still in Canada, are to be paid for by the home province at host province rates unless other arrangements for payment exist between the provinces. Also, services out-of-country are to be paid, as a minimum, on the basis of the amount that would have been paid by the home province for similar services rendered in-province. Prior approval may be required for elective services.

5. Accessibility—The health care insurance plan of a province must provide for insured health services on uniform terms and conditions and reasonable access must not be impeded, either directly or indirectly, by charges or other means. Also, there must be reasonable compensation to physicians and dentists for all insured health services rendered, as well as payments to hospitals for the cost of services. The notion of reasonable access to medical services is already covered by the principle of *universality*.

The Canadian government—federal and provincial—is the main source of payment for the health care program. At the federal level, funding for health insurance is derived from general tax revenues and increasingly from deficit financing (Northcott, 1988). The provincial governments use various combinations of tax revenues, premiums and, occasionally, user fees to finance the program (Northcott, 1988).

The federal government contributes to the operation of the provincial health insurance plans under the provisions of the Federal-provincial Fiscal Arrangements and Federal Post-Secondary Education and Health Contributions Act. Under the Act, provinces are entitled to equal per capita federal health contributions as "block funding" ($539.49 per capita in 1990–91) adjusted annually (Health and Welfare Canada, 1991).

On several occasions since 1977, the federal government has limited growth in the block of funds transferred to the provinces for health care. In 1986, it was reduced from the rate of GNP growth to GNP growth minus two percent. Bill C-69, in early 1991, froze federal transfers for two years (1990/91 and 1991–92) and after that, reduced it to GNP minus 3%. The February 1991 federal budget extended the freeze on the Established Programs Financing payments through 1994–95. Thus the cash portion of federal block funding has been shrinking over time (Saouab and Vance, 1992), and if this persists, financial pressures on the provinces to limit services will be strong.

While they cannot impose user fees or extra-billing without losing federal financial support, provinces have considerable latitude in determining how their shares of health care costs are financed. They may institute insurance premiums or sales taxes, use general revenue or adopt a combination of approaches (Saouab and Vance, 1992). Health insurance is the single largest program funded by provincial or territorial governments, but there is considerable variation in the amount of resources devoted to health care and the rate by which health care costs are increasing. Health care accounts for a large portion of provincial government budgets. New Brunswick spends approximately 25%, while Ontario and Quebec spend about 34.6 and 24.4% respectively. In Alberta, it is 33.2% while it is 23.3% in Newfoundland (Saouab and Vance, 1992).

Hospitals generally provide services according to government budget provisions. Physicians are paid on a fee-for-service system of reimbursement by the various provincial health care agencies. The provincial and territorial governments negotiate the fee schedules in conjunction with their respective medical association (Grant 1991; Northcott, 1988).

## Canadian Health Care Challenges:
## Aging Population and Shrinking Federal Funding

Rising health care costs, shrinking contributions from the federal government and a rapidly aging population, are major challenges facing the Canadian health care system. By linking the annual increase in the federal contribution to the growth in the GNP, the federal government has left the provinces to absorb more of the health care costs when the aggregate outlays for health grew faster than the economy as a whole. Health care costs have increased more rapidly than the growth of Canada's economy in eight of the past thirteen years (Iglehart, 1990).

In view of the declining federal contribution, some argue that the Health Act may have to be amended to allow charging patients for "non-essential" medical and hospital services to reduce health care costs. Others reject this solution because the definition of "non-essential" might become so broad and arbitrary and infringe on the basic universality of access principle.

To deal with the high costs of care, controversy continues around administrative charges, the definition of insured services and overall increases in the fee schedule. As much as 85% of the health care expenditure is for doctors and hospitals and they are being pressured by governments to help contain costs (Iglehart, 1990). It is feared that faced with fee constraints, physicians may increase the number of physician-initiated patient visits and the number of services provided. For example, the Ontario government estimated in its 1988 budget that during the 1980s, the cost of the province's health insurance plan had increased by 15%, of which 8% was actually attributable to higher costs and 7% to an increased demand for services.

The aging population poses further problems. Between 1901 and 1981, Canada's population grew four and a half times. During the same period, the older population (i.e., 65+ years) increased nine times. Moreover, between 1971 and 1981, the total population rose by 13%, while the segment of the population under 14 years decreased by 14%, and the older population grew by 35% (Novak, 1988). While in 1891 elders accounted for only 4.5% of Canada's population, in 1986 they constituted 10.7% of the total population (Chappell *et al.*, 1986). People over 65 years of age are heavy users of the health care system and there is concern that the aging population, projected to constitute 20% of Canada's population by the year 2031 (Statistics Canada, 1986), will overburden the system and further increase health care costs.

Research evidence indicates that older people tend to have more health problems than younger people (Novak, 1988:154). A study by the Alberta Senior Citizen's Bureau (1984) noted that while people 65 years and over constituted 7.3% of the province's population in 1981, they accounted for 18.4% of hospital discharge and used 36.7% of patient days. Other studies have shown that a small group of the elderly population, especially those who are eighty five years or older, account for a large proportion of health care utilization (Roos et al. 1984; Barer et al. 1987). "The elderly who receive medical care receive more of it than the young" (Barer et al. 1987, p. 858).

Efforts to forecast and simulate the likely impact of the aging phenomenon on the future cost of health care in Canada generally evoke a very bleak future. In their Ontario study, Gross and Schewenger (1981) estimated that the elderly will consume 46.5% of health services by the year 2001, and 56.6% by 2026. Woods (1984) has translated Canada's aging phenomenon into increased demand for major health care services including physician services, home-care services, mental-health facilities, and long-term care. Denton, *et al.* (1987) acknowledge that health care costs are sensitive to the aging, and prospective changes in the age composition will drive up the costs of health care in the future.

The majority of Canada's elderly reside in urban centers, with 40% living in centers of one-half million or more population (Health and Welfare Canada, 1983). Rural Canada has only one in twenty people over the age of 65 (Health and Welfare Canada 1982). However there are some small towns, notably in Manitoba and Saskatchewan, with very high proportions of elderly, some have more than 17% of their population over 65 (Novak, 1988). Major centers with high concentrations of elderly people in Canada include Victoria (17%), Vancouver (11.5%), and St. Catharines-Niagara (11.5%) (Statistics Canada, 1984).

These studies suggest that the aging population raises concerns for the future costs of health care in Canada. Also, provinces with higher elderly populations will tend to have higher health care costs than those with fewer elderly. In summary then, in addition to rising health care costs and a rapidly aging population with increasing health care needs, the provinces and territories have to cope with continually shrinking federal contributions to health care. Different provincial programs will respond to these challenges in different ways. The rest of this paper examines the health care system as it operates in Alberta, the cost reduction strategies implemented and the coverage available to the aged population.

## THE ALBERTA HEALTH CARE INSURANCE

The Alberta Health Care Insurance Plan (AHCIP) is a provincial government insurance plan which covers the costs of medical services and a number of related health care services for registered Alberta residents and their dependents. Residents who wish to be eligible for benefits must register with the plan and pay monthly premiums (except for exempt groups). Alberta and British Columbia are the only two provinces that levy premiums (National Council on Welfare, 1990) despite opposition from the National Council on Welfare. The Council has been critical of premiums as an unfair and inefficient way of raising money to help pay for health care because they are regressive and impose a heavy burden on the poor. Ontario has abolished monthly premiums, paid in roughly equal amounts by workers and employers, in favor of a payroll tax strictly on employers (Iglehart, 1990).

### Funding Alberta Health Care

Premiums, interests and penalties on late premium payments financed 31.4% of the cost of Alberta Health Care in the 1990-91 fiscal year. Monthly premium rates have increased steadily over the past few years as shown in Table 2. "The objective of these increases is to raise premium revenue so that it covers one half of the cost of basic health services, excluding services provided to seniors" (Alberta Health, 1992a, p. 6).

Between 1990 and 1992, premiums increased by 37.6% reflecting the pressure on the province to find additional funding for health care. It is especially significant that Alberta has chosen the premium increase approach despite criticism because it provides a "visible link" between the cost of health care and the benefit it provides (National Council on Welfare, 1990). The effectiveness of premiums as a tool for raising awareness of health care costs is difficult to determine and is beyond the scope of this paper.

**Table 2**
**Alberta Health Care Monthly Premium Increases 1990–1992**

| Year | Single Coverage | Family Coverage | % Increase |
|------|------|------|------|
| Pre-October 1990 | $19.75 | $39.50 | |
| October 1, 1990 | $23.00 | $46.00 | 16.75 |
| July 1, 1992 | $27.00 | $54.00 | 17.4 |

In 1990–91 fiscal year, Government of Canada contributions accounted for 14.1% of the cost as compared with 15% for the previous year. Thus premiums and federal government contributions covered 45.6% of health care cost in 1990–91. The Government of Alberta funded the remaining 54.4%, compared to 55.3% in the previous year. Thus, the premium increase has effectively covered the shortfall resulting from reductions in federal contributions and also reduced the Alberta government's contribution to health care by 9%.

Despite the premium system, no Alberta resident is denied coverage due to an inability to pay premiums. Eligibility for benefits is not linked to premium coverage (Health and Welfare Canada, 1991). AHCIP operates a premium subsidy and premium waiver program for residents with financial hardships, and provides premium-free coverage for seniors and their spouses; widows and widowers age 55 to 64 under the *Widows Pension Act*; recipients of certain social allowance, correctional or mental health programs and dependents of those receiving this premium-free coverage.

Revenue forgone due to the premium assistance program, exempt groups, and premium-free coverage to senior citizens and Alberta Widows' Pension recipients totalled $132,294,658 for 1990-91 fiscal year. The revenue forgone represents 27.6% of gross premium revenue (Alberta Health, 1992a).

## Accessibility

In 1990-91 fiscal year, Alberta had 128 acute care public hospitals and 38 stand-alone auxiliary hospitals operating throughout the province. These hospitals have an approved bed complement of 12,911 acute care beds and 5,593 auxiliary beds. The total number of acute care and auxiliary beds (18,504) provides a ratio of 7.52 beds per 1,000 population. Residents have access to health care facilities throughout the province. Physicians are encouraged to locate in under-serviced areas through a physician incentive program. For the province as a whole, there were 2,545,553 people, 4,441 physicians and a physician-population ratio of 1:573 in 1990–91 fiscal year (Alberta Health, 1992a).

Between 1988 and 1991, the number of physicians and other health practitioners grew at a faster rate than the rate of population growth (Table 3). The population grew by 6.3% while the number of physicians, pharmacists, and dentists grew by 8.5, 7.9 and 9.4% respectively.

**Table 3**
**Increases in Alberta Health Professionals 1988 to 1991**

| Health Professionals | 1988 | 1991 | % Increase |
|---|---|---|---|
| Dentists | 1,258 | 1,358 | 7.9 |
| Optometrists | 215 | 215 | 0.0 |
| Pharmacists | 2,078 | 2,275 | 9.4 |
| Physicians | 4,092 | 4,441 | 8.5 |
| Registered Nurses | 21,699 | 23,616 | 8.8 |
| Population | 2,395,000 | 2,545,553 | 6.3 |

Source: Alberta Health and Social Services Disciplines Committee (1992) Inventory of Health and Social Service Personnel, 1991; Health and Social Service Manpower in Alberta, 1988.

While there was no increase in the number of optometrists, the number of physicians increased at a higher rate than that of nurses. Alberta may have to take steps to curb a too rapid increase in the number of physicians to avoid a further escalation in health care costs, especially resulting from physician-initiated visits.

## SELECTED HEALTH PROGRAMS IN ALBERTA

AHCIP provides a number of creative and cost effective programs for its residents. A selected few are described for illustrative purposes.

### Family Health Services

Alberta provides a Community Health Nursing program available to all residents. Over 800 Community Health Nurses work with Albertans to provide health services ranging from prenatal counselling to bereavement support. They encourage health promotion and disease prevention, and screen for potential health problems. Community health nurses visit homes, contact new mothers and infants, provide health education and counselling to expectant and new parents, school children, adults and seniors, and provide communicable disease prevention and control.

## Screen Test

Alberta Program for the Early Detection of Breast Cancer opened sites in Edmonton and Calgary in October 1990. Several regional centers and an outreach program are being added to increase access for Alberta women in the future. Eligible Alberta women aged 50–69 are able to take part in the screening program whose goal is to reduce deaths from breast cancer by 30% within 15 years. The program is funded by Alberta Health Care and run by the Alberta Cancer Board.

In the United States, by contrast, Dr. Donald Henderson, former dean of Johns Hopkins School of Hygiene and Public health, maintains that it has been very difficult to get third-party payers to pay for mammograms, Pap smears or other preventive services (Skolnick, 1991). Mammographic screening for breast cancer can reduce mortality from this disease by as much as 30%. Yet in 1990, only 31% of women were being screened according to accepted guidelines (Bastani, Marcus and Hollatz-Brown, 1991). Studies in Los Angeles and Massachusetts found that cost and lack of insurance coverage were factors preventing women from obtaining mammograms (Zapka *et al.*, 1991).

## Communicable Disease Surveillance

The Public health Division operates a Communicable Disease Surveillance Unit. This unit monitors and controls all communicable diseases except sexually transmitted diseases (STD), tuberculosis and AIDS.[1] The unit receives information from health units, physicians, hospitals and laboratories, and ensures appropriate prevention and control activities. Surveillance is also maintained for non-notifiable diseases of particular concern. The Unit distributes approximately 750,000 doses of vaccine (excluding influenza vaccine) each year. Also, a surveillance system to monitor adverse reactions associated with immunizations continued in 1990. This is the only systematic, population-based surveillance program in North America and contributes over half of all such information collected in Canada (Alberta Health, 1992a).

The prenatal hepatitis B screening program screens almost all pregnant women in Alberta and identifies about 200 infants each year who require protection against hepatitis B. As a result of this, only 106 hepatitis B cases were reported in 1990–91, the lowest since 1981. The success of this program is evidenced by the fact that in Alberta, hepatitis B continues to be primarily a disease of adults with only four cases reported under 15 years of age and only one under 10 years in fiscal year 1990–91 (Alberta Health, 1992a).

**Sexually Transmitted Diseases Control**

This provides a comprehensive program for the control of STD in Alberta. Diagnostic and treatment services are provided through clinics in Calgary and Edmonton, as well as a clinic in Fort McMurray which operates under the auspices of the health unit serving that city and surrounding area. In 1990–91 fiscal year, 22,484 clients were seen, a 4% decrease from the previous year. STD Control disseminates information to both public and professional audiences and has responsibility for the STD information and tollfree AIDS Information Lines. STD Control also provides consultation to physicians and epidemiologic services that include contact tracing for STD, including HIV infections.

In addition to this, there is a Provincial AIDS Program which aims to limit or eliminate the spread of HIV infection/AIDS (primarily through direct and indirect educational activities), to monitor the spread of the infection, and to ensure that care and support for people with HIV infection/AIDS are available in institutional and community settings.

Through many such programs, AHCIP effectively controls health care costs. While no direct data is readily available for confirmation, it is presumably that the ensured free access to prenatal care, drastically reduces the number of low birth weight children. Dr. Robin Walker, Vice-President of the Canadian Council on Children and Youth, told the Canadian House of Commons Committee on Health and Welfare, on May 2, 1988 that the savings from reducing the low birth weight rate, even by 1%, would be millions of dollars a year. The cost of caring for each of Canada's surviving underweight babies is about $100,000 annually (Saouab and Vance, 1992). A 1988 study by the United States Congress-appointed National Commission to Prevent Infant Mortality estimated that hospitalization and medical costs for low-birthweight babies alone total more than $2 billion a year (Singh, 1990).

What is particularly impressive is the dedication and thoroughness with which these programs are run in Alberta. For example, the Public Health Division will contact a new mother to set up an appointment for immunization for the new baby through the Community Clinic nearest her home. At that appointment, subsequent appointments will be scheduled, and it is quite routine for personnel to call and remind mothers of an impending appointment. As a direct result of these and other measures, no cases of diphtheria were seen in Alberta in 1990 and no case of tetanus has been seen in Alberta since 1978. In addition, no cases of polio have occurred in Alberta since 1979 (Alberta Health, 1992a).

In contrast, in the United States in 1989, 55% of employment-based health insurance plans did not provide coverage for basic childhood vaccinations (Skolnick, 1991). The proportion of children from one to four years of age immunized against measles dropped from 66% in 1976 to 61% in 1985, and the number of measles cases rose from 2,800 in 1985 to 26,500 in 1990 (Rosenthal, 1991). According to the National Vaccine Advisory Committee, one factor contributing to this epidemic is the reluctance of insurers to include childhood immunizations among their health care benefits (Skolnick, 1991).

## Health Services for the Elderly in Alberta

AHCIP provides premium-free basic care for seniors, eligible widows and their dependents. This includes all medically required services of physicians and osteopaths and specific oral and surgical procedures performed by a dental surgeon. Additional dental coverage is available under the Extended Health Benefits program. Podiatric services, physical therapy, chiropractic services and optometrist services including eye glasses are provided. In addition, long term care centers provide room and board and a range of care services from personal care with nursing supervision to skilled medical and nursing care. These centers vary in size and are located throughout the province.

Through the Home Care program, health units provide health and support services to help people remain independent in their homes. Although 90% of clients are senior citizens, the program also serves individuals with acute care and palliative care needs. In 1990–91, a total of 23,500 clients were served.

The Alberta Aids to Daily Living (AADL) program enhances the independence of Albertans living at home who have a chronic or terminal illness or disability by assisting with the provision of approved medical equipment and supplies. In 1990–91, 66,645 Albertans aged 65 years and over received benefits under this program. Categories of benefits include bathroom equipment, walking aids, hearing aids, prosthetic/orthotics/footwear, respiratory equipment, oxygen, mastectomy prostheses and wheel chairs and wheel chair cushions.

In contrast, in the United States, Medicare covers only about 50% of medical expenses of the elderly (Rice and Gable, 1986) and 22% of Medicare recipients have no supplemental private medicaid coverage (Pepper Commission, 1990). Without supplementary insurance, Medicare patients have no coverage for most routine screening, immunizations, and care related to eyeglasses and hearing aids (Social Security Administration, 1991). In summary then, unlike their American neighbors, Alberta provides excellent quality of care for the elderly.

**Physician Benefit Programs**

In addition to the apparently cost-effective preventive programs, Alberta has special programs for physicians that help to keep health care costs down, and promote physician welfare and well-being. One of these is the liability insurance subsidy. Under an agreement reached between the Government of Alberta and the Alberta Medical Association, Alberta Health reimburses Alberta physicians for liability protection dues. Physicians practicing in Edmonton and Calgary receive 50% of their annual liability insurance above a base level deductible, while physicians practicing elsewhere in the province are refunded 100% of their premium fees above the deductible. The Department's contribution for the 1990–91 fiscal year was $4,780,000 (Alberta Health, 1992a).

The Incentive Payments Program encourages physicians to practice in rural communities by providing incentive payments. Expenditures for location incentives for 1990–91 fiscal year totalled $1,415,000 and applied to approximately 125 physicians.

By Agreement with the Alberta Department of Health, the Alberta Medical Association administers a Continuing Medical Education Program which is funded by the Department. This provides an allowance for fee-for-service physicians who wish to continue their post graduate medical education. Department funding for fiscal year 1990–91 totalled $1,870,000 and covered 3,204 full-time equivalent physicians.

The Alberta Physicians Disability Insurance Program, administered by the Alberta Medical Association, provides disability insurance for eligible Alberta fee-for-service physicians. For fiscal year 1990–91, the Department of Health contributed $1,357,000 covering the equivalent of 3,204 full-time physicians. Through these programs, Alberta has taken a collaborative and cooperative approach in dealing with physicians. The obvious question is how much all these programs cost. This is the focus of the next section.


HEALTH CARE EXPENDITURES

**Basic Health Services**

In 1990–91, total expenditures for basic health services provided in and outside Alberta increased by 6.5% to $853.5 from $801.7 million in 1989–90 fiscal year (Table 4). This included fee-for-service payments, as well as payments in respect of practitioners on salary, sessional[2] and contract arrangements. The 6.5% increase in total expenditures is modest considering the fact that the annual inflation rates for 1989 to 1991 were between 5% and 6% in major cities like Edmonton (Edmonton Economic Development Authority, 1991).

The average expenditure per person for basic health care in 1990 was $327.00. The total number of registered persons covered under Extended Health Benefits was 273,019 in 1990. Fee-for-service payments for Extended Health Benefits recipients amounted to $42,630,273, leading to a per capita expenditure of $156.14 per EHB registrant.

**Table 4**
**Breakdown of Total Expenditures for Basic health Services**

| Health Discipline | 1990-91 Expenditures $000 | Increase over 1989–90 (%) | Increase over 1989–90 ($) | Alberta Residents Only |
|---|---|---|---|---|
| Medical | 765,570 | 6.4 | 45,814,000 | 747,982,237 |
| Oral Surgery | 10,506 | 3.7 | 377,000 | 10,974,760 |
| Chiropractic | 29,323 | 6.2 | 1,708,000 | 29,176,338 |
| Optometry | 17,465 | 4.2 | 699,000 | 18,095,002 |
| Podiatry | 4,037 | 6.0 | 230,000 | 4,053,920 |
| Physical Therapy | 26,572 | 12.5 | 2,954,000 | 25,818,874 |
| Total | 853,473 | 6.5 | 51,782,000 | 836,101,131 |

Source: Alberta Health 1992a: p.7 and Alberta Health 1992b: p.1.

## Hospital Benefits

In 1990–91, total payments to hospitals in the province (active and auxiliary) for operating and capital expenditures are estimated to $2.07 billion. Expenditures for hospital services provided outside the province were $36.4 million (Alberta Health, 1992a). Total fee-for-service payments for basic health services provided to Alberta residents by practitioners in Alberta was $836,101,992. Of this, $747,982,237 was for basic medical services. The Plan paid approximately $13.2 million for physician services provided out-of-province to Alberta residents.

**Physician Payments**

The total fee-for-service payments for Basic health services provided to Alberta residents in Alberta increased by 8.19% to $836,101,131 from $772,810,992 in 1989–90. The total number of practitioners who received payments during the year and the average fee-for service payment per specialty are presented in Table 5.

The number of medical services per Alberta physician increased to 7,563 from 7,174 in 1989–90,  a growth of 5.42%. On the other hand, the number of discrete patients per practitioner decreased by 1.06%, from 566 in 1989–90 to 560 in 1991. This provides evidence of physician-initiated use of health care widely blamed as a major factor for the rising cost of health care. Visit services accounted for nearly half of the total fee-for-service payments in 1990–91 (48.08%). Approximately, one-quarter (25.87%) of the total payment was for pathology, radiology and other diagnostic related services (15.9%, 4.38% and 6.3%, respectively).

The number of medical services provided in Alberta per 1000 insured persons rose by 7.13% to 11,901. A large increase was registered in obstetric services (21.7%). Increases were also registered in office visits (14.63%), other diagnostic and therapeu-

**Table 5**
**Fee-for Service Payments for Basic Health Services by Specialty**

| Specialty | Number of Physicians | Average Payments (Canadian Dollars) |
|---|---|---|
| | Physicians | |
| General Practitioners | 2,255 | $137,487 |
| Medical Specialists | 1,039 | $137,550 |
| Surgical Specialists | 575 | $237,216 |
| Laboratory Specialists | 242 | $655,517 |
| Total Physicians | 4,111 | $181,947 |
| | Non-Medical Practitioners | |
| Dental Surgeons | 1,144 | $9,593 |
| Chiropractors | 364 | $80,155 |
| Optometrists | 222 | $81,509 |
| Podiatrists | 26 | $155,920 |
| Physical Therapists | 504 | $51,228 |

Source: Alberta Health 1992b, p. 1-2.

tic services (5.36%), consultations (5.00%), minor surgery (4.76%), major surgery (4.21%), radiology services (2.62%), anaesthesia (2.35%) and pathology services (0.94%). Decreases occurred for special visits (-1.52%), surgical assists (-2.86%), and hospital visits (-2.92%).

In conclusion, then, Alberta is providing excellent services for its residents at a small fraction of what it would cost in the United States. It is important to consider health care costs as a means to an end, or as the expenditure incurred in order to attain a desired goal (Angus, 1987). In this instance, the goal is the attainment of better health care for Albertans. Against this background, it is important to highlight the specific gains of the system using key health indicators. A direct correlation between health expenditure and improved health care is always hard to establish. Nonetheless, improvements in general health standards following increases in health care expenditure somehow justify the cost.

**Selected Highlights of Alberta's Gains and Programs**

1. Due to the hepatitis B screening program, the incidence of hepatitis B was at its lowest in 1990–91.
2. The percentage of low birthweight babies (under 2501 grams) has fallen drastically. For example, for the City of Edmonton, it fell from 7% in 1986 to 5.9% in 1990 and continues to fall further (Edmonton Community Trends Working Group, 1990).
3. No cases of diphtheria have been seen in Alberta since 1978.

## CONCLUSION AND LESSONS FOR THE UNITED STATES

The Province of Alberta has, in the face of rising health care costs, done a wonderful job of providing efficient, universally accessible health care to residents of the province. The quality and availability of care for the elderly, and the emphasis on preventive care through such Communicable Diseases Surveillance programs is especially laudable. Special physician benefit services such as liability insurance subsidy help to reduce overall physician costs and hence the total cost of health care. What is even more noteworthy is that Alberta is able to provide per capita basic health services to its population at $327.00 (Canadian) a year.

Definitely, there are lessons here for the United States. For example through the effective surveillance and preventive care (like prenatal counselling), Alberta is able to avoid or drastically reduce the need for more costly cures (such as low birth-weight children). Based on this examination of Alberta's Health Care system, the following recommendations are appropriate.

**Lessons for the United States**

1. Make primary care universally accessible. Controlling low birth-weight, ensuring and requiring universal access to immunization will save unnecessary and costly cures.

2. Encourage more primary care physicians and other less costly professionals such as midwives.

3. Keep physician numbers from increasing too rapidly to keep costs down. Research indicates that the over-utilization response is usually provider initiated. Without such controls, "a system that is awash with human and physician capacity and technical possibilities, and chafing under utilization constraints that, while ineffective in aggregate, are still onerous and offensive, might very well respond to the extension of coverage with a significant increase in recommended diagnostic and therapeutic interventions" (Barer *et al.*, 1987).

4. Physician benefit schemes might help to reduce cost of malpractice insurance, a basic source of high cost in American health care.

5. Provide better health care for the younger population. Ensuring relatively healthy adults of tomorrow might be an effective approach to controlling health care costs for the elderly in the future.

**Notes**

[1]There are special programs for these and especially STD.

[2]Sessional payments are an alternate form of physician remuneration to fee-for-service. Agreements are established and maintained between the Health Department, hospitals, and agencies. During the 1990–91 fiscal year, programs under sessional payment agreements included psychiatric services, out-patient diagnostic and treatment services for children, geriatric services, pediatric neonatology and intensive care, inner city community health clinics and two sport medicine clinics. In 1990–91, the total expenditure for sessional payments was $5,350,000.

**References**

Alberta Health. 1992a. *Annual report 1990–91.* Edmonton, Alberta, Canada.
Alberta Health. 1992b. *Statistical supplement: Alberta Health Care Insurance Plan 1990-91.* Edmonton, Alberta, Canada.
Alberta Health and Social Services Desciplines Committee. 1992. *Inventory of health and social service personnel, 1991.* Edmonton: Alberta Health.

___. 1989. *Health and social service manpower in Alberta, 1988.* Edmonton: Alberta Health.

Alberta Senior Citizen's Bureau. 1984. *Older persons in Alberta: Their use of programs and services.* Edmonton: Alberta Social Services and Community Health.

Angus, D. E. 1987. Health care costs: A review of past experience and potential impact of the aging phenomenon. In *Health and Canadian society: Sociological Perspective,* eds. D. Coburn and C. D'arcy, pp. 57–72. Markham, Ontario: Fitzhenry and Whiteside.

Barer, M. L.; Evans, R. G.; Hertzman, C. and Lomas, J. 1987. Aging and health care utilization: New evidence on old fallacies. *Social Science and Medicine* 24:51–62.

Bastani, R.; Marcus, A. C. and Hollatz-Brown, A. 1991. Screening mammography rates and barriers to use: a Los Angeles county survey. *Preventive Medicine* 20:350–363.

Beaujot, R. and McQuillan, K. 1982. *The demographic development of Canadian society* Toronto: Gage.

Bodenheimer, T. 1992. Underinsurance in America. *New England Journal of Medicine* 3274:274–8.

Chappell, N. L.; Strain, L. A. and Blandford, A. A. 1986. *Aging and health care: A social perspective.* Toronto: Holt, Reinehart and Winston.

Citizen's Fund 1991. *The seven warning signs: health insurance at risk.* Washinton, D.C.

Denton, F. T.; Neno, S. L. and Spencer, B. G. 1987. How will population aging affect the future costs of maintaining health-care standards? In *Aging in Canada: Social Perspectives,* ed. V. W. Marshall, pp. 553–568. Markham, Ontario: Fitzhenry and Whiteside.

Department of Health and Human Services. 1991. Health United States 1990: PHS91–1232.

Dickinson, H. D. and Hay, D. A. 1988. The structure and cost of health care in Canada. In *Sociology of health care in Canada,* Bolaria, S. and Dickinson, H.D., pp. 51–73. Toronto: Harcourt Brace Jovanovich.

Eckohlm, E. 1991. Health benefits found to deter job switching. *New York Times.* September 26, 1991, 1:12.

Edmonton Community Trends Working Group. 1990: *Tracking the trends: future directions for human services in Edmonton.* Edmonton: Social Planning Council.

Edmonton Economic Development Authority. 1991. *Edmonton report* (Spring). Edmonton: Economic Development Authority.

Friedman, E. 1991. The uninsured: from dilemma to crisis. *Journal of American Medical Association* 265:2491–5.

General Accounting Office. 1991. *Canadian Health Insurance: Lessons for the United States.* GAO/HRD-91-90 June 4, 1991.

Grant, K. R. 1991. Health care in an Aging society: Issues, controversies, and challenges for the future. In *Canadian society: Social issues and contradictions,* ed. S. Bolaria, pp. 198–221. Toronto: Harcourt Brace Jovanovich.

Gross, M. J. and Schwenger, C. W. 1981. *Health care for the elderly in Ontario: 1976-2026.* Toronto: Ontario Economic Council.

Health and Welfare Canada 1982. *Canadian Government Report on Aging.* Ottawa: Minister of Supply and Services.

Health and Welfare Canada 1983. *Fact Book on Aging in Canada.* Ottawa: Minister of Supply and Services.

Health and Welfare Canada 1991. *Canada Health Act*. Ottawa: Minister of Supply and Services.

Iglehart, J. K., 1990. Canada's Health Care System Faces its Problems. *New England Journal of Medicine* 3228:562–8.

Linton, A. and Naylor, C. D. 1990. Organized medicine and the assessment of technology: Lessons from Ontario. *New England Journal of Medicine* 32321:1463–1467.

National Council on Welfare. 1990. *Health, Health Care and Medicine* Minister of Supply and Services: Canada.

Newhouse, J.; Anderson, G. and Roos, L. 1988. Hospital Spending in the United States and Canada: a comparison. *Health Affairs* 6–16.

Northcott, H. C. 1988. Health-care resources and extra-billing: financing, allocation and utilization. In *Sociology and health care in Canada*, eds. S. Bolario, and H.D. Dickinson, pp. 38–50. Toronto: Harcourt Brace Jovanovich.

Novak, M. 1988. *Aging and society: A Canadian perspective*. Scarborough: Nelson, Canada.

Pepper Commission, Bipartisan Commission on Comprehensive Health Care. 1990. A call for action. Washington D.C.: Government printing Office, 1990. S. Prt. 101–114.

Rice, T. and Gabel, J. 1986. Protecting the elderly against high health care costs. *Health Affairs* 53:2453–4.

Roos, N. P.; Shapiro, E. and Roos, L. L. 1984. Aging and the demand for health services. *Gerontologist* 24:31–36.

Rosenthal, E., 1991. Measles resurges, and with far deadlier effects. *New York Times*. April 24, 1991 1:C23.

Saouab, A. and Vance, J. 1992: *Health policy in Canada*. Ottawa: Minister of Supply and Services Canada.

Singh, H. K. D. 1990. Stork reality. Why American infants are dying. *Policy Review* 52:56–63.

Skolnick, A. 1991. Should insurance cover routine immunizations? *Journal of American Medical Association* 265:2453–4.

Social Security Administration. 1991. *Medicare*. Baltimore: Department of Health and Human Services SSA 05-10043.

Statistics Canada 1984. *The Elderly in Canada*. Cat No. 99–932. Ottawa: Minister of Supply and Services.

Statistics Canada. 1986. *Age, sex, and marital status*. Cat. No. 93–101. Ottawa: Minister of Supply and Services.

Sullivan, C. B. and Rice, T. 1991. The health insurance picture in 1990. *Health Affairs* 102:104–15.

Wood, J. D. 1984. The population of Ontario: a study of the foundation of a Social Geography. In *A Social Geography of Canada*, ed. G. M. Robinson, pp. 92–137. Toronto: Dundurn Press, 92–137.

Woods, G. 1984. *Investigation of the impact of demographic change of the health care system of Canada*. Final Report on the Task Force on the allocation of health care resources. Toronto: Woods Gordon, Management Consultant.

Yeates, M. H. 1977. *Main Street: Windsor to Quebec City*. Toronto: MacMillan.

Zapka, J. G.; A. Stoddard, A.; Maul, L. and M. E. Costanza. 1991. Interval adherence to mammography screening guidelines. *Medical Care* 29:697–707.

# Chapter 10

## Health Care Reform In the United States
## The Canadian Health Care System
## What Should We Adopt?

*Ralph J. Anderson, M.D.*
*Professor and Chairman*
*Fort Worth Affiliated Programs*
*Obstetrics and Gynecology Consultants*
*of the Southwest, P.A.*
*Fort Worth, Texas*

The need for health care reform in the United States has been realized by patients, providers, and financial supporters of the health care system as being necessary and urgent. The confluence of ever expanding technology, an aging population, and increasing demands of the public has created increasing costly care of uneven quality that is provided to only a portion of our citizens. The Untied States government has used market mechanisms to balance the pressures of demand and supply. However, the accelerating health care costs have forced it to investigate other systems including Canada's system of Medicare. In developing health care reform ten ideal principles of a health care system must be included. Firstly, the services must be comprehensive. Secondly, services must be reasonably accessible to all residents. Thirdly, services must be universal. Fourthly, services must be portable. Fifthly, the rights of the patient to choose their medical providers must be preserved. Sixthly, the style of practice must supply high quality treatment in a practical and efficient system with guaranteed access to state of the art technology. Seventhly, the bureaucracy developed to manage the system must be comprehensible, efficient and relatively simple to manage. Eighthly, the health care system must be affordable and be financed fairly. Ninethly, medical liability insurance reform must be enacted. Tenthly the health care plan must be supported by the patients, the providers, and the financial supporters of the plan in order to be successful. The Canadian Medicare plan does have broad public support and does guarantee fairness and equality of care. It seems to provide a rational approach with enhancement of professional equity and allowance for other social needs. It has shown some weaknesses, however, including conflict between physicians and government regulators, concern by the medical profession over compensation and autonomy, restrictions on state of the art technology, a reduction in the time the physician can take for the psychological treatment of disease, and medical inefficiency as determined by misuse of medical facilities and beds.

The Canadian system combines national and provincial funding, allows fee for service, and professional autonomy within certain financial limits and encourages patient autonomy. Canadians are proud of their system which generally provides good medical care to all of its citizens at a lower cost than in the United States—averaging $1,915.00 American dollars for 1991, the latest year for which figures are available, compared with $2,868.00 in the United States. However, spending over the last 5–7 years has grown rapidly and the increase approaches that occurring in United States. It is causing quite significant financial distress and has necessitated the cutting of Federal transfer payments to the ten provinces and two territories which run the health system for 27 million Canadians since the Federal government, which initially funded approximately one-half of the health system cost now funds 30% of the plan, the provinces have been forced into even larger deficits to finance health care and health care finance now consumes approximately one-third of the total spending of the provinces. The fact that the government, Federal, and provincial, is the only payer for services has been successful in controlling expenses and containing administrative overhead costs. However, it has also led to increased confrontation between the providers of health care and the government and it has also led to the notion that the Canadian system is characterized by resistance of competition and innovation.

## Services Must Be Comprehensive

For a health care system to truly provide what is expected of it, it must cover all services including active treatment, preventive treatment, long term care, and ancillary services. The Canadian Medicare System originally did cover a wide variety of services; however, recently with financial constraints becoming increasingly more of a problem, reducing covered services has become a popular approach to shifting the burden of financial constraint to the users.

The Ontario Health Insurance Plan has reduced fees to commercial laboratories and allows them to bill patients directly. Ontario, which insures ten million people, approximately forty percent of Canada's population, has reduced costs by stopping payment for certain services in connection with employment, insurance, pensions, legal proceedings, recreation, and education, by ending coverage of electrolysis, used for the removal of unwanted hair, sometimes the result of hormonal disorders, by reviewing coverage for forty other items including psychoanalysis, vasectomies, newborn circumcision, in vitro fertilization, and chiropractic, podiatric, and osteopathic services, and by increasing patient payments for drug prescriptions covered by the Ontario Drug Benefit Plan which chiefly serves people over sixty five. The Canadian government could at one time afford to be comprehensive and cover all medical services but now must reexamine what it can and should finance. The lesson to be learned involves the fact that the plan needs to be comprehensive, but to expect taxes to totally fund the system is unrealistic.

**Services Must Be Easily Accessible to all Residents**

Routine medical services are reasonably accessible to all residents of Canada; however, state of the art technology and subspecialty care are either not available locally or are available but with significant waiting periods. For many years government limits of medical spending have resulted in long waiting lists for costly non emergency procedures. Patients have had to wait as long as eighteen months for hip replacement surgery, twelve months for cardiac surgery, and three to six months for elective coronary bypass surgery. In some cases, provincial governments have sent patients outside the system to the Untied States for their treatment in order to reduce the backlog. The problem does not involve those needing urgent service because they do get that service; however, the problem does arise in the are where the service is not considered an urgent need but where it is safe to wait a reasonable period of time. The question arises as to whether the time the people do have to wait for these procedures is reasonable.

In some ways the Canadian system over services its residents. The government has attempted to supply inpatient hospital services in many small communities to a degree that some people consider excessive. An attempt must be made in the United States to properly balance the delivery of care. On the other hand, subspecialty services, with state-of-the-art technology, is so regionalized it is unavailable or available with long waiting periods.

**Services Must Be Universal**

In an ideal health care system every American must be covered according to medical need and not ability to pay. It must be regarded a benefit of being a citizen of the Untied States and not viewed as a commodity. This is the major feature of the Canadian System. However, the universality must not preclude efficiency and a structure must be established so the universality is guaranteed in a bureaucratic system that is relative simple, comprehensible, and efficient. In addition, universality does not mean that all services must be offered in all areas. Medical treatment is categorized as primary care, secondary or specialty care, and tertiary, or subspecialty care. Primary care clearly must be available quickly, easily, and efficiently to all citizens in all areas. Specialty care for the most part can be regionalized within a reasonable drawing area so that it would be available within certain health districts but not necessarily in every town. This might vary in different areas where traveling distances would be a problem. Subspecialty care needs to be regionalized and offered with efficient use of man power and technology. The Canadian system clearly offers primary care extremely efficiently; however, it is far less organized in it's delivery of specialty and subspecialty care in that it offers too much in some areas and not enough in others. As a result, often hospitals are supplying hospital care in small places where it is extremely costly. For example,secondary obstetrical care is being offered in hospitals where less than a thousand babies are being delivered per year. On the other hand, state of the art technology which in the United States is considered part of the active management of the patient often is unavailable except in university centers where there are long waits for the procedures including MRI scans CT scans. Our health care system should certainly look at the mechanism utilized in Canada for the delivery of primary care but should look for a regionalizaton of specialty or subspecialty care, with state-of-the-art technology so that the delivery of the care is both beneficial to the patient and cost effective.

**Services Must Be Portable**

It is mandatory that each citizen have coverage that is portable, meaning that a resident of any state must be covered for services received in any other state or country. This is supplied by the Canadian Medicare System.

**The Right of the Patients to Choose Their Medical Providers
Must Be Preserved**

It is mandatory that the patient be allowed freedom of choice of doctors or hospitals for their medical treatment. Patients in Canada do have this freedom of choice.

The Style of Practice Must Supply Preventive Medicine as well as High Quality Active Treatment in a Practical and Efficient System with Guaranteed Access to State of the Art Technology.

*The Medical Team*

To determine the appropriate service to provide for a patient, one has to begin with a clear understanding of the needs of the patient. Often these needs can be met more effectively and more efficiently by paramedical personnel rather than by physicians. Many analysts of the Canadian Health Care System believe the explosion in Canadian health costs has been encouraged by an over supply of doctors and the fee for service system that rewards them for seeing more patients and doing more procedures. In 1964 there was one doctor for every 800 people in Canada. Today there is one doctor for every 450 people in Canada. Growth in the United States has been comparable where in 1965 the ration was one doctor for 720 persons compared with one for 411 persons now. The World Health Organization recommends one doctor for every 600 patients. Ontario's Deputy Health Minister, Mr. Michael Decter, states that each new doctor that goes into practice costs the province $500,000 per year. In Canada, approximately eighty percent of the doctors work under the fee for service system as opposed to salaries. Critics say that this system creates incentives for doctors to provide more services than may be needed. In fact, the over supply of doctors by itself is not the problem. Patients, without any financial restrictions, tend to very much over use the medical system and if more doctors are available, then more patients will go to those doctors. In Canada in order to reduce the number of physicians trained, at the encouragement of the Ontario Department of Health, the University of Toronto has announced a thirty per cent reduction in enrollment in its medical school. Medical schools in other provinces have also announced cut backs. The American system must follow the lead of Canada in reducing the number of doctors being trained and allowing paramedical personal, physician assistants, and nurse practitioners, to manage those problems compatible with their level of training. It should be noted, however, that physicians cannot bill Medicare for services provided by nurses in the Canadian system. If we are going to adopt such a system in the Untied States, it is clear that there must be reimbursement for those supervising the nurses, physician assistants, and nurse practitioners.

*Appropriate Use of System by Patients*

The Canadian Medicare System is significantly overused by patients who seek medical attention for conditions that do not require medical attention, who insist on prolonged stays in the hospital that are unnecessary, and who overutilize nursing homes and other chronic care facilities when those patients could be more efficiently and better cared for in a home setting. Because the system is free and because there have been no user fees, patients tend to seek medical advice quickly for minor ailments that are very self limited. Education of the patients is vital in helping them to decide at what point they should enter the medical system. No such educational system exists in Canada and no attempt is made to educate the patients in this regard. In addition, until recently no user fees have been utilized. In fact, user fees would contravene the Canada Health Act of 1984, which reaffirms the fundamental principle of universal access to comprehensive care unabated by financial barriers. This act is currently being challenged by many politicians who are suggesting that wealthier Canadians would be willing to pay fees to ensure that the poorer Canadians continue to get free health care. Quebec's Ministry of Health has already proposed a user fee of $5.00 each time a patient uses an emergency room but has not yet adopted it. It does require a $2.00 service charge for prescriptions for those over sixty five who normally get prescriptions free. A ceiling limits the fees to $100.00 per year. The experience of the Canadian system would indicate that without user fees and without education of the patient, the patients do overutilize the system. This needs to be noted and avoided as we develop our system in the United States. It is mandatory that patients be educated about when to use the system in order to control the costs.

*Appropriate Use Of Beds*

A major lesson to be learned from the experience of the Canadian health care system refers to inefficient bed utilization. In Canada there are 4.4 acute care beds per 1000 population and 2.4 long term beds per 1000 population. The average occupancy rate is 85.4% and patients utilize bed days at a rate of twelve hundred bed days per year per 1000 population. In comparison, patients with third party insurance carriers in the United States use 800 bed days per year per 1000 population and patients enrolled in HMO's use 400 bed days per year per 1000 population. In terms of chronic care hospital utilization whereas 10% of Canada's over sixty five population are in chronic care hospitals or nursing homes, only 6% of such patients in the United States and Australia and 5% of such patients in England are in chronic care hospitals or nursing homes. It is estimated in Canada that 20—25% of all patients in acute care hospitals do not need to be there, and that 30% of residents of nursing homes should be at home if a rational system of home care or elderly day care services was in place in their community.

In addition to patients in Canada being admitted too frequently they stay too long in Canadian hospitals and there is little use of same day admissions for surgical procedures. It is clear that in developing health care reform, utilization of beds is a key factor in keeping costs reduced and the Canadian system would only serve as a negative role model.

*State Of The Art Technology*

Diagnostic equipment such as MRI and CT scans is critical to the physician in making diagnoses and developing treatment plans. In Canada most physicians complain that it is very difficult or impossible to utilize adequate scanning techniques in the investigation of patients. In the United States this technology is easily available and some critics believe it is overutilized. It is clear that some balance between the two must be reached.

## Prescription Drugs

The Canadian government pays for approximately one half of all prescription drugs through a variety of provincial benefit programs that cost tax payers approximately 1.2 billion dollars per year. The governments do nothing to ensure that these products are used wisely with educational programs for physicians and patients. Patients are often over demanding in their use of drugs and doctors often too lenient in their supplying of these drugs. It is mandatory that in addition to medications being available, education for proper administration or utilization of the medication is important.

## Outcome Management Quality Assurance

The Canadian Health Care System has been very slow to adopt any system of accountability for medical care carried out in either the office or hospital. In the adoption of the health care reform in this country it is mandatory that accountability be established so that physicians and hospitals are aware of their outcomes. These outcomes and complications must be available to patients as they make decisions needed for the treatment of their medical problem.

## Education

Physicians, hospital administrators, and patients must be more extensively educated on all matters related to the practice of medicine. In addition to understanding the pathophysiology of disease processes and outcomes, physicians must be better educated in alternate forms of delivery of health care so that they can then determine whether they or a paramedical member of the team should deliver the care, whether it is appropriate that acute care be carried out to in a hospital or at home and when chronic care is best administered at home or in the hospital. Similarly, hospital administrators must be educated along the same lines so that the patients receiving treatment in acute care institutions where costs are high truly need to be there. Patients need to be educated as to when to seek medical assistance, when treatment should occur as in inpatient as opposed to an out-patient, when acute care might be better done at home than in a hospital, when chronic care might better take place in the patient's home rather than a chronic care hospital, and when to appropriately utilize pharmaceutical preparations in the management of their disease.

*Prevention of Disease*

It is clear that medicine has only a small and minor influence on the health status of a patient. Genetic, environmental, social, and economic conditions play a much greater role in prevention and causation of disease. Poor diets leading to heart disease or cancer, smoking habits leading to cardiovascular disease and cancer, lack of proper hygiene for prevention of infection, loss of the feeling of well being, poverty, employment hazards, excessive use of alcohol, violence, and loneliness all are major contributors to an increase in disease which results in excessive costs to the tax payer. Investments in social programs to try to reduce some of these problems would be very helpful. In spite of the fact that the Canadian government has been very active in developing social programs, they have stopped short of doing what must be done to affect the onset of disease. The Canadian government has been remarkably negligent in addressing these problems; the government of the Untied States has even been worse. Health care reform must include addressing these very serious problems in attempting to improve them so that the prevalence of disease will diminish.

## The Bureaucracy Developed to Manage the Health Care System Must Be Reasonably Simple, Comprehensible, and Efficient

One of the mistakes of the Canadian government in establishing their health care program was not having a strong and effective organization. The Federal government, the regional government, the medical profession, business and other financial supporters of health care, and patients all have a significant role to play to ensure that the system is established properly and runs efficiently. Health care reform is very complicated and it will take the input of these various groups in order to make it successful. Above all, it needs an effective manager. The Canadian system is not well organized and does not have a clear leader. It is very much like a baseball team without a manager. All the individual parts are attempting to work but there is no coordinator of the entire system.

The Federal government clearly must play a major role in establishing short term and long term goals and must enact the laws, rules, and guidelines to oversee the organization of the delivery of health care. They must establish a mechanism to ensure that these goals are realized and that the laws, rules, and regulations are followed. By doing this they will avoid crisis management.

The regional government must have the authority to adapt the laws, rules, and guidelines to the specific needs for their region and must establish a mechanism to ensure that the goals are realized and that the laws, rules, and guidelines are followed.

The medical profession must be aware of the laws, rules, and guidelines and must realize that the problems must be addressed and solutions reached. They must offer constructive criticism and work with the organization whose charge it is to develop an effective system of health care. Above all, they must look at the global situation as it relates to health care and not just their own personal needs.

The financial payers of health care must have their views considered and work with the government and the providers to develop the system.

Finally, patients must also understand the laws, rules, guidelines, and restrictions under which the health care system will operate and be aware that the delivery of health care system will be changed. They must work with the government, the providers, and the payers to develop the system. They must be prepared to change their habits of seeking health care, be willing to be educated about common disease, and when they should seek medical assistance and be prepared to alter their living habits and attempt to live a healthier life style. If they are not willing to do that thee must be prepared to bear a higher portion of the cost of the health care system.

Whereas administrative costs of health plans in the United States represent approximately 10% of expenditures in health care, the rate in Canada is 2.5%. The cost of hospital administration and accounting are considerably higher in the United States than in Canada. In addition the paper work in the American system is overwhelming and we could learn a lot from our Canadian neighbors in the reduction of these costs through a more simplified system.

The proportion of overhead expenses of physicians related to gross income is also much higher in the Untied States than in Canada. This is partly because of a higher incidence of group practice and shared expenses that takes place with Canadian physicians. American physicians must realize that they are not going to be able to continue to operate in isolation from one another and look more into shared expenses and group practices.

**The Health Care Sytem Must Be Affordable and Be Financed Early**

The participators in the health care system including the Federal government, the regional government, the physician, the payers in the business world and elsewhere, and the patients all must realize that the delivery of a excellent health care system with state of the art technology involves considerable expense. The Canadian system generally provides good medical care to all of its citizens at a lower cost than in the United States. However, spending in recent years in Canada on health care has increased almost as rapidly as it has in the United States. The Canadian system is reaching the point of not being able to function and several factors have been considered in an attempt to make it solvent. Although, the establishment of user fees has been widely discussed, the Canadian Health Care Act of 1984 would forbid them because it reaffirms the fundamental principle of universal access to comprehensive care unimpeded by financial barriers. However, several politicians are calling for his issue to be reassessed.

The Canadian government has learned that although at one time it could be comprehensive and cover all medical services, with new economic realities, it needs to re-examine what it will cover. In establishing our health care system it is important to learn the lesson that the government cannot pay for everything. The Federal and Regional governments must combine to cover as many of the costs as possible. However the other payers must realize that they are going to have to make their fair contribution to the system. The providers, including the Doctors, para-medical personnel and the hospitals must reduce their overhead and expenses and very likely receive less remuneration than they have in the past for the management of medical care. Businesses must incorporate health care costs as benefits for their employees. Finally the patients must also realize that they are going to have to make a contribution through taxation, possible user fees and more reasonable expectations and more intelligent usage of the health care system.

**Medical Liability Insurance**

Another means of reducing costs relates to the problem of medical liability insurance. In Canada the problem of medical liability insurance is minimal compared with that of the United States. The physicians are insured through the Canadian Medical Protective Association at premiums that are considerably less than those of their American counterparts. Canadian Medical Protective Association rarely settles out of court and most cases are pursued to the end, thus effectively eliminating nuisance claims. In most cases the lawyers do not take a case for a percentage of the settlement. Those involved with health care reform in the United States must recognize that the medical liability problem is serious and results in law suits being common and often frivolous, in high premiums for medical liability insurance, and in physicians being forced then to practice more costly defensive medicine. We could learn a great deal from the Canadian system regarding medical liability and reduce the cost of health care proportionately by adopting a more aggressive approach to frivolous law suits and by reforming the legal system so that a fee instead of a percentage of the settlement would serve as remuneration for the lawyers. The practice of having a board representing patients, providers and payers to adjudicate many of these cases instead of pursuing them in the more expensive court system should also be investigated. Real tort reform is mandatory.

**The Health Care Plan Must Be Supported by the Patients, the Providers, and the Payers**

SUMMARY

The accelerating cost of the health care system in the United States has necessitated the investigation of alternate forms of health care delivery including the system of Medicare in Canada. In an ideal system services must be comprehensive, accessible to all residents, universal, and portable. The patients must be allowed their choice of providers. The style of practice must supply high quality treatment in a practical and efficient system with guaranteed access to state of the art technology. The bureaucracy developed to manage the system must be comprehensible, efficient and relatively simple to manage. The health care system must be affordable, be financed fairly, and be supported by the patients, the providers and the payers of the plan in order to be successful.

The Canadian system does have some significant strengths. It is a system that is very ethically defensible in that it does supply comprehensive services that are relatively accessible to all patients, it is universal, and it is portable. The Canadian government could at one time afford to be totally comprehensive and cover all medical services. However, economic realities have forced it to re-examine what it can and what it should finance. The lesson to be learned involves the fact that the plan needs to be comprehensive but to expect taxes to completely fund the system is unrealistic. The Federal government, the regional government, the providers, the payers and the patients must all contribute to make the system financially solvent. The Canadian system is very successful in supplying primary medical services to all residents and their approach to this needs to be studied carefully. However, specialty and subspecialty care needs to be better organized. In some cases it is overly available in institutions where it is not practical to deliver that type of care while in other cases it is unavailable or available with unreasonably lengthy waiting periods.

Another major strength of the Canadian system is a significant attempt to control costs. This is reflected by a decreased cost of the bureaucracy in Canada compared to the United States. Much can be learned by planners of health care reform in the United States from the more simplified Canadian system that results in lower hospital administration and accounting costs and lower overhead expenses of practitioners. The Canadian system has attempted to control fees paid to those who deliver health care. There is little doubt that there has been exploitation of the American system by many physicians to the point where some physicians are viewed as doing obscenely well. However, in contrast the Canadian system of reimbursement of physicians and other medical personnel has again been exploited by the government because it is an easy place to reduce costs. The increase in reimbursement of physicians does not even closely approximate the elevation of costs that the physicians have encountered over recent years in practice expenses. The Canadian government has been very liberal in supporting the unions to increase the costs of paramedical personnel that works in hospitals and offices while at the same time it has been very restrictive in increasing the budgets of either the hospitals or the reimbursement of the physicians to cover those costs. It is clear that some form of cost containment of fees must take place but it must take into account the realities of inflation and increasing costs for doing business. The Canadian government has worked hard to keep costs a reasonable level. In Canada there seems to be an unwritten law that health care expenditures should stay at 9% of the gross national product. This idealistic approach should be encouraged providing the reduction in the cost is shared equitably by the payers, the providers and the patients.

While the Canadian system has some very distinctive strengths it also has some very outstanding weakness. Firstly, the fact that the government is the only financial supporter of services has been quite successful in controlling expenses and administrative overhead costs. However, it has lead to significant confrontations between the providers of health care and the government and has lead to the notion that the Canadian system is characterized by resistance of competition and innovation.

Secondly, in establishing their health care program the Canadian government did not establish a strong and effective organization. It does not have an effective manager and the government has played an increasingly restrictive roll and has destroyed any competitive influence. It has followed the lead of all nationalized health care delivery systems that attempt to destroy private medical sectors, not because they are inferior but because they are superior and the existence of an alternate system is an affront to the bureaucrat who is running the system. In the development of health care reform in the United States it is important to realize that not only the Federal and regional government but also the providers, the payers, and the patients must be part of that development and must be satisfied with that development in order for the system to be successful.

A third weakness of the Canadian system involves internal contradictions. Physicians feel very much caught between the government and the patients. The government actively encourages health care utilization by all of its citizens while the public perceives the medical care as being free. The physicians are then abused for driving up the costs and feel very much caught in the middle of a three sided vice. The health care system must decide if it is going to allow all services including state of the art technology to be used or if it is going to ration care according to age and disease specific conditions. The Canadian system has never been able to make that decision. The health care system has forced the doctors into trying to make this decision and then criticizes them when the costs inevitably increase. The American health care system and not the providers of health care must make that decision.

A fourth deficiency relates to inefficient utilization of beds in the Canadian system. Acute care beds and chronic care beds are both heavily utilized by patients that could be treated in other facilities where the costs would be considerably less. In Canada there are too many admissions, patients stay in hospitals too long, and there is very little use for same day admission for surgical procedures. The American system must learn from these deficiencies.

A fifth deficiency relates to the extreme restriction on use of technology in Canada. Many physicians in Canada feel that a lack of access to medical technology reduces the effectiveness of their ability to practice. They believe they do not have adequate access to CT scanners, MRI scanners, x-ray equipment and sonography equipment, cardiac stress monitors and gastroscopes. In hospitals and clinics in the United States there are in excess of 2000 MRI scanners whereas in Canada there are between 15 and 20 and these are all hospital based. Patients needing this technology either are not offered it or have to wait long periods to obtain it. Whereas American practice seems addicted to technology, restrictions imposed by Canadian politicians put the physicians in an extremely difficult position and suggest that if the technique is not available it is not needed. In addition many of the hospitals in Canada have great difficulty repairing or replacing obsolete or worn out equipment so that machines that are being utilized are often not state of the art.

Finally the notion that the government can provide everything for everyone in health care is obsolete. In order for the health care system to be effective the Federal government, regional government, physicians, the payers and the patients all must realize that on excellent health care system is expensive and must be supported by everyone. Federal and regional governments must set up an efficient organization, must be prepared to change laws such as those that relate to medical liability, and must supply reasonable funds through taxation of its citizens. The physicians must be prepared to practice good medicine and not extravagant medicine and must be prepared to accept lower fees for their services. The payers must be prepared to properly finance insurance programs within their industry and educate their employees as to the proper use of the health care system. Patients must be prepared to pay appropriate taxes and to utilize the system so that they only seek medical care for conditions that truly require medical attention, so that they assume more responsibility of health care for themselves and their families in less expensive institutions, and so that they alter their lifestyles so that illnesses produced by less than ideal lifestyles could be reduced.

It will be difficult but not impossible to develop an ideal health care system that can combine the best of the Canadian and American systems. We must strive to combine the American focus on freedom and market forces with the Canadian devotion to fairness and equality. It is clear that we must shift from a system that is focused on treatment of illnesses to one that promotes wellness and prevention and must strive to develop a system that provides state of the art medicine in the most practical atmosphere possible.

# Chapter 11

## The Rocky Trail of Acceptance
## of Medicare by Canadian Physicians
## A Short History

*Robert A. H. Kinch, M.D.*
*Fort Worth Affiliated Programs*
*Obstetrics and Gynecology Consultants*
*of the Southwest, P.A.*
*Fort Worth, Texas*

Writing in 1992 a special report in the Canadian Medical Association Journal entitled "Medicare turns 30" Malcolm Taylor leads off—

> July 1992 marks the 30th anniversary of Saskatchewan's introduction of the first universal, tax-supported program of medical care insurance in North America. It is hard to believe that an entire generation has grown up under its protective umbrella and, given current nationwide popular support for Medicare, it is equally difficult to recall its horrendous birth pangs.
>
> But, despite the heavy costs for the participants and for much of the public, Saskatchewan had pioneered again. Eleven years after the province introduced hospital insurance in 1947, a national program was initiated; it would take only half as long for national Medicare to arrive once Saskatchewan first offered it in 1962.

Although Saskatchewan holds the honors there was an ongoing ferment of discussion. After 10 years of discussion, the Canadian Medical Association (C.M.A.) Committee of Seven under the chairmanship of Dr. T. C. Routley in co-operation with the Hafferty committee of the Department of Health gave a unanimous endorsement of the following historic resolutions in 1943:

> The Canadian Medical Association approves the adopting of the principle of health insurance. The Canadian Medical Association favours a plan of health insurance that will secure the development and provision of the highest standard of health service, preventative and curative, if such a plan be fair both to the insured and to all those rendering the services.

During these 10 years, Norman Bethune, a daring but too dashing a surgeon at the Royal Victoria Hospital in Montreal, a man regarded either as a hero and a genius by some, or an outcast by others, was passionately putting together the Manifesto of the Montreal Group for the Security of the Peoples' Health. He was attempting to jolt the conscience of his conservative colleagues. On April 17th, 1936 he got his chance in front of the Montreal Medical Chirurgical Society taking as his title "Take the Private Profit out of Medicine."

He strongly advocated adopting a system of socialized medicine and spared no effort to berate his colleagues.

A few random quotes:

"Medicine, as we are practicing it, is a luxury trade. We are selling bread at the price of jewels."

"Let us say to the people not—'how much have you got' but—'how best can we serve you.' Our slogan should be 'we are in business for your health.'"

"The people are ready for socialized medicine. The obstructionists to the people's health security lie within the profession itself. Recognize this fact. It is the all-important fact of the situation. These men with the mocking face of the reactionary or the listlessness of the futilitarian, proclaim their principles under the guise of 'maintenance of the sacred relationship between doctor and patient,' 'inefficiency of other non-profit nationalized enterprises,' 'the danger of Socialism,' 'the freedom of individualism.' These are the enemies of the people and make no mistake. They are the enemies of medicine too."

This speech was received with hostility by this Montreal audience. Nevertheless Bethune was frequently invited to speak on serious scientific subjects all over the U.S. and Canada. He always stunned and shocked his colleagues by ending his talk with his Manifesto.

A provincial election was called for 1936. The Manifesto of the Montreal Group for the Security of the People's Health was delivered to election candidates in Montreal, to the Premier of Quebec and to hospital, health and religious authorities.

He was unprepared for and depressed by the hostility and indifference of those who read his Manifesto. Few took it seriously.

After a visit to Soviet Russia, he joined the Communist party and in October 1936 set out for Spain. Fighting on the Republican side he organized the first mobile blood transfusion service supplying blood to the wounded front line troops. This served as a model for the second world war.

Disgusted again by the political changes in Spain, he joined the People's Republic of China under Chairman Mau Tse Tung. Here he at last found his metier, operating in caves, Buddhist Temples, stables and anywhere he could find shelter. At the height of his fame as a hero in China, he died in 1939 from Septicemia from an infected needle stick.

Fighting for losing causes, this man is still a hero to millions of Chinese and their children, an evangelist who thrived on war. In 1971—he was ultimately deified—to cement Canadian Chinese diplomatic relations in a ceremony in the Royal Victoria Hospital—Montreal, his nemesis, still to the chagrin of some. His statue can be seen in a small park in the center of Montreal.

The next historical landmark was the election in 1944 of the Socialist Cooperation Commonwealth Foundation (C.C.F.) government under Tommy Douglas in Saskatchewan.

He launched a Hospital Services Plan in which all recipients of old age pensions and mother's allowance, as well as wards of the province, were entitled to medical, hospital, dental and drug benefits. Despite his party's 15-year commitment, Tommy Douglas realized that he did not have the finances to cover the whole population of the province.

Meanwhile, the Federal government passed the Hospital Insurance and Diagnostic Services Act (HIDS) in 1957. This was the first of the twin legislative pillars on which the Canadian health insurance system was built. The key feature of the HIDS act was that public insurance coverage for hospital services was universal, across the population as a whole, rather than as on the American pattern in the mid-1960s, covering only selected population groups.

Saskatchewan already had a hospital in place. This act provided the financial windfall which Tommy Douglas needed to pass his Provincial Health Care Plan.

In 1960 Tommy Douglas faced a provincial election and the issue was Medicare. He won.

He started negotiations with the Saskatchewan Medical College, whose president at the time was a surgeon, Dr. Harold Dalgleish.

Negotiations become acrimonious, enraging Dr. Dalgliesh and the medical profession, that, with their support, he instructed the members to withdraw their services as of July 1st 1962.

The plan produced a fully fledged doctors' boycott, with this notice pasted on physician's doors:

TO OUR PATIENTS
THIS OFFICE WILL BE CLOSED AFTER
JULY 1ST, 1962

## WE DO NOT INTEND TO CARRY ON PRACTICE
## UNDER
## THE SASKATCHEWAN MEDICAL CARE
## INSURANCE ACT

Emergency doctors were imported from Britain to break the boycott, only to have an injunction placed on them barring them from hospital privileges. Eventually it was settled in the government's favor in 25 days.

This resulted in an extremely bad press for the physicians. The plan was put in effect on July 26th, 1962.

In 1964 Judge Emmett Hall was appointed by John Diefenbaker, a Conservative Prime Minister to prepare a brief for a national Medicare plan. This plan was accepted by the Federal government and negotiations were started to pass the Medical Care Act of 1966.

Lester Pearson-Canada's Prime Minister was ruling a shaky minority Liberal government. Snapping at his heels was David Lewis, the leader of the socialist National Democratic Party whose promise of support depended on the implementation of this National Medicare plan. Lester Pearson was encouraged to accept this plan and later Prime Minister Pierre Trudeau implemented it.

In 1970 the second withdrawal of services was organized under the leadership of a radiologist named Lougheed and included all the Specialists in the Province of Quebec. Again, the press was against the doctors. Massive fines were leveled against the physicians. The government ordered them back to work. This boycott coincided with a National Emergency in which a British Diplomat named James Cross, was kidnapped by a small revolutionary cell named the Front Liberation de Quebec. This cell, or series of separate revolutionary cells, used friendly radio stations to convey written messages to the authorities. These messages were usually picked up from trash cans or phone booths. No one knew their numbers, or support, but they were determined, militant, and in the view of the Federal and Provincial governments, a danger to the security of the country. They had been responsible for the rash of letter box bombings in English speaking Montreal in 1968 and 1969. For these reasons Mr. Trudeau declared an enactment of the War Measures Act. Many anti-government Nationalists were arrested without charge, soldiers patrolled the streets of Montreal and Quebec city. Those arrested were suspects of revolution activities together with sympathetic authors, actors, chanteuses and writers; a very vocal minority ever since. The doctors, already losing heart, returned to work because of the National Emergency. The fines were never paid.

As far as the specialists were concerned, they set up a war-room to direct the physicians withdrawal of services. Only emergency and obstetric services remained open. My hospital, the Montreal General remained open for obstetrics. To increase the chaos, my staff obstetricians were sent to the Canadian Medical Association headquarters in Ottawa, together with all nonessential physicians.

They were replaced by the staff of the Jewish General Hospital, who knew nothing about my department.

After 16 days, when Pierre Laporte was murdered, the physicians were certain that there would be a National emergency—They were already losing heart and enthusiasm in the face of insistent media and community attack. They returned to work. The heavy fines were never paid. Again this withdrawal damaged physicians esteem with futile results.

The next crisis occurred in 1984. Pierre Trudeau the Liberal Prime Minister enacted the Canada Health Act which banned extra billing by physicians and the charging of extra fees by hospitals.

In passing the Medical Act the weak Liberal Government hoped to bolster its waning popularity by accusing the Conservative opposition that it was against Medicare. That it did not take the bait is shown by the following excerpt from a book written by a Liberal cabinet member, Mr. Donald Johnson. It did not work, as all the conservative M.P.'s forsook their principles, and together with every other M.P. voted for the measure.

It was April 9, 1984. The House was in session and about to vote on [Health and Welfare Minister] Monique Begin's controversial Canada Health Act which denied extra billing. It was an historic moment. Conservative free market doctrine dictated that they [The Progressive Conservatives] support doctors in charging over and above the fee set by Medicare. They had argued long and battled hard in committee against the bill. The speaker called the House to order and the poll of members began. A strange scene unfolded. Not only were Liberals and, predictably, the NDP [the socialist leading New Democratic party], voting yes but one by one every Tory in the House, including Brian Mulroney, the leader of the opposition, was voting yes, too. Many of our members were incredulous. Then it dawned on them: the public opinion polls. The Tories realized that public opinion was so solidly behind what Monique was suggesting that they dared not vote the courage of their political convictions. When the final vote was counted not a single Tory had voted no.

The Federal Government stated that provinces which allowed doctors to extra bill would lose Federal grants, dollar for dollar, of the amount extra billed. The Liberal minority government of Ontario had become the target for fevered rhetoric and promptly barred extra-billing. The physicians in Ontario—the only province really affected by this act, waged a 25 day withdrawal of services under the leadership of a urologist, Lionel Reese, then President of the Ontario Medical Association. Their argument was that it interfered with professional freedom and the doctor patient relationship. Having lost the boycott, they felt that the public perception despite their efforts to depict it as revolving around professional freedom, was that the withdrawal of services was a struggle over money. The boycott understandably saved the government a considerable amount of money. This was both from physicians' services not billed and from all reduced hospital expenses during the boycott. It cost the physicians income and loss of considerable public sympathy.

The Ontario Medical Association had acted without prior agreement of the doctors in the negotiations to refuse to ban extra billing. After withdrawing their services, the doctors received nothing in exchange for the loss of their right to extra bill.

To bring history up to date—the present case is about user fees.

To quote Heiber:

> The defenders of Medicare worried that a trend towards reliance on direct charges—both extra-billing and hospital user fees—might ultimately endanger public health insurance by impeding reasonable access to services, one of the basic principles of Medicare. These fears were generally voiced as accusations of providers greed rather than criticism of provincial government activities. The potential for "two-tier medicine," with better service reserved for those able to pay, was repeatedly invoked. Whereas physicians might argue that society considered it acceptable for only some to be able to afford Cadillacs (e.g., approved of "two-tier transportation"), and permitted inequalities in the allocation of housing, food and other necessities, their position had little political appeal; indeed, it strengthened the determination of the "friends of Medicare" (especially in the labour movement, among senior citizens, and in the Liberal and NDP parties) to ensure that universal Medicare was "preserved."

The whole concept of Canadian Medicare is embodied in equal access, undeterred by income or ability to pay. This will mean a means test.

The small fees, which are proposed, appear minor—but the destruction of a "holy" principle may well result in a backlash, which will defeat this method of deterrence.

The U.S. Constitution states that education is the right of every citizen. It does not give the same right to health care.

As we proceed to a National Health Care System, if it is to be successful, a bold philosophical change of attitude to health care must take place. Health must be given the same right as education.

American physicians, individualistic as they are proud to be, will not stoop to withdrawal of services to achieve their ends. Consequently it is hoped that the necessary changes will take place without the "horrendous birth pangs," accompanying the history of the birth of the Canadian Medicare System.

# Section 3

# U.S. Needs and Directions

# U.S. Needs and Directions

The papers in this final section will examine the values of the U.S. that will shape health care reform and examine the directions that reform could take.

The first chapter, "The A, B, Cs of Medical Care: America, Britain and Canada," by Derek Gill, examines rationing of health care as it is implemented in the three countries. Dr. Gill is a British sociologist and is currently Professor and Chair in the Department of Sociology and Anthropology at the University of Maryland Baltimore Campus. He argues that the three systems practice rationing, with Britain and Canada holding down the supply of medical care through reimbursement rates, and the U.S. rationing according to ability to pay for care using insurance or cash. Dr. Gill first examines the effects of the concepts of individualism and collectivism, and of equity, uniformity, distributive justice and public accountability on the organization for the health care delivery systems in the three countries. He outlines the principals of managed competition, and then uses the Canadian and British systems to provide criteria for evaluating the managed care competition model. Major criteria identified include sources of revenue to finance the model, whether direct or indirect taxation; the balance between individual and societal responsibility for providing for health care; and the degree to which the system can be cost efficient.

In "International Convergence in Health Care Systems: Lessons, from and for the USA," Professor Rex Taylor examines recent health care reforms in the Britain, Sweden, France and Canada and suggests ways these reforms could be instructive for health care reform in the United States. While all four countries have some form of national health insurance and have eliminated financial barriers to use of health care, all four have recently reviewed their health care systems to determine ways the systems could be reformed to hold down spending, as well as to make the systems more efficient in terms of allocation of health care resources, to reduce discontinuities in levels of care, and to increase consumer choice. For a solution to their problems these countries have adopted the American principles of managed care as espoused by Alain Enthoven. Prof. Taylor notes the irony that the United States is looking at the possibility of adopting a national health insurance at a time when the countries that have such schemes are weakening their systems and adopting systems more like that in the United States.

David R. Smith, M.D., is currently the Commissioner of the Texas Department of Health. His co-author, Ron J. Anderson, M.D., is President and CEO of Parkland Memorial Hospital in Dallas. In their article, "Feudal vs. Futile Medicine: Can We Have Cost Containment Without Prevention," Dr. Smith and Dr. Anderson argue that health care reform must include comprehensive health care that includes prevention and primary care as essential elements. They describe and discuss the advantages of the Community Oriented Primary Care model in delivering comprehensive services to targeted populations in specific neighborhoods. Specific advantages discussed include reduced barriers due to transportation needs, reduced financial barriers, and the convenience of one-stop shopping for related health and social services.

In the chapter "Health Assurance Development: A Unique Partnership," Daniel J. Schneider, M.D., M.P.H., with Katye Kowierschke, M.S., and Janice Smith, M.B.A., describes a model in which prevention is aimed at the underlying social and behavioral causes of health problems. HAD is a community based program that is based on a partnership between general education and health care that focuses on educating children in prevention of unhealthy behaviors including delinquency, smoking, drug and alcohol abuse, consuming high fat diets, and teenage pregnancy. Dr Schneider argues that resources invested in prevention would result in decreases in money spent for health care to treat illness later in life.

Gerald J. Middents, M.Div., Ph.D., describes a method of educating student for their future roles in policy making as citizens and as influential policy makers in his chapter, "Lessons for Citizen Policy makers in Canada and the United States on Health Care Policy." Dr. Middents is currently Professor of Psychology and Director of Contemporary Policy Studies at Austin College in Sherman, Texas. In the first part of the chapter, Dr. Middents briefly outlines a history of the development of the current health care system in the U.S. and discusses four major problem areas with the system, including access to care, cost of care, quality of care and ethical considerations. In the second half of the chapter, Dr. Middents describes a course for junior and senior students at a four year liberal arts program that incorporates a creative problem solving model in which students work in teams to analyze problems and develop policy solutions, and are graded on written and oral reports that are presented to community leaders.

In the final chapter, "Canadian Health Care System: Implications for Nursing in the United States," Patricia N. Dzandu, M.S., M.A., R.N., C.N.A.A., examines the role of nurses under health care reform. She argues that nurses, especially nurse practitioners, can have an expanded role as primary care givers. She cites examples in Canada where nurses are the major primary care giver for isolated populations of native inhabitants. At the time of the conference, Ms. Dzandu was Director of Nursing at a hospital in the Dallas-Fort Worth Metroplex. She is currently on the staff of the Peninsula Psychiatric Hospital in Hampton, Virginia.

# Chapter 12

## The A, B, Cs of Medical Care
## America, Britain and Canada*

*Derek G. Gill, Ph.D.*
Professor and Chair
Department of Sociology and Anthropology
University of Maryland—Baltimore County

## INTRODUCTION

The organization, management, delivery but above all cost of medical services represent significant charges upon the GDP of the industrialized world. In the U.S., where the private sector (predominantly by corporations but also including payments by individuals) finances about 60 per cent of the expenditure, Fein has suggested that "As a result, American companies have proportionately less capital to invest, thereby jeopardizing the country's international competitive position" (1992, p.46). In addition an estimated 37 million Americans are without health insurance (and must therefore purchase medical care from their own, often limited resources or seek charity care) and millions more are inadequately insured. This sorry state of affairs is achieved currently at the cost to both the private and public sector of almost 14% of the GNP, the highest in the Western World. Comparative figures for the costs of medical care based on gross domestic product in 1991 were: America 13.4%, Britain 6.6% and Canada 10%.

The Clinton administration has already declared reform of the American medical care system to be one of its top priorities and in this circumstance it is essential to produce a set of theoretical concepts by which ensuing reforms may be evaluated. Such concepts must include comparisons of the principles or values which underpin a given societies' choice of medical care system as well as the actual mechanisms through which medical care is delivered. Although in its infancy, cross-cultural and comparative studies of various countries' medical care systems are attracting more attention and

*I am grateful for the comments of Tim Diamond and Bill Rothstein on an earlier version of this paper.

generating increasingly valuable analyses. Even more interesting is the exchange of ideas across national boundaries concerning methods for the restructuring of specific medical care systems. In 1985 the Nuffield Provincial Hospitals Trust published Enthoven's 'Reflections on the Management of the National Health Service (NHS),' in which Enthoven proposed the introduction of the principle of competition to the NHS through the generation of "internal markets" which would encourage providers, hospitals and G. P.'s, to compete, hospital against hospital, G. P.'s against G. P.'s for "customers," i.e., patients and by so doing improve operational efficiency and lower costs in the NHS. This document, Day and Klein (1991) suggest, must have strongly influenced the Thatcher administration's reform of the NHS outlined in Working for Patients (HMSO, 1989). Whether or not Enthoven's "Reflections . . ." influenced the proposals in Working for Patients, Day and Klein conclude that the introduction of "internal markets" will do little to promote market principles within the NHS and may distort clinical judgment to the ultimate disadvantage of patients.

Rather than a sudden splurge into a competitive health care system, the NHS's "internal market" for hospital care will be a special kind of market, with managers trading with each other and with the consumer conspicuous by his or her absence. Moreover, the trading may have more to do with the reliability, accessibility, and timeliness of services provided than with the price. Managers will be seeking not the cheapest form of intervention for individual patients, but the services package that appears to offer the best value and the services *required* (emphasis added) by their populations. (Day and Klien, 1991, p.52).

And in the primary care sector Day and Klein argue:

> . . . it is clear that most GPs will have no pressing reason to engage in competition for patients. Similarly, it is likely that the most contentious component in the government's package—the introduction of budget holding for GPs—will also dampen competition. Specifically, budget holding permits GPs to shop around, on behalf of their patients for the kind of diagnostic and elective procedures that are the core of the waiting list issue. At the same time, it gives them an incentive to deal with patients' problems themselves, instead of passing them onto the hospital service. Budget holding GPs thus will be forced to examine the financial implications of their clinical decisions. The judgement of GPs . . . would become corrupted. Instead of thinking only about the patient, they would be worrying about their bottom line (Day and Klien, 1991, p.54).

Currently the notion of 'managed competition'—a concept close to the idea of 'internal markets' which was a focal component of Enthoven's Reflections on the

Management of the National Health Service—is being strongly advocated as the principle upon which the Clinton reforms should be based. For the U.S. the cost savings, improvements in risk sharing and efficiency which managed competition is expected to provide will help to cover the cost of incorporating the un- and under-insured into the reformed system. For the U.K., where universal coverage has been in effect since 1948, internal markets are expected to free-up additional resources which can be plowed back into the system to, in part, assuage the underfunding of the NHS which most authorities believe to have been the case since its inception (Gill, 1980. Klein, 1989). For the U.K., such aspirations are clearly unrealistic in the light of Day and Klein's conclusions (see also Navarro, 1991 for additional criticisms of attempts to introduce competitive principles into primary care in the U.K.) and in the U.S., as I shall argue, the principle of "managed competition" will similarly be found to be wanting as a procedure for reducing medical care costs.

For those who support a less radical solution (i.e., which does not include taking into public ownership the major providers of medical care-hospitals) to reform American medical care, the Canadian system of a monopsonistic payment mechanism and global budgets as procedures for controlling costs are preferred. Organizations as disparate in membership and structure as the General Accounting Office, the American College of Physicians, and Physicians for Social Responsibility call for a national health plan similar to Canada's (Bodenheimer, 1989, 1990; Woolhandler and Himmelstein, 1991).

While there are radical differences, already apparent, among the three systems—universal coverage v. limited access—there is one commonality which all three share: rationing. In America rationing is achieved through the purse—those unable to purchase (or have purchased for them) health insurance are denied access or are dependent upon 'charity' care, the costs of which are often passed on to the affluent or borne by public sector hospitals (National Association of Public Hospitals, 1991). Both Britain and Canada ration access to medical care by providing in some instances, but subject to correction in Canada, insufficient resources to treat all patients who might benefit from a given procedure (Gill, Ingman & Campbell, 1991; Naylor, 1991) and by the system of the queue, whereby patients may have to wait their turn for elective surgery.

In effect, Britain and Canada also 'ration' providers by holding down rates of reimbursement to the supply side of the medical care provider/patient relationship, particularly doctors. Physicians are reimbursed much less generously in both Britain and Canada than in the United States. In what follows, therefore, the issue of rationing will figure prominently in the attempt to generate theoretical positions and proposi-tions to evaluate proposals, both imported and indigenous, for the reform of the U.S. medical care system. It should also be emphasized that rationing, or a more neutral phrase, cost-containment, was also embraced by six other OECD countries in the 1980s: Belgium, France, Germany, Ireland, the Netherlands and Spain (Hurst, 1991).

The argument will proceed in four steps: 1) a distinction will be drawn between the notions of individualism and collectivism and related to Weale's (1990) distinction between institutional (well developed) and residual (less developed) forms of the welfare state and the medical care systems embedded therein; 2) the concepts of equity, uniformity, distributive justice and public accountability will then be explored as they apply to the provision of medical care; 3) the principle of Health Insurance Purchasing Cooperatives (Health Alliances, HAs) and managed competition will be outlined and related to the previous discussion of values and 4) aspects of the British and Canadian systems of medical care will be abstracted, insofar as they are relevant, to provide additional criteria for evaluating the proposed HA and managed competition model for the reform of the U.S. system.

**Individualism, Collectivism and Medical Care**

The distinctions between individualism and collectivism have already proven useful in analyzing the forms in which medical care and other social services are delivered in a variety of national settings (Clark, 1991; Gill, Ingman & Campbell, 1991; Gill & Ingman, 1994; Ingman & Gill, 1986; Ingman, Gill & Campbell, 1986). In general, societies which support, albeit to varying degrees, collectivist principles in their overall societal value systems tend towards a relatively highly developed welfare state apparatus and provide universal access to medical care. Societies which endorse individualistic principles tend towards a limited welfare state apparatus and limited access to medical services. Clark (1991, p.632), has noted that ". . . The United States has always been a country that has emphasized personal autonomy or independence. . . . Indeed, even early observers of the Republic like Tocqueville noted the penchant for individualism." Clark goes on to demonstrate the relevance of individualism in the U.S. today by summarizing Bellah *et al*'s (1985) major findings of their work entitled 'Habits of the Heart' which studied attitudes of Americans toward basic principles or values which guide social and political action. "Their conclusion is that rampant individualism poses a significant threat to our ability to live together in a national community, a "commonwealth" in which the common good has a real significance for its members." Clark also notes that two influential books by Lipset, 'The First New Nation: The United States in Historical and Comparative Perspective' (1963) and 'Continental Divide: The Values and Institutions of the United States and Canada' (1990) supports the conclusion that an emphasis on individualism versus collectivism are "seen as a significant barrier to the acceptance of social policies responding to the needs of the larger community."

In terms of medical care, a society which operates with a predominantly individualistic orientation may be defined as one which emphasizes the duties and responsibilities of individuals to provide for their medical care needs, while a social system which operates with a collectivist orientation emphasizes the responsibility of the society at-large to provide medical care for all. Under a collectivist orientation the financing of medical care is partially or completely decommodified. An individual does not generally have to enter the market place to purchase preventive, curative, or ameliorative medical services, directly or indirectly, by purchasing health insurance. Services are made available at zero cost at point of delivery so that those unable or least able to bear the cost of medical care necessary for the maintenance or restoration of health are not barred from access.

In practice, the dichotomy between individualist and collectivist orientations is never complete. The elite in all societies reserve the right to access the 'best' and most expensive forms of medical care through their ability to use their wealth or power to purchase or direct services to meet their needs (Reinhardt, 1993, p.186). Moreover, in the American context, one of the advocates of reform of the medical care system through the introduction of HAs and managed competition explicitly acknowledges the need to placate the interests of the elite:

> Reform will meet fewer objections if its financing resembles the current, employer-based system of insurance premiums. A tax-based system might well be simpler, more efficient, and more progressive. Nevertheless, converting to a tax-financed system would create large numbers of losers as well as winners—and the losers would be affluent and powerful. Health care reform is hard enough without stirring upper-income taxpayers to opposition. (Starr & Zelman, 1993, p.116)

One might also add to this list of potential losers physicians, on average the highest paid M. D.s in the Western world (Fein, 1992, p.51), senior executives and managers of Blue Cross/Blue Shield, the private-for-profit health insurance industry and its shareholders and the hoards of white-blouse/white-collar workers who process the 'paper jungle' consequent upon the multiplicity of payers, private and public involved in the generation and collection of charges for medical services.

In Britain the elite is similarly isolated from some of the rationing devices of the NHS. A small private sector persists, providing medical care for those wealthy enough to afford private insurance premiums, or who have their premiums paid by their employers as a fringe benefit. This does not, however, purchase access to 'better' medical care. Most private insurance covers relatively simple medical procedures and the treatment of costly medical care interventions, including chronic care, is left in the hands of the NHS. Private insurance provides more attractive hospital environments—

single rooms, better food, choice of surgeon, but the major benefit is that privately insured patients can choose the time of hospitalization to suit their own schedules and therefore jump the queue for predominantly elective treatments. In the public sector prescription charges, a regressive tax, clearly antithetical to a collectivist orientation, were originally introduced at the behest of international money-lenders who insisted on the measure to reduce, albeit in token fashion, government expenditure if Britain was to be bailed out of one of its many post-war balance of payment crises. Subsequently, prescription charges were raised to dissuade both patients and primary care providers from over-utilizing drug therapies for the treatment of what were defined as minor illness episodes. Despite the regressive nature of this 'health tax' receipts are minimal since approximately 60% of all prescriptions are exempt from charges; pregnant and nursing mothers, children and the elderly and those requiring constant medication for the treatment of chronic conditions.

In the American context, however, the commodification of medical care continues to exert an upward pressure on the price charged for medical care since in both the hospital sector and the third party payer market a significant proportion of insurance coverage and medical services are offered on a private-for-profit basis. Costs for medical care are driven upwards by the need to generate and maintain healthy profits for the investors who provide the financing for profit-oriented health insurance companies and proprietary hospitals.

The search for profits adds further impetus to rising costs by encouraging a switch from community to experience ratings to calculate health insurance premiums. Insurance companies and even pre-paid medical service providers are often tempted and often succumb to the attraction of covering low-risk populations to whom they can offer lower premiums compared with companies that must continue to cover high-risk patients, such as Blue Cross and Blue Shield if they are to continue to operate as quasi-public insurers. Consequently, high-risk groups, including those with on-going medical problems, are denied access to health insurance or faced with draconian premium increases if they are to continue to be covered. Again the quasi-public insurance sector and the public hospitals are required to absorb the additional costs of covering high-risk patients while private-for-profit insurance companies and providers could generate profits from covering low-risk populations.

One further conceptual clarification is necessary before entering upon discussion of the second part of the fourfold argument outlined earlier; an examination of the issue of choice in relation to medical services. In a market system medical care providers charge what the market will bear and consumers are expected to choose between alternative providers in accordance with the usual principles of economic exchange; quality, cost and effectiveness. It is now, however, generally recognized that the consumer, *i.e.*, the patient in medical care exchanges, has little ability to recognize real choices (Gill, 1978; Gill & Horobin, 1972; Waitzkin & Stoeckle, 1976,). Physicians control an esoteric body of knowledge that is difficult for most patients to penetrate and fully understand which enable M. D.s to determine both input and outcomes in doctor/ patient exchanges. Physicians decide not only what is wrong with the patient but what treatment modalities are appropriate to ameliorate or cure the disease condition. Under these circumstances the costs of the income/outcome equation are determined by only one party to the relationship, the physician; in effect, physicians ultimately determine both the demand and supply of medical services. In these circumstances patient choice is mostly a chimera.

The introduction of D.R.G.s and a prospective payment system to reimburse hospitals for services to Medicare patients is an explicit acknowledgement of the factors outlined in the previous paragraph. The price that Medicare will pay for hospital treatments is no longer determined by the varying market conditions in different parts of the United States. Rather, reimbursements are set on a national average for the services needed to treat sets of conditions grouped under the D.R.G. system but with adjustments permitted for local variations and extra costs incurred, such as the training of future generations of doctors. In effect, the freedom of hospitals to charge what their local markets can bear has been partially eroded. Indeed, it will be argued, both in steps 3 and 4 of the argument, that the proposals for reform of American medical care through HAs and managed competition implicitly if not explicitly support a partial decommodification of medical service provision.

But the next step is to consider other value propositions and one procedure which necessarily follows if the ethical positions underpinning these values prove acceptable.

### Distributive Justice, Equity, Uniformity, and Public Accountability

One ethical principle must be discussed at the outset, the principle of distributive justice; a principle which ultimately can only be resolved at the level of simplicity, even naivety. No one should be barred access to a medical service or procedure which can prevent the onset of a disease or illness, can cure an acute condition or can ameliorate a chronic illness. Ultimately the condition of access is determined objectively (scientifically). Currently, we cannot, nor ever are we likely to be able to, cure anencephaly, neither can we be sure that we can effectively screen and therefore abort fetuses which might otherwise survive, but without the ability to become functioning human beings. Under these circumstances, therefore, a condition of medical uncertainty prevails.

The basic principle of distributive justice can now be reduced to the statement— no one should be barred from access to medical services or procedures which can be prevented, cured or ameliorated through currently extant medical knowledge and technology. This proposition is clearly supportable theoretically since objective criteria (scientific knowledge) can distinguish between effective and ineffective medical interventions. At the margin, of course, certainty slips back into uncertainty but again the only appropriate resolution would seem to be a form of public account-ability where a collectively-based judgment permits or curtails the application of scarce resources to procedures with unpredictable outcomes.

But let us return to the more mundane arenas in which illnesses currently can be prevented, cured or ameliorated. Since 37 million Americans have no access to regular medical services, then prevention, cure or amelioration are unavailable to this popu-lation and a further unidentified proportion of the population have insufficient insurance coverage to afford certain forms of curative and ameliorative medicine. To resolve these problems, the principles of uniformity and equity should determine the way in which medical resources are made available to the population to be served.

Uniformity implies the provision of a uniform quality and quantity of medical services in all geographic locations and all social classes wherever need exists; inner-city ghettos, sparsely populated districts, pockets of rural poverty, immigrant laborers, the unemployed, the homeless and so on. The principle of equity, already stated, requires that medical services should be supplied at zero cost at point of delivery and throughout the plethora of medical services necessary to prevent, treat or ameliorate existing medical problems so that all who are sick are equally treated.

To achieve these objectives, which are derived from the principles of distributive justice, uniformity, and equity, the providers of medical care, the medical profession and its collaborators in the medical enterprise, drug companies, the medical technology industry, hospitals, hospital administration, nurses, laboratory technicians, etc., etc., must be accountable, through the body politic, to the general population and to the nation's sick, ill and debilitated.

The body politic must, therefore, accept the responsibility of ensuring that the principles of distributive justice, equity and uniformity are adhered to in the delivery of medical services since it (the government) is finally responsible for the well-being of the population it serves. In the final analysis the state itself is dependent on the preservation of hegemony (Gramsci, 1985) through the implementation of social policies which attract the support of the population if the state is to survive. Opinion polls in the U.S. indicate clearly the disaffection of the majority of the American public with the current medical care system (see Navarro, Altman, & Navarro, 1992, pp.23–30). It is therefore not surprising to note that the current administration expresses a real commitment to reform the present system of medical care provision.

The minimal conditions under which the medical care industry must be publicly accountable are now quite clear—the body politic must ensure that the principles of distributive justice, equity and uniformity control the way in which currently effective medical services are delivered to the American public. But the government must undertake an additional responsibility under the rubric of public accountability; that of resolving the dilemmas associated with the certainty/uncertainty dichotomy in medical care. When the scientific and medical communities cannot agree upon the relative effectiveness or the predictable outcomes of a specific medical regimen or procedure, whether it involves inexpensive or expensive allocation of resources, then the conflict must be resolved within an alternative framework. This situation necessarily reinvokes the notion of rationing. When uncertainty prevails, it is the responsibility of the political process to determine the limits of expenditures upon medical procedures whose outcomes are unpredictable. What other authority could fairly and reasonably be expected to undertake such responsibility other than the body politic? It is the duty of government, through its responsibility to promote the well-being of the population it serves and represents, that alone can determine the rationing of scarce resources.

The argument can now proceed to step 3; an outline of the way in which Health Alliances and managed competition are designed to resolve the conceptual and value propositions outlined thus far.

### Health Alliances and Managed Competition

Before considering the arguments in favor of HAs and managed competition outlined in, for example, the special issue of Health Affairs entitled 'Managed Competition: Health Reform American Style' (1993) it seems reasonable to review Clinton's campaign proposals outlined in 'Bill Clinton's American Health Care Plan' (1992), also presented in the September 10, 1992, issue of the *New England Journal of Medicine*. These proposals, as outlined by Families USA (October 1992), included the following:

> The establishment of a National Health Board that would establish annual budget targets to assure that health care costs do not go up faster than the average American's income. To meet such global targets, individual states would establish rates applying to all payers other than managed care networks and set ceilings on premiums for managed care. Managed care networks would compete based on prices and services offered. The National Health Board would establish a core benefit package for all plans that would include ambulatory care, in-patient hospital care, prescription drugs, basic mental health care, and important preventive benefits, such as pre-natal care and screening mammography. Employers would be required to purchase either private health benefits directly or participate in publicly sponsored, privately operated alternatives that provide the specified core benefits package. Those members of the population not covered through their employers would participate in the publicly sponsored, privately operated alternatives. Insurance companies would be required to guarantee

access to health insurance to all groups and to all persons within those groups regardless of their medical condition. Insurers would be required to use community rating principles so that premiums are based on the expected costs for all policyholders, not a particular group's cost based on previous medical history. Governor Clinton's plans also included provisions to establish local health networks responsible for the total care of the patients served; to reduce malpractice litigation through the availability of alternative mechanisms for resolving disputes and through the development of medical practice guidelines to help eliminate improper care; to reduce administrative costs for the simplified billing system; to slow price increases for prescription drugs; and to control proliferation of duplicative technology.

It is immediately apparent that these proposals include a mix of increased regulation, alongside a commitment to continued involvement of the private health insurance sector, since 'managed care networks' would be expected to compete with each other to attract potential patients by offering premiums whose rates are based on the prices and services to be offered. But the basis for this competition on prices and services is constrained by the requirement that all plans must offer an equivalent care benefit package whose components would be determined by the deliberations of the National Health Board.

Further, this care package of medical benefits which must include ambulatory care, in-patient hospital care, and important preventive benefits (an arena notoriously difficult to identify), must be provided under two additional constraints—insurance companies would be required to guarantee access to health insurance to all groups and all persons within these groups, regardless of their medical condition. And insurers would also be required to base their premiums on community rather than experience ratings so that the ultimate premiums charged reflect the costs of medical coverage for the total population insured and eliminates the selection into insurance coverage of groups of 'low-risk' patients. The other components of the Clinton plan to reduce the costs of medical provision—the reduction of malpractice litigation by introducing alternative mechanisms for resolving disputes, unspecified except for the development of medical practice guidelines to help eliminate improper care; the reduction of administrative costs through simplified billing procedures; slowing price increases for prescription drugs and controlling the proliferation of duplicative technologies—are all most likely to be achieved through regulatory procedures other than price competition.

Clearly, the Clinton proposals are designed 'to control health costs' or more accurately, medical care costs, since health is determined more by factors extrinsic to medical procedures—including standards of living and control of pollution—rather than direct medical intervention. Moreover, the proposals outlined above have their major impact on the 'supply side' of the medical industry. These proposals, in effect, attempt to control certain aspects of the provision of medical care by eliminating the profit component in insurance coverage from experience rating rather than community rating, the introduction of medical practice guidelines to eliminate improper medical care (i.e., the elimination of unnecessary and therefore costly procedures), controlling the proliferation of duplicative (and often very expensive) technologies and so on. In other words cost-containment strategies to reduce the supply side (rationing of medical resources?) of the doctor/patient exchange.

But the proposal to establish, through a National Health Board, a core (minimum?) benefit package of insured medical services is, in effect, a rationing device this time applied to the patient side of the doctor/patient exchange. A minimum care benefit package, by very definition, implies the identification of medical services which, while technically and scientifically available, are unavailable to those whose coverage is restricted to the core (minimum) medical care package. Those who wish medical care coverage above the minimum package must purchase extra medical insurance or pay for each additional unit of medical care at market prices. Inevitably a two-tiered medical care system will ensue; rationing by the purse will continue but at least those currently un- or under-insured would be covered.

At present, there is limited information of the broad structure for the reform of American medical care emerging from Hillary Rodham Clinton's task force and the current Congressional debates which will continue through much of 1994. Nevertheless some aspects of the proposals are already apparent; both the views of Starr and Enthoven seem to be influential. Major aspects of the proposed framework would appear to be:

> The purchasing cooperatives are not intended to provide insurance, much less medical care. . . . they contract with health plans and offer consumers a choice. HIPCs are the managers of managed competition. The first line of defense is an empowered consumer. Many principles of managed competition . . . reflect an interest in promoting informed, cost-conscious consumers. . . . A second defense against high costs and low quality is the management of the HIPC itself, which yields the combined purchasing power of its large blocks of consumers in negotiations with plans. . . . The third line of defense is "upstream" regulation at the national level, including technology assessment for cost-effectiveness, development of practice guidelines, changes in training for primary care, and global limits on expenditure growth. Besides supporting consumer decisions and performance, their own countervailing role, HIPCs would be responsible for keeping spending within global budgets and adapting national policy to

local circumstances. It is essential to managed competition that participation be mandatory for employers or at least a broad base of employers. Without mandated membership, high-cost employee groups [mining, fishing, construction, chemical manufacturers and many other hazardous industries] will be attracted to the purchasing cooperatives, low-cost groups will stay away, the growth of the cooperatives will be slow, and they will never reach the size they require to function effectively. The surest way to kill managed competition is to make the purchasing cooperative voluntary or to create loopholes that allow low-risk employee groups or associations to self-insure. (Kronich,1993, p.94)

It would appear from the above and the preceding discussion that regulation and control is as much if not more significant for the cost-containment component of the proposed reforms than the savings through increased efficiency and administrative economics which are expected to flow from managed competition.

Currently it is assumed that Medicare will continue and Medicaid will be folded into the new system. Those currently employed but whose income is insufficient to purchase health insurance and whose employers cannot afford to provide insurance for their employees will have to be subsidized from public funds if they are to be able to join the new provider groups. Most single parent families and the unemployed will also require subsidies, probably at the level of 100% of costs. Some savings might accrue if Medicare rates were means tested, charging the affluent elderly more than the average for coverage, but this suggestion and the subject of subsidies for the poor may be politically difficult to accomplish. Kronich is probably referring to these problems when he suggests that

> . . . there are strong political and administrative arguments for maintaining a separate program and for delaying the folding in of the acute care portion of Medicaid into the HIPC. Although there are many complaints both from beneficiaries and providers about the Medicare program, proposing a massive change would be extremely disruptive and likely would impede passage of a reform program. (1993:94)

It is also not clear what role, if any, HAs and managed competition would play in relation to the Veterans' Administration Hospital System or the Indian Health Service. Are they to be included and if so, how? What special arrangements will be necessary to provide medical care coverage for the chronically ill (outside the Medicare population), the disabled and, end-stage renal disease patients? It is also unclear what role HAs and managed competition can play in providing medical care to part-time workers. A wide variety of service industries employ high proportions of part-time workers who are not eligible for benefits of any kind, insurance, retirement and medical care. Clearly, part-time workers could not be expected to contribute more than a token amount to the cost of medical insurance. For many, perhaps most, coverage may be available through relatives, parents or spouses, but for socially isolated singles and single parents a public subsidy would be necessary if they are to obtain medical insurance.

Funding of the HAs may also present a problem. Their administrative costs might be passed on to the medical care provider groups in proportion to the number of patients enrolled in the group(s). Alternatively HAs costs could be born by state or federal authorities out of general revenues. A further complication, could arise where state boundaries (lines drawn on a map) do not coincide with geographic on social reality; Kansas City, St. Louis, or in rural areas such as the Appalachian mountains which (in the U.S.) include the jurisdictions from Maine to Northern Alabama. Clearly in some areas, if HAs are to achieve administrative rationality their boundaries will have to cross state lines.

But enough of problem identification. If managed competition between provider groups, promoted and over-seen by HAs can contain costs (realistically, maintaining the increase in medical costs to at or below the average increase in inflation and GDP growth) the savings realized might address some of the gaps outlined above, for example, "folding in of the acute care portion of Medicaid into the HAs."

For the proposed system to work HAs must persuade a number of provider groups to compete against each other to offer an identical core medical package at the lowest possible price which must not exceed (*i.e.*, *capped*) a global budget in a given period—a year, two years or how long? The implication is that one 'best' provider would be endorsed. For HAs with a large catchment area a number of provider groups could be endorsed if the variations in premium rates were small—say plus or minus 5%. In sparsely populated regions or for industries whose operations include 'difficult areas' such as urban ghettos, it may be difficult to attract enough provider groups to make competition possible. But suppose such difficulties could be overcome and a small variation in premium rates was acceptable; what savings could be expected?

At present, there are approximately 1,500 insurance companies operating in the American medical care system. It is obvious that the intent of HAs and managed competition is to reduce, drastically, this number. But remember a sufficient number of provider groups must survive if competition is to be effective. It would seem that the true paradox between managed competition and cost containment is beginning to emerge. There are too many companies at present, because of distortions of the market, such as experience rating, denial of coverage for high risk groups, unconstrained fee-for-service, but many provider groups (medical companies) must survive if competition is to survive. How many?

New York State has a population of roughly 20 million people—if transients and illegal immigrants are included. How many HMOs, IPAs or PPGs would be necessary to serve this population? Five, ten, twenty, fifty? How many HAs would be necessary to oversee these producer groups? While competition over premiums may help to contain medical insurance costs, economies of scale and reduced administrative costs are likely to produce as much or even more dollar savings. One would therefore conclude that the lowest possible number of provider groups would offer the best chance of cost-dollar savings. However, competition requires the survival of a number (unknown, undefinable) of providers who must adjust to the population densities of New York City and the sparsely-populated Adirondacks. Moreover, each plan must offer a core package of medical benefits at competitive prices across the population and geographic vagaries of New York State. Such problems are likely to occur, to a greater or lesser degree, in the remaining 49 states. Are there alternative forms of medical care delivery which could assuage these difficulties? Possible solutions to the problems of medical care delivery in the U.S. may be provided by consideration of the basic principles which underpin the delivery of medical services in Britain and Canada. The final section of this paper will address this possibility.

## Alternative Frameworks from Britain and Canada

In both countries medical care is financed through a monopsonistic—single payer-payment system funded predominantly through government sources. In Canada the central government and the provinces share the cost of medical care, as is the case for Medicare and Medicaid in the U.S., whereas in Britain medical care costs are overwhelmingly borne by the national government. A single payer system can obviously maximize the advantage of community over experience rating since the cost, often very expensive, of caring for the sickest members of the population, can be spread across the total risk pool, the nation state. Moreover, the responsibility of central government or a combination of central and local government for sole responsibility for the funding of medical care maximized opportunities to spread the costs as equitably as possible. Government sources of revenue are extremely broad but it is reasonable to argue that the major categories are direct or indirect taxes on individuals and institutions within the nation state.

In general, indirect taxes tend to be set at a particular rate, for example, a 5% sales tax applied in many American states, and a 17.5% value-added tax in Britain, levied against all but a small number of exempt goods such as basic food stuffs and, customs and excise duties and user fees such as marriage or car licenses. Generally sales and value-added taxes are regressive taxes, particularly when applied to 'essential goods and services' since they represent a bigger bite from a disposable income of $10,000 compared with an income of $50,000. In principle, however, indirect taxes could include a progressive component by raising the rate for 'luxury goods' such as cars with engines above a defined cubic capacity or cost, leisure boats above a prescribed size, houses beyond a specified square footage and so on. The issue is not what is possible but the extent to which governments are prepared to inject a degree of fairness into the indirect tax structure.

Similar arguments apply to direct taxation. When governments become responsible for the funding of medical care the relevant contributions of different segments of the population to the overall costs of medical services becomes more visible. Today, in the U.S., the cost to general taxpayers of the mechanism through which large companies are able to deduct considerable funds from pre-tax profits as an allowable expense for providing medical insurance for their employees is almost completely hidden from the public. Within a single-payer system, governments would be under no obligation to companies to provide tax relief for medical care since the costs would be borne by the society at large, not particular components of the productive sector.

Moreover, tax rates could be adjusted to inject a fair and visible contribution from all members in the social system related to their ability to pay. In other words the tax system would include a steeply progressive element of deductions from earnings (both earned and unearned) in which the proportion absorbed by direct taxation would increase with increased ability to pay.

In practice both the British and Canadian taxation systems are only mildly progressive, which in turn, limits the amount of revenue which they can collect. Therefore, within a single-payer system to finance medical care the stark realities of the actual or potential disequilibrium between government revenues and the costs of medical care becomes very apparent. The circumstances of real choice now become operationalized and obvious. Additional allocation of resources to medical care can only be financed by reducing government expenditures on other socially rewarding services: education, low-income housing, pensions, defense, transportation and communications infrastructure and so on *or* by increasing government revenues, i.e., raising taxes. Ultimately, therefore, the battle for the allocation of scarce resources is joined in the political arena where the battle belongs. Medical care, if it is to be rationed, and the factors driving up medical care costs—technological innovation and increasing proportions of elderly persons in the population make this inevitable—suggests that a monopsonistic payment system as a rationing device is to be preferred against the impersonal and unfair forces of the market place where wealth ultimately determines access to medical resources.

We have now returned to the distinction, even the conflict, between individualistic and collectivist value principles. A medical care system which operates with a predominantly individualistic orientation is one which emphasizes the duties and responsibilities of individuals to provide, if at all possible, for their medical care needs. A social system which operates with a collectivist orientation emphasizes the responsibility of the society at-large to provide medical care for all so that no one is barred from access to medical services.

In 1948 when the NHS Act was passed, Britain clearly endorsed the principles of collectivism, although for pragmatic political purposes, the architect of the NHS, Anueran Bevin, allowed a small private medical care sector to persist. While Thatcher attempted to reduce the collectivist orientation, a policy continued under Major, Day and Klein have suggested that even the injection of internal marketing principles to the operation of the NHS is unlikely to seriously disrupt the continuation of a collectivist orientation. In Canada, even without taking into public ownership the hospital sector and continuing with a fee-for-service reimbursement system for physicians, collectivist principles have been entrenched. Annual growth of medical care expenditure has been held within reasonable bounds and although it is the second most expensive medical care delivery system in the Western world, expenditure on medical services in Canada is still almost four percentage points in terms of GNP below that of the U.S. The cost of Britain's NHS is even lower, with only a little above 6% of GNP absorbed by medical care. Clearly the collectivist principles which predominate in the provision of medical services in Britain and America have been markedly successful in limiting medical care costs in both countries *and* are still popular among the populations they serve if the results of opinion polls are to be believed. Why?

Obvious savings emerge from the reduced administrative costs of monopsonistic payment systems and economies of scale consequent upon spreading medical risk across the total population to be serviced. Both the G.A.O. and Woolhandler and Himmelstein estimate these savings to be in the range of $60–$90 billion dollars, a sum which would easily cover the cost of covering the estimated 35–37 million Americans without medical insurance coverage.

But other aspects of the British and Canadian systems probably contribute significantly (how much is difficult to estimate but better data collection and analysis of medical procedures and outcomes may cast additional light upon the problem) to cost-effectiveness; the higher proportion of general practitioners compared with specialists in Britain and Canada in contrast to the U.S. With the exception of medical emergencies, patients in Britain and Canada can only access medical specialists if their G. P.s decide that such referrals are objectively appropriate. Given that most patients may have some idea of what is wrong with them—they are in pain, they cannot perform their usual range of employment activities, leisure pursuits, or other social roles—they nevertheless do not know what procedures will be necessary to return them to a previously existing state of health, or in the worst scenario, chronic illness, what treatments will best ameliorate their condition. Patients are therefore not in a position to make a rational choice between treatment alternatives or even decide whether the possibility of a successful treatment outcome is feasible. In effect, G.p.s make these decisions. In practice, G. P.s determine what treatments are applicable and effective in the treatment of minor illnesses and diseases and refer conditions beyond their capacities to specialists who have the higher level esoteric skills and technical facilities (hospitals) to diagnose and treat more complex maladies.

The critical element in this decision tree is clearly the competence of the G. P. and her/his ability to exercise humility and therefore refer patients whose conditions are beyond her/his competence to diagnose and treat to medical specialists who can. How is this best achieved? By subjecting G. P. decisions to continuous monitoring of their clinical behavior in accordance with the ever-changing body of scientific and medical knowledge which should inform their decisions. [The same criteria should also be applied to the next and subsequent levels of medical expertise in the specialist sectors; continuous monitoring of secondary and tertiary care physicians' decisions and treatments so that their outcomes are also subject to scientific scrutiny.]

Now it would seem that a position has been defined which can begin to direct the best choice between different forms of medical care provision. Competitive forces can only intervene indirectly upon the scientific credibility of clinical decisions in the medical care sector. Since patients are ultimately not in a position to choose between the effectiveness/ineffectiveness of particular medical procedures some organizational component in the system of medical care delivery must undertake this responsibility. A third party must be interjected into the doctor/patient exchange whose responsibility is to monitor the effectiveness of medical decision-making procedures.

At the margin of medical decision-making procedures sits the dilemma of uncertainty and certainty. Moreover, the significance of this dilemma often represents a choice between expensive procedures whose outcomes are unpredictable. The ultimate decision-making principle in a medical care system in which an individualistic orientation prevails is the ability of the system to absorb the costs of the high-risk procedure. In the real world, where scarce resources are limited, the allocation of scarce resources to medical procedures whose outcomes are uncertain means that other more effective medical interventions or resource allocations to other forms of desirable public expenditure are curtailed. Clearly such a circumstance raises the probability that the general public, if not the body politic, will detect a degree of unfairness, of inequity in these circumstances. Under a medical care system which operates under a collectivist principle which includes the administrative advantages and the cost-sharing principles of universal access and risk-sharing across the total population the problem of inequity is eliminated. The principle of uncertainty is ultimately settled by the public accountability through the body politic of the medical profession to the population it serves.

But above all the adoption of a monopsonistic payment system creates the motivation for a government to introduce a system for monitoring medical decision-making criteria since the cumulative costs of medical care impinge upon the government's ability to allocate resources to other forms of public expenditure which effect the well-being of the population. Ultimately, it is only a third party to the doctor/ patient exchange that can adjudicate between effective and ineffective medical procedures. The final court of appeal must rest with objective criteria which stem from the application of currently prevailing scientific criteria. Such objective criteria can only be imposed through a system of government which if it is to retain authority must ultimately represent the interests of the collectivity, the whole population it governs. However imperfectly, Britain and Canada have advanced further along this path than has the United States of America.

## References

Bellah, R. N.; Madsen, R.; Sullivan, W. M.; Swidler, A. and Tipton, S. M. 1985. *Habits of the heart: individualism and commitment in American life.* University of California Press.

Bodenheimer, T. 1989. Payment mechanisms under a national health program. *Medical Care Review* 46 (Spring):3–43.

Bodenheimer, T. 1990. Should we abolish the private health insurance industry? *International Journal of Health Services* 20:199–220.

Clark, p. G. 1991. Ethical dimensions of quality of life in aging: autonomy vs. collectivism in the United States and Canada. *The Gerontologist* 35(5):631–9.

Day, p. and Klein, R. 1991. Britain's health care experiment. *Health Affairs* (Fall):40–59.

*Families USA.* 1992 (Oct). A comparative analysis of the presidential health plans. Washington, D.C.

Fein, R. 1991. Health care reform. *Scientific American* (Nov):46–53.

Gill, D. G. 1978. Limitations upon choice and constraints over decision-making in doctor-patient exchanges. In *The doctor patient-relationship in the changing health scene*, ed. E. B. Gallagher, pp. 141–154. U. S. DHEW Pub. No. (NIH) 78–183.

____. 1980. *The British national service: a sociologist's perspective.* U. S. Department of Health and Human Services, NIH Publication No. 80-2054.

Gill, D. G., and Horobin, G. W. 1972. Doctors, patients and the state: relationships and decision-making. *Socological Review* 20(4):505–20 (New Series).

Gill, D. G. and Ingman, S. R. 1994. *Elder care, distributive justice and the welfare state: retrenchment or expansion.* Ithaca, New York: S.U.N.Y. Press.

Gill, D. G.; Ingman, S. R. and Campbell, J. 1991. Health care provision and distributive justice: end stage renal disease in Britain and America. *Social Science Medicine* 32(5):565–77.

Gramsci, A. 1985. *Selections from the prison notebooks.* Edited and translated by Hoare, Q. and Nowell, G. New York: Smith International Publishers (Eighth Printing). See especially State and Civil Society.

Hurst, J. W. 1991. Reforming health care in seven european nations. *Health Affairs* (Fall):7–21.

Ingman, S. R. and Gill, D. G., eds. 1986. Geriatric care and distributive justice: cross-national perspectives. *Social Science Medicine* 23:1205–1369. See also the introductory article to this special issue: Gill, D.G. and Ingman, S. R. Geriatric care and distributive justice: problems and prospects, 1205–15.

Klein, R. 1989. *The politics of the NHS*. 2nd ed. London: Longman.

Kronich, R. 1993. Where should the buck stop: federal and state responsibilities in health care financing reform. *Health Affairs* Supplement:87–98.

Gage, L. S.; Weslowski, V.B.; Andrulius, D. P.; Hunt, E. and Camper, A. B. 1991. *American safety net hospitals: the foundation of our nation's health system*. National association of public hospitals. Washington, D.C. 127.

Navarro, V. 1992. A response to conventional wisdom, 23; Altman, D. E. What do Americans really want? In Navarro, V., ed., *Why the United States does not have a national health program*, ed. V. Navarro. Baywood Publishing Company.

Naylor, C. D. 1991. A different view of queues in Canada. *Health Affairs* Spring:110–28.

Reinhardt, V. E. 1993. Reorganizing the financial flows in U.S. health care. *Health Affairs* Supplement:172–93.

Secretary of State for Health, 1989. *Working for patients*. London: Her Majesty's Stationary Office, Comment 555).

Starr, P. 1993. Design of health insurance purchasing cooperatives. *Health Affairs* Supplement:58–64.

Starr, P. and Zelman, W. A. 1993. Bridge to compromise: competition under a budget. *Health Affairs* Supplement:7–23.

Waitzkin, H. and Stoeckle, J. D. 1976. Information on the micropolitics of health care: summary of an ongoing research project. *Social Science Medicine* 6:263–76.

Weale, A. 1990. Equality, social solidarity, and the welfare state. *Ethics* 100:473–88

Woolhandler, S. and Himmelstein, D. V. 1991. The deteriorating administrative efficiency of the U.S. health care system. *New England Journal of Medicine* 324:1253–8.

# Chapter 13

## International Convergence in Health Care Systems
## Lessons from and for the USA

*Rex Taylor*
*Visiting Professor*
*School of Community Service, University of North Texas*

This paper challenges the presumption implicit throughout this volume that it is the American health care system that will have to change and become more Canadian- or European-like. Evidence is presented from a number of countries which shows that these health care systems are already moving closer to the American. Thus, instead of America learning from others, a one-way traffic of ideas, there seems to be an international convergence on a common set of ideas and structures. At the same time, while the American health care reforms have still to be announced, it is likely that they will result in increased central control.

From an American perspective countries like Canada, Britain, Sweden, and France have eliminated most of the financial barriers to health care and their citizens enjoy comparable health status at lower costs—in individual expenditure on health care and as a percentage of GDP. It must therefore come as a surprise for Americans to learn that all of these countries have recently undergone extensive reviews of their health care systems, and in Britain and Sweden these have already led to fundamental changes. All of these countries have had to respond to a macro economic imperative to reduce spending but they have also become dissatisfied with the ways in which their systems of health care were functioning. The most salient common problems were and are: inefficiencies in the allocation of health care resources, discontinuities between levels of care and insufficient opportunities for the exercise of consumer choice. Faced with such problems, these countries have turned to the American concept of the HMO and various forms of managed competition. The diffusion of these efficiency producing proposals owes a good deal to the phenomenal influence of Alain Enthoven but it also has to be acknowledged that the oil crisis of the mid 1970s left European politicians and health planners very receptive to his ideas. Indeed, it is only evident in retrospect the extent to which the mid-seventies marked a social policy break-point. Oil shocks, inflation and economic growth challenged the capacity of most European governments to maintain previous growth rates in health and welfare spending. There was a political shift to the right and the trade winds of policy ideas changed direction. Up until the mid-seventies the flow was mainly from Europe, especially Britain and Scandinavia, to the USA. Since then European politicians and planners have increasingly turned to the American free market thinkers—Milton Friedman, Albert Hirschman, Michael Novak and Alain Enthoven (Glennerster and Midgley, 1991).

The extent to which market competition has been introduced into health care varies from country to country, and it is to such a review that we now turn.

## Britain: The Purchaser-Provider Split

Margaret Thatcher was elected in 1979 with a mission to curb public spending. She was devastatingly successful. The rate of spending on health and social services was cut to less than half that of the GDP. These tight limits put great pressure on the NHS and prompted a radical overhaul, essentially designed to get more health care out of the existing budget. Alain Enthoven spent a sabbatical in London in 1985 and left a closely worded critique of the NHS, claiming that it suffered from perverse incentives, inefficiencies, over-centralization, lack of accountability, and unresponsiveness to consumers (Enthoven, 1985). He argued that the health authorities should cease to have direct responsibility for managing health services; instead they should become purchasers, buying services from the most efficient agencies they could find. This is in effect what has happened.

The central idea that underpins the new NHS is the division between the *purchaser* and *provider* of services (LeGrand, 1992). The providers compete with each other for contracts set by the purchaser. There are two classes of purchaser in the new system: the health authorities (as suggested by Enthoven) and the general practitioners. Each health district receives a grant from central government based on a capitation formula- so much per head, weighted by age and aggregate mortality and social deprivation indices. It is then the responsibility of the districts to asses the health needs of their populations, to determine spending priorities and to draw up contracts with hospitals and other service providers. The hospitals, meanwhile, are becoming independent trusts, receiving capital from central government but having to earn their current revenue from contracts won from the health districts and general practitioners. If the system works as intended, and it is still to early to judge, the more expensive and inefficient hospitals will close (Glennerster, 1992).

Groups of fund-holding general practitioners also act as purchasers. They receive a budget, also based on a capitation fee, and from this they purchase drugs, diagnostic tests and a range of straightforward treatments for their patients. Overspending may be penalized in the next allocation but underspent funds can be used to improve services.

There is an obvious similarity between fund-holding general practitioners and the American HMO. The major difference is in size: most HMOs having around 100,000 members, ten times larger than the average fund-holding practice. This size difference may be critical since the larger HMO is better able to average out the high risk and cost cases. However, unlike the HMO, the fund-holding practice retains control over much of its work, so that if the budget looks like overspending it can refer fewer patients for treatment by using the waiting list (Glennerster, 1992). A similar division between purchaser and provider is beginning to operate in long-term social care, where the social work department is the purchaser and the providers are increasingly non-profit organizations and even new for-profit agencies (Pinker, R. 1992).

## Sweden: The County-led Internal Market[1]

Historically, Sweden has spent more on health than any other country in Europe, and more than any other country in the world except Canada and the USA. The financial crisis of the mid-1970s affected Sweden as it did Britain, and the search for ways of containing costs coincided with growing criticism of the health care system (Saltman and von Otter, 1992). While Swedish primary care is organized around local health centers (staffed with general medical practitioners, nurses and some specialists), most patients use hospital-based specialists without being referred by the health center doctor. The implications for cost control and service planning are obvious. Without an effective gatekeeper, the bias towards hospital care has been unchecked; hospital spending accounted for about three quarters of the total health expenditure. A further consequence has been the comparative unattractiveness of work in primary care settings. General practitioners are well paid but they have low status vis a vis their hospital colleagues and they have little control over their work. Moreover, there is little choice for the patient, patients being seen by whoever happens to be on duty (Matsaganis, 1992).

The Dagmar Reform of the mid 1980s replaced the previous fee-for-service system with a capitation payment from the national insurance fund. This money is paid directly to the 26 county councils and it has given them the power to decide on which services they want and from whom. In effect, 26 internal health markets have been created within Sweden (Saltman and von Otter, 1992). The way in which these internal markets operate can be got from a review of developments in the Kopparberg and Stockholm county councils.

In Kopparberg the county council retains overall financial and planning control but it has delegated all other responsibilities for health care to 15 Medical Care Areas (coinciding with municipalities and neighborhoods). The Board of each Medical Care Area draws up contracts with its local health center to provide primary care. In turn, each health center is required to submit a health care plan, based on needs assessment, for the provision of services to its catchment population. Once the plans are approved by the Board, hospitals are invited to submit tenders for their services. The overall similarities with the British fund-holding general practice will be obvious, although there are some minor differences (Matsagamis, 1992, p. 13).

In Stockholm the county council retains overall responsibility but it has delegated resources to nine Local Area Boards. Each Board places contracts with its local health centers, the contracts specifying details of the service required (i. e., staffing, opening hours). Unlike Kopparberg, the Stockholm Local Board works with the health center to determine health care need, and they have more complex arrangements with the eight city hospitals. They use DRG's to determine prices, and contracts specify price, volume, and quality of the service to be provided. One further noteworthy feature of the Stockholm model is that health centers are required to draw up "cooperative agreements" with hospitals to improve integration between primary and secondary care (Matsagamis, 1992, p. 11).

Thus, while there are local variations, the new Swedish health care system is characterized by the same distinction between purchaser and provider which now pertains in Britain. Production is separated from finance, resources are devolved, the counties regulate the internal market, and the hospital and health centers compete with each other—at least in theory, it is too early to determine practice. Since September 1991, when elections produced non-socialist majorities in the parliament and the county councils, the movement towards managed competition has quickened. The new Minister of Health favors the extension of competition to primary care doctors and he has appointed a commission to explore fund-holding for all services. The Commission is expected to report in 1994 (Lewis, 1992).

### France: *Les Réseaux de Soins Cordonnés*: The HMO by Another Name[2]

France combines NHI with fee-for-service private practice in primary care and a mixed public-private hospital system. Reimbursement takes three separate forms: primary care doctors and those in private hospitals on the basis of a negotiated fee schedule, public hospital doctors on a part- or full-time salary basis, and those in private hospitals on a negotiated per diem fee (Rodwin, 1981).

As far as economic efficiency is concerned, there are well-publicized problems, both on the demand and supply side (Berthold-Wurmser, 1987). On the demand side there is a strong tendency for overutilization, stemming from the lack of incentives— for both doctor and patient—to balance marginal changes in risk with marginal increases in cost. On the supply side the fee-for-service encourages doctors to oversupply so as to maximize their income. Similarly, the per diem reimbursement in private hospitals is an incentive to increase the average length of patient stay. There is also, as in Sweden, little incentive to shift the balance of resources from hospitals to various forms of community-based provision.

Early attempts to contain the increase in health spending involved higher co-payment charges on the patient and the imposition of global budgets on the system as a whole.

A more thorough-going HMO-type reform has recently been proposed (Lannois *et al.*, 1985.) It was inspired by Alain Enthoven's Consumer Choice Health Care Plan for the USA (Enthoven, 1980). But whereas Enthoven's plan was devised to *create* a NHI, the French plan has been devised to achieve greater efficiency within an *already established* NHI system. The proposal has 5 principal elements. The first element is the preservation of existing NHI entitlements. The current level of benefits would become a minimum benefit package under the new plan. The second is the creation of a network of medical services (Réseau de Soins Cardonnés). The RSC's, like the HMOs, would recruit through open enrollment and they would require primary care doctors and hospitals to provide cost effective medical services. The third element is the promotion of integrated care. The RSC would assume a contractual responsibility to provide its enrolled population with all medical services covered under French NHI and patients would retain free choice of doctor. The fourth element is repayment on a capitation basis. The RSC would receive a prepaid capitated fee directly from the beneficiaries NHI fund. Its annual budget would therefore be the annual capitations payment multiplied by the number of its enrollees. Finally, the fifth element would be competition between RSCs. There would be competition on three levels; between RSCs and traditional NHI, between RSCs themselves, and between the health care providers to whom the RSCs send their patients.

**Canada: Publicly Financed Competition**

In Canada, as in France, neither the hospital, doctor, nor patient have an incentive to be economical in their use of health care resources (Rodwin, 1992). Since patients benefit from what is perceived to be "free" tax first dollar coverage, they have no incentive to choose cost-effective forms of care. Equally, doctors lack incentives to make efficient use of hospitals. Stoddart (1983) has characterized the problems of the Canadian health care system as "financing without organization." In his view, Canadian provinces adopted a "pay the bills" philosophy, in which decisions about service provision—which services, in what amounts, produced how, by whom and where—were viewed as the legitimate domain of physicians and hospital administrators (Stoddart, 1985).

As in France, there have been two traditional strategies for cost constrainment: control over supply (e. g., hospital spending and rationing medical technology) and, increasingly, reliance on market forces to reduce demand (e. g., various forms of user co-payments). Rodwin (1992) has questioned the effectiveness of both approaches: the former because it exacerbates confrontation between providers and the state, the latter because it provides no encouragement of more efficient practice styles. Stoddart's proposal for more thorough-going reform (Muldoon and Stoddart, 1989) takes the form of publicly financed competition based on four principles.

The first principle is the creation of three payment modalities for primary care. Physicians would have the choice of renumeration by fee-for-service, capitation fee or salary. Fees in the fee-for-service mode would correspond to the current fee schedule, the capitation rate would be based on the average cost of insured service per patient and salaries would be determined nationally.

Second, the tax-based financing on NHI would remain unchanged.

Third, while patients would have freedom to select particular doctors they would have to commit themselves to one payment modality for their primary care.

Fourth, the premium for each modality would be adjusted at the end of each enrollment period and based on total cost. The least costly modality would then become the baseline for coverage under NHI, and patients enrolled in the two more costly modalities would have to pay the difference.

Rodwin (1992:275) notes that although the Stoddart plan is not as elaborately developed as the French RSC model, it represents a serious challenge to the status quo. However, it has to be acknowledged that the Stoddart proposal has only attracted government interest in Ontario, and more generally, outside the academic community there is little public support for this extreme form of managed competition.

Having reviewed the changes and projected changes in the health care systems of Britain, Sweden, France and Canada, it will be apparent that there are a number of important commonalities.

First, Alain Enthoven's ideas and proposals are all pervasive. In the U.K. one has to go back to Beveridge, or possibly Titmuss, to think of a single individual who has had more influence on policy development.

Second, most of the changes and proposed changes are profoundly controversial and they are, and will continue to be, subject to political swings. It is not accidental that they have coincided with a general swing to the political right, and any future swing to the political left would probably result in their emasculation.

Third, they are largely untried and, as yet, unevaluated. There is relatively little evidence available to estimate their full consequences—intended and unintended.

Fourth, and this is the major thesis, they all exemplify a move away from traditional state support and control toward various forms of managed competition.

The remaining task of this paper is to assess the probability that U.S. reformers will move the U.S. health care system in the opposite direction, i.e., from its current free market stance to one in which competition is increasingly managed and regulated by the state.

## U.S.A.: Managed Competition and the Probability of Increased Central Control

Whatever the details of the eventual health reform package, it is widely assumed that they will involve a form of managed competition.

The Congressional Budget Office's specially commissioned study, *Managed Competition and its Potential to Reduce Health Spending* (CBO, 1993) defines the goals of managed competition as follows:

> The managed competition strategy . . . seeks the efficiency, flexibility, and innovation that characterize competitive markets without the undesirable cost and coverage problems of the present system. (CBO, 1993, 12)

Many different proposals have been put forth under the managed competition umbrella, they include Alain Enthoven's *Universal Health Insurance Programme* (Enthoven, 1991).

Enthoven's proposal begins with *mandated* private coverage of all full-time employees, plus a payroll tax on wages of part time and seasonal employees. With these revenues, plus 8% of income contributed by the self-employed, early retirees and other non-employed persons, the federal government would make payments to the states. Each state would then establish an agency which would contract with the private sector managed care plans to enroll former Medicaid patients, the self-employed and workers whose small business employers think they can get a better deal from the public sponsored agency.

The major strength of this and similar "play or pay" schemes is that it builds on the employment base and it would eliminate Medicaid as a separate scheme. (A program for the poor is generally a poor program). For present purposes it is another feature of Enthoven's proposal which requires elaboration—the creation of a new tier of regulation and control. The specially commissioned CBO study (1993) identifies the creation of such regional organizations as the single most important feature of managed competition. Whatever form such organizations take, they will provide a base for regulation and control analogous to the British health authority; both setting conditions and standards but not providing any services themselves. The detailed kinds of regulations which could evolve are set out in the CBO study and include:

a) rules for periodic open enrollment;
b) guidelines for the production of standard packages based on community risk rather than an individual's experience rating;
c) standardized information disclosure by all competing health care organizations; and
d) spot checks and quality monitoring.

Taken together, these regulations amount to a substantial increase of public involvement in the American health care system. Even so, it is extremely doubtful that the proposed regulatory framework will be sufficient to counter the built-in incentives and achieve the required reduction in health care spending[3]. There are good grounds for this skepticism. The Director of the Congressional Budget Office recently testified to the Ways and Means Committee on this vital question:

> We are convinced that even if a managed competition approach with all the critical elements described above were carried out, its effects would [only] occur over an extended time. Significant savings in national health expenditure would probably not occur within the usual five year time horizon of CBO estimates (CBO, 1993:15).

A candid acknowledgement of the lack of sound empirical data, but an astonishing one given the importance attached to managed competition.

By itself, it is unlikely that managed competition will achieve the required savings. If so, additional regulatory mechanisms will be necessary. These will probably fall short of global budgeting along British or Canadian lines, and they are more likely to involve the strengthening of existing government mechanisms. The first obvious possibility is an extension of DRGs. They represent a form of partial global budgeting because they replace retrospective reimbursement with a prospective lump sum. They were introduced for in-patient treatments in 1983 and there are already plans to extend them to out-patient services. A second possibility could be a reintroduction of the Certificate of Need. Originally introduced in the late 1970s to slow down proliferation of hospitals and expensive treatments, they were discontinued in the 1980s. The present proliferation of ICUs and sophisticated diagnostic imaging facilities (e.g., the USA has 2000 MRIs, four times as many as Germany) will proceed unabated unless capital grants are limited or regional consortia of users encouraged. Capacity controls are a third possibility. The USA already has one of the highest physician to population ratios in the world and since it is the individual physician who determines about 70% of the system's expenditure, a reduction in medical school admissions would result in future savings (Ginzberg, 1990). But even if the government prefers to let the market determine the overall number of medical students, there is a separate case for it intervening to obtain the desired balance between specialists and generalists (currently 84:16 and the proportion of specialists is still growing). A similar case could be made for robust intervention to achieve a more equitable geographical distribution. Whatever the cost-control mechanisms eventually chosen, it seems inescapable that they will result in *more rather than less* federal regulation. If so, Americans will have to accept greater public involvement in their health care system, just as the British and Swedish publics are having to accept greater involvement of the market.

The convergence being proposed for health care systems is clearly analogous to the convergence in industrial systems which Clark Kerr (1962), Daniel Bell (1960), and Harold Wilensky (1975) claimed to detect in the 1960s and early 1970s. They argued that as capitalist societies adopted some of the collectivist features of socialist societies, so would socialist societies adopt some of the free market and pluralist features of capitalism. (Having lived through the remarkable transformations in Eastern Europe in 1991, it is difficult not to add the rejoinder "And how!"). The engine driving this earlier convergence was the logic of industrialism. By contrast, the engine driving the present day convergence in health and social care systems is largely demographic. Keeping people alive who would otherwise have died and keeping everyone alive for longer is expensive. In the United States it is probable that part of its cost escalation derives from the high expectations that Americans have for their own health and for what doctors can do for them.[4] The "do something" ethic of American medicine is a natural consequence, with obvious consequences for cost escalation. It could transpire that these deep-seated expectations will frustrate rather than strengthen the attempts of the reformers; in which case, the convergence thesis proposed in this paper will only be partly fulfilled.

## Notes

[1]The best recent treatment of changes in the Swedish health care system is provided in Howard Glennerster and Manos Matsaganis' excellent monograph, *The English and Swedish Health Care Reforms: The Welfare State Program*, LSE, November 1992. The following section draws heavily on their account.

[2]Victor Rodwin has worked extensively on Franch and Canadian health care reforms. This section draws on his excellent chapter, "New Ideas for Health Policy," pp. 265–285, in Mark Field's *Success and Crisis in National Health Systems*, Routledge, New York, 1989.

[3]The secret to the success of any health care reform in the U.S.A. lies in the extent to which the existing incentives are removed. I am grateful to Dan Johnson for emphasizing this fundamental point in a seminar at which this paper was first presented.

[4]De Tocqueville was the first to make this observation when he wrote:
"In America the passion for physical well-being is not always exclusive
. . . but it is general. The effort to satisfy even the least wants of the body
and to provide the little conveniences of life is uppermost in every mind."
Almost 200 years later, Talcott Parsons made a similar observation when he wrote:
"Illness is a kind of alienation in American society: alienation from a set of
expectations which puts particular stress on individual achievements."

## References

Bell, D. 1960. *The end of Ideology*. Glencoe, Illinois: Free Press.

Burthold-Wurmser, M. *et al.*, eds. 1987. *Systeme de sante, pouvoirs publics et financeurs: qui controle quoi?* Paris: Documentation Francaise.

Congressional Budget Office. February 2, 1993. *Statement of Robert D. Reischauer, Congressional Budget Office, before Subcommittee on Health*. Committee on Ways and Means.

Congressional Budget Office. May 1993. *Managed competition and its potential to reduce health spending*. Washington.

Enthoven, A. 1980.*Health plan: the only practical solution to the soaring costs of medical care*. Reading, Massachusetts: Addison-Wesley.

—. 1985. *Reflection on the management of NHS*. London: Nuffield Trust.

Enthoven, A. and Kronick, R. 1991. Universal health insurance through incentives reform. *Journal of the American Medical Association 265* 19: 2553.

Ginzberg, E. 1990. *The medical triangle: physicians, politicians and the public*. Boston: Harvard Press.

Glennerster, H. 1992. *The English health reforms: why and wherefore?* Paper WSP/79 in LSE Welfare State Programs: London.

Glennerster, H. and Midgley, J. 1991. *The radical right and the welfare state*. Harvester/Wheatsleaf.

Kerr, C., *et al.* 1962. *Industrialism and industrial man*. London: Heinemann.

Launois, R., *et al.* 1985. Les Réseaux de Soins Cardonnés (RSC) propositions pour une reforme du systeme de sante. *Revue Francais des Affaires Sociales,* 37–61.

Le Grand, J. 1992. *Paying for or providing welfare?* Paper given to Social Policy Association Annual Conference. Nottingham.

Lewis, A. M. 1992. Sweden reforms primary care. *British Medical Journal* 605:601.

Matsaganis, M. 1992. *Reflections on health care reform in Sweden*. Paper WSP/79 in LSE Welfare State Programs. London.

Muldoon, J. M. and Stoddart, G. 1989. Publicly financed competition in health care delivery: a Canadian simulation model. *Journal of Health Economics* 8 (3): 313–38.

Pinker, R. 1992. Making sense of the mixed economy of welfare, *Social Policy and Administration*, 26 (4): 273–283.

Rodwin, V. G. 1981. The marriage of national health insurance and la medicine liberale in France: a costly union. *Millbank Memorial Fund Quarterly* 59:16–43.

—. 1984. *The health planning predicament: France, Quebec, England and the U.S.A.* Berkeley: University of California Press.

—. 1989. New ideas for health policy. In M. G. Field ed., pp. 265–285. *Success and crisis in national health systems.* New York: Routledge.

Saltman, R. B. and Otter, C. von. 1987. Revitalizing public health care systems: a proposal for public competition in Sweden. *Health Policy* 7: 21–40.

Saltman, R. B. and Otter, C. von. 1992. *Planned markets and public competition.* Milton Keynes: Open University Press.

Stoddart, G. 1983. *Publicly financed competition in Canadian health care delivery: a viable alternative to increased regulation?* Proceedings of the Conference on Health in the '80s and '90s. Toronto: Council of Ontario Universities.

Wilensky, H. 1975. *The welfare state and equality.* California: University of California Press.

—. 1985. Rationalizing the health care system. in T. Courdien, *et al.*, eds. *Ottawa and the provinces: the distribution of money and power.* Ontario Economic Council, Toronto.

# Chapter 14

## Feudal *vs* Futile Medicine:
## Can We Have Cost Containment Without Prevention?

*David R. Smith, M.D.*
*Commissioner of Health, Texas State Department of Health*

*Ron J. Anderson, M.D.*
*President and CEO*
*Parkland Memorial Hospital*

### INTRODUCTION

The 1980s were expected to be the decade of cost containment where spending constraints would bring health care expenditures in line. Instead, this ten year period witnessed unprecedented growth as national expenditures for health care more than doubled (Levy & Waldo, 1986). A large proportion of this growth was realized in the high-tech and tertiary components of health care. Investment in preventive health services—often a component of primary care—has not been a priority. Less than three percent of all health care expenditures were devoted to government public health activities. A substantial percentage of these expenditures was directed to nonpreventive tactics and categorical programs (Sofaer & Kenney).

This trend of advancing technologies and subspecialization has provided unparalleled advancement in medicine and the creation of new knowledge. The outcome of these forces has pushed medical science to unprecedented accomplishments—medical knowledge and therapeutics have profited by these trends. The application of this new knowledge and technology has not been uniformly applied to the populations of greatest risk.

The debate over budget deficits and the adequacy of the current health care delivery system has raised questions about our curative model of care. For many, including some leaders in the business community, opportunity for restructuring the existing system has been seen in the fertile soil of prevention and primary care (Bacon, 1991 & Warner, 1987).

As issues, health care and prevention are rapidly becoming topics of debate in the arenas of public policy, industry and politics. This is perhaps best illustrated by an analysis of precipitating factors which have lead to significant labor disputes over the last two to three years. During this period, approximately 4/5 of all labor disputes have been precipitated by disagreement over health care benefits (The Economist, 1991). As this nation searches for solutions to the inadequacies of the existing health care system, one factor remains undeniable—change. Existing problems in financing, access and content of care will be debated and system reform is inevitable (Smith,*et al.*, & Relman, 1983).

## Historical Perspective

History has much to teach us, and the present push for reform should not proceed without at least a cursory review of the past. The distinct and separate evolutions of curative and preventive medicine have their roots in Greek mythology. Aesculapius, the Grecian father of medicine, had two daughters—Panacea and Hygeia.[1] Panacea grew to represent curative medicine while her sister (Hygeia) went a separate and distinct path and embraced the practice of preventive medicine and public health. The two arms of this family have remained distinct and divided throughout time.

While medicine primarily evolved through the legacy left by Panacea, some notable exceptions did evolve. The ancient Chinese fostered some novel approaches to preventive strategies. The mandarins of this time bolstered preventive efforts by paying physicians only if their patients were well (Sofaer & Kenney). It has only been in the last several years that serious consideration has again been given to similar strategies.

In this country, the separate pathways of preventive and curative medicine were accentuated by the Flexner Report of 1910 (Flexner). This report created the impetus to develop a medical model which adopted the curative approach to health care delivery. This report firmly anchored medicine within science and highlighted the disciplines of anatomy, physiology and biochemistry. Prevention and its related disciplines of epidemiology, bio-statistics and public health remained distinct and outside of the science of medicine.

While the medical model remained within science, prevention fell under the purview of public health and the public sector where it has often languished because of poor funding, limited leadership and limited efforts of advocacy. In a recent study evaluating the content of medical education, prevention consumed less than 1.5% of the medical curriculum (Bishop, 1983). Despite our increasing concern over nutritional determinants of disease and health, only 24 of 126 medical schools require courses in nutrition (Manber, 1985.

Until recently, reimbursement and financing strategies have failed to foster the proliferation of preventive health services. Instead, the rewards in financing and reimbursement remained in curative and high-tech approaches to medical care (Waldo, *et al.*, 1986 & Smith). The incentives created through financing reinforced the pathophysiologic model thus promoting the development of large centralized medical centers and medical curriculums integrating the discipline founded by Panacea and Flexner. From these roots, and the external incentives created by existing reimbursement strategies and grant priorities, the delivery system has further evolved to become more compartmentalized - often by organ system. This trend has predicted the specialization of medicine which is dependent on expensive technology (Smith, *et al.*)

**Cost and Benefits**

The cost of not providing primary or secondary preventive services can be staggering. In a country and society which believes in the wisdom of investment capital and long term strategies for investment return, one might think that prevention, as a strategy which invests in individuals and communities, would be second nature. This has not been the case and while Americans have watched the Fram Oil Filter commercial parade its slogan "you can pay me now or pay me later" this nation has failed to weave this theme into the fiber of our health system. Instead, this nation remains a "pay me later society" that has continued to be enamored with catastrophic and resurrection medicine.

The price of this decision to "pay later" can be staggering. An analysis of the recent outbreak of measles in Dallas county perhaps best elucidates the failure of implementing preventive health services. The 1989-90 outbreak of measles in Dallas county captured almost 2500 victims—twelve died. A recent study was designed to look only at the inpatient charges that were generated by admissions to local hospitals from the outbreak. The study reviewed the inpatient charges of all area hospitals during the period of the epidemic. The accumulated charges exceeded 3.5 million dollars.

Conservatively, it has been estimated that the cost of immunizing 10,000 more individuals (in an effort to target those at greatest risk prior to the onset of the epidemic) would have cost approximately $150,000 to $200,000. For comparison purposes, the figures do not include the cost of providing ambulatory care to patients who contracted the virus and presented to hospital emergency rooms, public sponsored health centers, or private physician offices. As an investment strategy, the community could have saved almost $25.00 in inpatient costs for every dollar invested if it had appropriately immunized susceptible individuals.

This case study of the failure to practice prevention clearly underscores the need to embrace the paradigm of prevention represented by Hygeia. This case study also uncovers a medical system which often defies logic. It reveals a medical system which reinforces costly interventions and cures while neglecting prevention or early intervention. A medical system which continues to pay for: hysterectomies, but not pap smears; admissions for strokes, but not anti-hypertensives; mastectomies, but not mammograms; sick baby care, but not well baby care; measles but not a measles vaccine, will fall short of producing significant cost savings. Such a policy will *not* realize cost-containment without a reversal in present policy and a commitment to logic.

## Change and Incentives

The labor force is changing and the competitiveness of any nation is dependent upon the skills and capabilities of its workers. Demographers point out that the workforce will parallel the changes in our population—more Hispanics, African American and women. The word "minority" will be replace by the terms "emerging majority." This transition in population dynamics places an added requirement on states and communities to address the disproportionate needs of these risk populations who die earlier and have increased rates of preventable disease such as measles, diabetes, cancer and strokes (Brooks, *et al.*, 1991). To not do so will erode the financial and economic foundations of our communities.

Business and labor have become significant participants in the debate on health care financing an delivery and both are demanding change. While labor disputes increasingly focus on health care issues, the Washington Business Group on Health has surveyed managers and CEO's of large and small businesses and the majority are calling for reform (Bacon, 1991).

Proposed changes in health care financing are just beginning to set the stage for reform. While the intended effect may not be to create a health system where now a medical system exists—the end result may produce a health system which "front loads" our investment in care with resources to change current medical practices. An example that illustrates the failure to incorporate preventive services into the existing medical model is the reduction in the number of immunizations being provided within certain portions of the private sector, with a concomitant shift of the burden to the public sector (Haley, et. al., 1988). The implementation of relative value scales (designed conceptually to increase reimbursement for cognitive skills) could improve reimbursement and an impetus to provide preventive services. This will occur slowly due to the relatively small percentage of real dollars being invested or shifted from procedurally oriented medicine. Similarly, the reformulation of methods to allocate Medicare dollars to undergraduate and graduate medical education should foster a behavior change in academia which promotes primary care training and incorporates prevention within medical school curriculum (Smith, *et al.* & Boumbulian, *et al.*).

Other factors will influence the incorporation of prevention into the existing medical model, such as the increased sophistication of purchasers of care and the development of health promotion and disease prevention as a product line for many health care providers. This will include hospitals trying to position themselves for the anticipated change. The impact of these trends have begun to be appreciated by payers such as Blue Cross and Blue Shield which recently released its list of reimbursable preventive services. Managed care has successfully marketed preventive health in some areas of the country.

Innovative approaches designed to create incentives for providers of care and patients to practice preventive health are already in place in some systems (Smith, *et al.*, Boumbulain, *et al.*, Breken, *et al.*, & Logsdon, *et al.*, 1989). Reductions of co-pays and deductibles for patients who remain compliant with prescribed regimens are gaining favor. Increasingly, private practices, clinics and HMO's are installing patient help systems designed to "case manage" patients with the aid of reminder files, phone calls and home visits (Breken, *et al.*, 1989). Numerous demonstration programs often funded through granting agencies are utilizing incentive programs designed to change patterns of patient behavior (Breken, *et al.*, 1989). Finally, in some areas, such as the Community Oriented Primary Care Program at Parkland Memorial Hospital, physician incentives are being installed to enhance the effects of patient based incentives.

Incentive-based programs can be created to link an incentive program to the achievement of health outcomes. Health status objectives can be selected based upon prevalent health problems identified by the health center staff. Outcomes to be tracked should be linked to known effective strategies for preventive health care. The targeted outcome, such as the reduction of breast cancer related to morbidity and mortality in the targeted community by 10% through the application of breast self examination and screening mammography, is monitored through data sources such as a hospital or state tumor registry and hospital discharge data. Initially, it will be more appropriate to track the appropriate application of processes or interventions such as breast self examination and screening mammography in an effort to measure increasing compliance with established guidelines and targets.

**Changing Venues**

The trend to shift patient care from the inpatient to the outpatient setting will continue—if for no other reason than the payers desire to move care from a more expensive (better reimbursed setting) to a less well covered setting. This change in venue provides opportunities for hospitals and their medical staffs to develop and implement new models of care which embrace preventive strategies and positions these systems to capitalize on changing incentives.

The current patterns of health care delivery, specifically emergency rooms and walk-in clinics, by-pass the most cost-effective and health effective services that can be provided within a community based ambulatory setting. To overcome the existing inertia which promotes reactive care, a new model must evolve. Changes in incentives will not be sufficient to promote wellness unless models of care are developed which practice these concepts. These models need to challenge existing paradigms and embrace a health model which promotes prevention and early intervention through a continuum of care that is accountable for assessing the appropriateness of care, the place of care and the ability of the system to maximize functionality and autonomy.

Significant steps have been taken in several communities to implement a community based strategy that embraces the concept developed by Dr. Sydney Kark and promoted through the World Health Organization and the Institute of Medicine of the National Academy of Science (Institute of Medicine, 1983). COPC is a way of practicing medicine that blends traditional primary care with public health services. The program is designed to pinpoint at-risk populations in order to improve the health status of individual patients as well as the community in which they reside. Whereas the traditional medical practice or hospital based care is oriented toward the number of patients seen, procedures and dollars, COPC is an outcome oriented program which defines success from measurable epidemiologic results (Smith, *et al.*, & Institute of Medicine, 1983).

COPC creates a framework to provide integrated care on a one-stop shopping basis, thus minimizing repetitive administrative costs and fragmentation of care. The one-stop concept also reduces barriers, such as transportation, by co-locating related services at one place, such as well child, sick child, immunizations and health screening and education services.

The concept is predicated on the ability of a health care entity to understand and take responsibility for the health care needs of a population or a defined community. Epidemiologic principles are applied to identify areas of need and populations at risk. The community participates actively in the process designed to identify and give priority to community health needs. Resources are focused on health problems which are prevalent, preventable and which most adversely affect the target population. The system is structured to deliver a comprehensive array of health services within a preventive framework.

**Rural and Regional Systems**

To be viable on a larger scale, this model will require a regional approach to planning that establishes rural and urban coalitions (Institute of Medicine, 1983). The partnership will collaborate in efforts to identify resources and ensure continuity of care for rural patients in this expanded system of health services. This will also enable rural communities to benefit from new technologies and reduce barriers due to distance and limited resources. Such needs are particularly apparent in the areas of perinatal and trauma care where only limited efforts at regionalization have been initiated.

Through legislation, grants and private foundation support, several COPC demonstrations could be developed in the state and linked with appropriate transportation services to regional tertiary care centers. The Robert Wood Johnson Foundation, the Kellogg Foundation and the National Rural Health Association have undertaken several collaborative initiatives to establish community-based primary care systems in rural areas throughout the country. Liaison with the state Medicaid program may foster the development of prepaid systems of care for the working poor and medically indigent and provide the impetus for more rural sites to obtain the designation of Federally Qualified Health Center (FQHC).

More creative programs and opportunities should be sought and developed. Legislative reform such as the Rural Health Act, which improved ambulatory reimbursement, must be expanded to include enhanced cost-based reimbursement for preventive health services. Additional opportunities include the development of affiliations with Area Health Education Centers (AHEC) funded through the U. S. Department of Health & Human Services. These centers link academic, medical and health professional programs with communities by supporting training opportunities in these settings. Such affiliations bring expertise, prestige and resources to the community while supporting the comprehensive health center. Through existing affiliations between the Texas Department of Health and the United States Public Health Service rural communities should develop strategies to take advantage of recent expansions in the National Health Service Corps appropriations in order to develop increased capacity and capability in selected rural communities. An aggressive plan to support new health professionals must be a part of this package to prevent the isolation that can occur in such settings.

To effect change in rural health, there needs to be an aggressive approach to meet the unique challenges and the vision to build a system of care that is contained within a regional unit. Rural America is not isolated from the devastating effects of substance abuse, AIDS, measles, trauma, occupational hazards, diabetes or strokes; therefore it should not be isolated from the resources necessary to improve quality of life or to reduce preventable morbidity and mortality.

## CONCLUSION

We can no longer afford a health-care system based on sickness rather than on health—one in which the imbalance between primary care and prevention leaves both modes incapable of fulfilling Americans' health and medical needs.

The popular health-care reform debate becomes meaningless, unless our system has the capacity to care for those who currently lack access to the system. Even if we issued every medically indigent American a magic plastic card labeled "National Health Care Insurance," the needs of many would go unmet.

Solving the health-care problem in America must begin by building capacity—for both primary care and prevention. And in doing so, we must take advantage of the opportunity to correct the ancient inequity between treating diseases and preventing their occurrence and to create a new vision that links primary care and public health. It could be the beginning of a long-term reconciliation between Panacea and Hygeia.

Attempts at such a reconciliation are not without precedent. The concept of integrated care has been labeled community-responsive medicine and Community Oriented Primary Care (COPC). COPC minimizes fragmentation by reducing barriers such as transportation and by co-locating services, such as laboratory; pharmacy; radiology; health education; Women, Infants, and Children (WIC) services; and immunizations, in one site. It is a way of practicing medicine that blends traditional primary care with preventive public health.

While primary care focuses on the individual patient or "user" and does not assume responsibility for the health status of the community at large, COPC is driven by the defined need for health services identified within the target community.

This nation has a vested interest in the health of its citizens as we speed toward the 21st century with an aging population, a potential shortfall in our labor force, and the next public health crisis that will test our system of care. We must protect our investment by building health-care capacity wherever it is needed. For the health of our citizens, for the future of our labor force, and for the economic imperative to curb the uncontrolled growth of health-care costs, we also must change the fractured way health care is delivered in America.

We must seize this opportunity to end the wasteful discord between Aesculapius' daughters, to reunite Hygeia and Panacea by building capacity in both preventive and therapeutic medicine and by promoting the concept of Community Oriented Primary Care.

## Note

[1] The author has requested poetic license from the reader: Hygeia is the Goddess of Preventive Health; however, Panacea is a term, not a Goddess of Greek mythology.

## References

Bacon, J. 1991. Uncle Sam wants you to talk about community health. *Business and Health.* September.

Bishop, R. 1983. Preventive/community medicine curriculum time in United States medical schools. *Journal of Community Health* 9(1):3–6.

Boumbulian, P. J.; Smith, D. R. and Anderson, R. J. COPC Model creates environment for prevention. American Hospital Association. *Outreach* Vol. 12 (1).

Breken, D.,*et al.* 1989. Improving preventive care of a medical clinic: How can the patient help? *American Journal of Preventive Medicine* 5 (6):353–9.

Brooks, D. D.; Smith, D. R. and Anderson, R. J. 1991. Medical apartheid an American perspective. *Journal of the American Medical Association* 266:2746–9.

The Economist. 1991. *Health Care* July 6:5–18.

Flexner, A. *Medical education in the United States and Canada.* The Carnagie Foundation for the Advancement of Teaching, 1910. New York.

Haley, C.; Schulte, J. M.; Brown, G. R. and Zetzman, M. R. 1988. *Changing immunization referral patterns among pediatric and family practice physicians in Dallas County, Texas* 87:204–7.

Institute of Medicine. 1983. *Community-oriented primary care: new directions for health service delivery.* Conference Proceedings. Washington, D.C.

Levy, S. The triumph of equivocation. *New England Journal of Medicine* 321:25 1750.3.

Logsdon, D.; Lazaro, M. and Meir, R. 1989. The feasibility of behavioral risk reduction in primary medical care. *American Journal of Preventive Medicine* 5 (5).

Manber, M. 1985. Evolving medical schools curricule. *Medical Schools World News* 26:141–3.

Relman, A. 1983. Reforming the Health Care system. *New England Journal of Medicine* 323 (14):991–2.

Smith, D.; Anderson, R. and Boumbulian, P. Community responsive medicine: defining an academic discipline. *American Journal of Medical Sciences* 302 (5):313–18.

Sofaer, S. and Kenney, E. The effect of changes in the financing and organization of health services.

University of Texas Southwestern Medical School Department of Pediatrics and Parkland Memorial Hospital. 1991. Unpublished Data.

Waldo, D.; Levit, K. and Lazenby, D. 1986. National Health Expenditures: 1985.*HCFA Review* 8 1:1–21.

Warner, K. 1987. Selling health promotion to corporate America: uses and abuses of the economic argument. *Health Education Quarterly* 14 (1):39–55.

# Chapter 15

## Health Assurance Development—A Unique Partnership

*Daniel J. Schneider, M.D., M.P.H.*

*with assistance from*

*Katye Kowierschke, M.S.*
*Janice Smith, M.B.A.*

*Health Assurance Development:* An original concept for discussion of
assuring health vis-a-vis health care cost occurrence in strategic health
policy planning and funds allocation in Canada and the U.S.

". . . medicine . . . [has]. . . itself created new kinds of disease."

—Illich

"Infancy is the eternal Messiah, which continuously comes back to the arms
of degraded humanity."

—Emerson

### INTRODUCTION

Pursuing health through medicine dominates discussion of health care organization and costs. We have become willing, trusting, and even preoccupied customers of
medicine because it has successfully increased our average life expectancy. Simulta-
neously, we intuitively look forward to inevitable disease, disability and death while
society at large has necessarily become progressively and collectively more responsible for both defining the services and allocating the resources necessary to deliver
whatever cure or care we aspire to have on hand when our time of ultimate need arrives.
This preoccupation with "curing" ourselves into health by means of "medicalization"
has been seen as an oxymoronic aberration by Illich, with others (i.e., Horrobin,
Ingman, Waitzkin) debating modern medicine as cause of an artifactual, not real,
decrease in medical ills; even causing more disease in the long run than has been cured.
The discussion surrounding Illich's view argues that ameliorating disease at one stage,
circumstance or time in life simply sets the timer for the disease clock to strike its toll
at another stage, circumstance or point in time. Thus, accomplishment of lower cost

256

cures of acute diseases earlier in life sets man up for increases in frequency of more costly chronic, debilitating and degenerative diseases later in life. Increased life span through the healing arts inevitably forces increased incidence of hopelessly unrecoverable disease beyond the reach of the healing arts regardless of cost caused Illich to call the legitimacy of medicine into question. As more presently underserved citizens access services, this process will compound.

Emerson's observation and perception focuses on the stable, seemingly predictable for all time, regenerative potential in each infant at birth seemingly independent of and without regard for any degradation of parents and adults. The deliberations of both Illich and Emerson tacitly deal with the biological and psychological reality of our DNA's somatic and germinal duplicity. Looking at health from Illich's focus, the natural aging limits of our somatic DNA are imposed on medicine, and thereby, onto society, resulting in inescapable escalating expenditure of money, time and frustration in pursuit of evanescent health as somatic DNA becomes ever more damaged or ravaged over time. The regenerative bloom and promise at infancy, insightfully observed by Emerson, on the other hand, is accomplished through germinal DNA meiotic recombinant repair and outcrossing complementation (Bernstein). Germinal DNA, with special means for regenerative repair, supplies the somatic DNA for the biology and personality codes of each conceptus (Reiss, Innis). Arguably, because of the regenerated, robust nature of each human's apparent potential at birth, we expend a disproportionately small portion of health care dollars, comparatively almost nothing, culturing the healthy development of children. Thus, the Illich and Emerson views come together in the reality of our DNA endowment encoded at conception; to wit: given whatever somatic DNA with which we chance into life, we must protect and make best use of before our health potential is all to quickly degraded and dissipated, our fondest hopes and Faustian fantasies notwithstanding, for surely each of our DNA's days as servant to each of us are numbered by nature—and our own learned actions.

Neglect to fully develop the DNA critical period coded potential in early life (our development years) for each of us is paid for both as reduced productivity while that potential should still be useful to us (our independent years) and as heightened and/or accelerated, even futile, costs during life's inevitable degradation (either premature or natural old age years). This neglect is both individual and collective within our society, and is manifest as neglect in caring for the aged and neglect to provide and care for learning environments for youth in our communities. To remedy this neglect, health culturing requires society's collective action (Dalley, Alexander) across family, neighborhood and social class lines. We argue for general education group dynamic community learning environments to overcome this neglect in order to allay much of the cost and morbidity of aging through health inducing learning in early life. It is our goal to diminish and postpone the cost of ill-health for as long a time as possible through assuring early development of healthy lifestyles and practices and productive liveli-hoods. This is achievable through healthy culturing of children such that each grows to adopt healthy lifestyles that cause as little somatic damage and thereby as little demand for health services as possible with the largest proportion making maximum productive contribution during as long and healthy life span as possible before the inevitable end arrives with as little cost and fuss as possible.

Thus, I have coined the term *Health Assurance Development* to describe *the deliberate provision within society whereby culture is designed to assure a high probability of lifelong healthful decision-making by as many individuals within the population as possible.* Establishment of *Health Assurance Development* for both the U.S. and Canada will require adoption of an appropriate goal and will require unique, new alliances and partnerships between health care professionals, especially by those within public health, and general education professionals.

## Cost Justification

If health care costs in the United States continue to increase at the current rate, by the year 2000 our nation will spend at least $1.7 trillion annually. In a February, 1993, speech, President Bill Clinton made this projection and also predicted that 20 percent of our Gross National Product will be spent on health care in the year 2000. That's up from about 14 percent of GNP today. Increased access will possibly drive the cost even higher. The American College of Preventive Medicine estimates that 60 percent of our annual health care cost is used to care for conditions caused by preventable behavior.

Canada's approach to health care delivery is often referred to as a cost efficient model for application to U.S. health care organization. In a recent report (Redelmeier), this position is apparent. In an interview reported in the Wall Street Journal (Anders) on March 18, 1993, Redelmeier states that the U.S. would save about 5% ($40 billion of $838 billion annual) of current health care costs by employing the Canadian system. Thus, if we were to modify our organization of health care services in the U.S. such that we save about 5 percent of our health care costs, given our current projections for the year 2000, this 5 percent reduction would be about $100 billion ($0.1 trillion) per year. On first look, this may seem like a lot of money, and in fact is a lot of money. But examination of the output side shows that a 5% saving would only reduce the total projected health care cost to $1.6 trillion from the present projection of $1.7 trillion. In these terms, the 5 percent does not seem like much. And what is important to recognize is that 60% of the "reduced" health care cost of $1.6 trillion would still probably be due to preventable behavioral risk factors. These behavioral risk factors, therefore, leave lots of room to work on inducing health to save a big part of $1 trillion. That's a potential savings of $1 trillion through assuring healthy behavior as compared to a potential savings of $0.1 trillion through health care services reorganization. Have we really focused our attention to the appropriate issue in controlling health care costs? Or, should we not focus on both better health care organization AND *Health Assurance Development*?

**Behavior Justification**

Our current U.S. working hypothesis about health care costs in Canada is: The health care cost advantage in Canada results from better, more efficient organization. In fact, this is in large part probably a valid hypothesis; one that should be vigorously and energetically analyzed and considered, as is being accomplished through contemporary studies and conferences. But, could this 5 percent cost savings also reflect that the Canadian health care cost advantage may be the "tip" of a healthier behavior "ice berg"? For example, could the willingness of Canada, and the tendency for Canadians, to sustain original cultures help preserve family centered values that favor healthier patterns of behavior development? Could cultural determinants of health related behavior be significant to the difference in health care costs observed between the U.S. and Canada? A careful analysis of these questions could help understand effective ways to make appropriate health care savings through *Health Assurance Development*.

Recognition that behavioral risk factors play important roles in health is not a new or recent observation. Many cultural practices seek to govern behavior at least in part to assure health outcomes. Monogamous marriage; fasting; avoidance or restriction of meat or certain meats; and many other behavior practices, often as religious dogmas, share health as well as broader cultural foundations. Hippocrates is credited with advising physicians to carefully observe the habits of patients on entering their households, considering various intemperances in the diagnosis of ailments. Mencius, a disciple of Confucius, is credited with observing that man can survive all calamities of heaven and nature but we can have a great deal of difficulty surviving calamities we bring onto ourselves. From ancient times, man has recognized the importance that behavior plays in the health outcome that each human has for all time experienced. Their wisdom is no less applicable today. We must now focus on the individual and collective roles played in determining what each persons' behavior, as well as forces in the learning environment of individuals contributes to health care cost in our society.

Neither rationing of health care nor looking for fixes in organization will correct the fundamental and significant human behavior component to health care costs. Without a doubt, trying to fix what we do as professionals that contributes to health care costs is justified and is terribly important, but the big gains in reducing health care costs are to be found in inducing healthy behavior.

Thus, there are two parties that influence the health care cost equation:

the learned behavior of human beings, individually and as groups; acting together with, the acquired behavior of the health professionals, individually and within organizations.

Unfortunately, we tend to place most of our attention in pursuit of solution to our health care cost crisis on the role and organization of health professionals in the illustrated vector diagram. The greatest health cost gain, a gain of as much as 10:1 however, can come only by focusing and intensifying our interventions on the determinants of, and the development of, lifelong healthy behavior of individuals. The gain can be large. As mentioned earlier, it is estimated that 60% of our health care costs are due to preventable behavioral risk factors. Today, behavioral risk factors are associated with about $0.5 trillion; and are predicted to double to $1 trillion by the year 2000 if not vigorously attacked.

**Learning Foundation**

When the term "preventable behavior" is used today, drug abuse, violence, unwanted teen pregnancy or HIV/AIDS jumps into the minds of most people. The same group of people often do not associate "preventable behavioral risk factors" with the biggest killer in the country—heart disease—though physicians constantly point to the contributing behaviors that cause it: Overeating, Under exercising, Stress, High-fat diets . . . and a lack of learning to drink an adequate amount of water to reduce the risk of hypertension. Now there is the real culprit—lack of *learning* to "behave" in healthful ways. Lack of **learning** healthful habits; **learning** healthful beliefs; **learning** healthful practices; all adding up to **learning** healthful lifestyles and **learning** healthful decision-skills. For example, the cost of failure to learn suitable healthy behavior cost the U.S. more than $135 billion in 1991 for coronary heart disease according to Department of Commerce data.

In looking at the causes of the Number 1 killer by itself, it becomes apparent that children learn proper nutrition and physical activity, beginning at birth, from within culture and social environments (WHO). Behavior patterns, such as eating and exercise, are set by the time children start school. When the Number 1 Killer is added to all the other diseases caused by preventable behaviors, the result in terms of both human   suffering and dollar costs is overwhelming; human suffering and loss of opportunity being proportionally larger costs than the actual dollar cost of focal disease.

But "learning" within society is a prime order function of culture and education. Learning by virtue of culture is mostly an informal process...learning at home, on the street, from movies, at church, from television, from peers, from parents and all sorts of other sources in all sorts of settings while engaged in all sorts of family, neighborhood and social class activities. And much of this informal learning has significant impact on health behavior. Informal learning has a far greater impact on health behavior than formal learning.

It is true that much of health behavior can be leaned in formal education settings; at public or private schools and other organized settings. But it is the composite of informal learning and formal learning that formulates the health related behavior of each of us. So, putting these two kinds of education together—informal education and formal education; informal learning and formal learning—collectively I refer to these as "*General Education*." The learning environment of each human consists of components that come from each part of this composite - General Education. Every child is born human. Each**learns**, through the specific**general education** environment to which exposed, to become "Black," "White," "Hispanic"; or to become kinder/ gentler vs. violent, promiscuous vs. monogamous, literate vs. sub-literate or illiterate, productive vs. burdensome, criminal vs. law abiding, antisocial vs. social, abusive vs. nurturing, sharing vs. greedy, etc., etc.

But, how do we create change to make a big dent in the 60 percent of health care costs due to preventable behavioral risk factors? To do this, *We must forge a partnership between general education and health care!* A partnership to foster intergenerational and transgenerational health literacy in heart disease, cancer and stroke, drug abuse, tuberculosis, unwanted pregnancy, child abuse, and environmental pollution. *Each* a national problem in human misery and countless loss of dollars. A partnership to induce health will also reduce scholastic under achievement and criminal behavior by virtue of the common natural history and etiology of these problems. And will increase total life productivity potential as well.

One logical starting point is to articulate, and then crusade for, a health and general educational partnership around a clear macrocultural *Health Assurance Development* goal, such a goal would be added to goals for education already in existence. In 1990, President George Bush convened the Governors of all the U.S. states to define national education goals. The Governors specified six goals, which were launched in April, 1991, as America 2000. In 1993, President Bill Clinton retained the six goals, changing the name to "Goals 2000." It is my argument that the most expedient way to ignite the needed partnership between health and general education is through the addition of a health assurance goal. I have crafted, and energetically crusade for, such a specific seventh goal, the *Health Assurance Development* Goal, as follows:

> The **learning environment** of all children, all citizens, in America shall **assure** the **development of** lifelong **health**ful skills, practices, attitudes, beliefs, and habits.

The adoption of this goal will require provision of appropriate conditions for the accomplishment of three criteria against which the behavioral health effectiveness of community program trials can and must then be measured. These criteria are:

a)   Clear definition of suitable *"learning environments"* vis-a-vis associative, value-based and cognitive learning modalities;
b)   Clear definition of expected health behavior outcomes desired from that environment (*assure* correlated with *health*);
c)   Clear definition of the learning processes operative within the learning environment needed to accomplish the desired health outcomes (*development* correlated with *health*).

Adopting this goal as a national goal mandates open debate and trial of ideas and opinions, and forces sound epidemiological modeling and testing of options, ecological models, and methods and measures conceived to achieve the goal. The research objective of setting the goal is to test community-based healthy behavior learning environment trials with research vigor and rigor similar to biomedical bench testing and clinical trials as historically employed in public health.

This *Health Assurance Development* goal is an entirely new, fresh and positive approach to curtailing health care costs. It is much more than health education per se . . . it is not only another part of the kindergarten through grade 12 formal curriculum. It is a broad general education, cultural strategy applied to both formal and informal education environments. It is family-oriented, group dynamic, community-based learning locally managed to overcome underlying health ignorance at the root of our escalating health care and cost crisis. As a seventh National Education Goal, it can be implemented through state and community councils organized and charged as local innovators of general education reform.

*Health Assurance Development* must create group dynamic, community-based means to **induce** health as an integral function of society. Only through local self-control accomplished by community group dynamics can community action come to gripes with family, neighborhood and social forces in the learning environment of all community members, especially of children;—this is the challenge for general education. In this fashion, *Health Assurance Development* as means to affect health cost containment is entirely different than dealing with health care costs through manipulation of health care organization, placing caps on services, administering health care rationing schemes, etc., etc., or hoping for traditional medical care programs to reduce disease costs. *Health Assurance Development* can make a real difference now so that down the line, health care costs decline.

*Health Assurance Development* is much more than, and entirely different from, tort reform, national health insurance, rationing, Medicare, Medicaid, and current changes to the health care system which only treat the symptoms, while the "tumor" continues its "metastatic" unchecked growth. At the end of this paper, a natural history diagram illustrates the process by which *Health Assurance Development* already occurs naturally within many families in many segments of our communities.

## Health Crisis Driving Force

The *Health Assurance Development* goal-setting concept has far reaching consequences for Texas, the U.S. and Canada. Just look at its potential significance here in our home state of Texas. The following quote is taken directly from the Texas Health Policy Task Force Report released in 1992 by Texas Governor Ann Richards:

> Texas faces a crisis in health care the proportions of which are so great that
> its delivery system could collapse before the turn of the century . . . the
> existing health care system is broken.

Texans tend to blame much of this crisis on the health care delivery system. But, how much of this current crisis should really be blamed on the association between health ignorance, risk taking behavior and disease; that is, disease occurrence that is causally associated with ignorance about health protective behavior and unhealthy lifestyles, practices and activities of both individuals and society? The answer is: Quite a bit. For instance:

- Texas teens, ages 12 through 19, gave birth to over 50,000 newborns in 1991.
- Suicides by teens trend upward, and increased in number to 183 in 1991.
- Investigations of child abuse are up six fold during the last decade.
- Referrals to juvenile probation for violent offenses are up by 122 percent since 1988.
- The prevalence of substance abuse among secondary students in Texas is reflected by a marked increase in alcohol and tobacco use.
- Promiscuous sexual exposure has resulted in a dramatic increase of pediatric HIV/AIDS, and,

- Behavior intermixed with cultural and socio-economic factors has reversed historic downward trend in incidence of tuberculosis.

Incidence is how sharply rising with increased frequency of drug resistant and avian strains; and in 1991, the Texas Hispanic population experienced a 116 percent higher incidence than the Black and White populations combined.

Further, we must remember that, while Texas has dense city populations, it also has large rural populations. By Census Bureau definition of urban/rural populations, 19.7 percent of Texans are rural. With the 10 P.M. news, and tomorrow's headlines, usually depicting life only in the inner city, it is sometimes easy to forget that problems exist in the "country" too. For example, compared to urban Texas, in rural Texas:

- The rate of arrests for certain drug-related crimes, particularly those involving alcohol use, is almost doubled in rural Texas;
- Births to mothers under the age of 18 years is about 20% higher in all ethnic groups;
- The poverty rate is consistently higher;
- About one out of every six rural persons has no health insurance, and almost 11 percent of the rural population is enrolled in the Medicaid program.

## Considerations on *Health Assurance Development* needed

And when we think of two of the top four causes of death in the U.S.; heart disease, and stroke; we have to wonder how adult health care costs would be different if children were assured health behavior development with healthful learning from birth. Learning as simple as drinking enough water. Or being cultured from birth to eat healthful foods (WHO). How would the years into ripe old age be influenced if we began insisting today that grades pre-K through four drink three to five cups of water each day while at school? Could we remove part of the cost of these top diseases from the health care system while improving the quality of life?

Or consider the matter of obesity. Eating lunch with first-graders will show you they frequently are allowed fifteen minutes in which to eat. Yet we tell overweight children to eat slower so their stomach has time to notify their brain that hunger is sated.—the stomach takes longer than 15 minutes to respond. And what about the nutritional habits most school and mealtime menu choices teach? How would the health care costs and quality of life into old age be influenced if we began today insisting that grades pre-K through four take a full thirty minutes to eat a healthy lunch? Could we remove another part of the chronic cost weight from the sagging health delivery system?

Let your imagination run free for a moment. Think about the opportunities that abound for **parenting** activities to emphasize learning good health habits. Books, music, art and entertainment for families that tell about families; or families hiking, picnicking, enjoying parks, working and playing together; or simply exercising together: or studying together, doing chores together. . . . Or doing projects together with **groups of families**; how about raising gardens of healthy foods? Or community improvement projects; clean-up projects; recycling projects—even cottage industry projects. Not only the physical exercise is healthy, but the habits and associations learned are healthy; and the morals, character traits and values learned contribute to health. And better nutrition and healthy sustainable natural environments and health inducing societal environments are important results.

Of most important concern are steps to be taken by the community. Perhaps the most difficult step is finding the means by which community leadership can achieve group dynamic control over informal learning environments that occur in media, on the street, in entertainment and in the promotion of many products with unhealthy features. The goal setting and community council action approach established within the America 2000 strategy is a very big step in a direction that should work. Addition of the goal as set out in this paper would enhance this vital effort.

These are just a few *Health Assurance Development* activities that come quickly to mind and address some of the worst killers and disease circumstances modern nations face.

## CONCLUSION

Behavior modification is not new. We have already seen its success in anti-smoking programs and progress being made in drug-free programs. But healthy behavior development, tied to a general education/health care partnership that induces health is needed to reduce health care costs. Unfortunately, we commonly use the same old medical model—"don't worry about what caused the predisposition for premarital promiscuity, just deliver the baby"—is still being used. Society has changed and the old "cures" must change also. We must develop a New Paradigm . . . its time we deal with the real natural history which results in susceptibility for unwanted pregnancy, HIV and violence; its time to worry about the cultural causes of our preventable risk factors resulting in heart disease, stroke, hypertension and many other behavior-related diseases. Its time we define just what cultural epidemiology and cultural modification can do to induce health. Culture is manageable. Culture is modifiable. But clear societal goals are the only means to initiate and make culture modification rational; and epidemiology is the means to assess progress in achievement of those goals.

We must become "physicians to our culture." Culture is always changing. Madison Avenue knows very well how to make culture change to satisfy commercial interests. We can develop similar skills to stimulate and support the family, neighborhood and community learning environment—the culturing environment—needed to assure healthy behavior development of all citizens. Recognizing the societal and cultural changes which have occurred in our state, in our nation and in the modern world, we strongly propose adoption of our goal for *Health Assurance Development*. By this means we can use epidemiologically valid methods to modify the health outcomes of society commencing with behavior development of children in their formative years—in anticipation of conception, infancy, through pre-school, and up— and thereby use the learning environment of children as the conduit for educating the adult.

This concept is complimentary to certain aspects of the 4H program and intergenerational literacy programs prominent throughout the U.S. However, because a partnership has never been forged between health and general education, the two disciplines have never recognized their common strands infrastructure to develop their uncommon strengths and destiny once allied.

Is such an alliance possible? After all the years of silence and autonomy on the part of each with respect to the other, can a partnership that will equip our children and grandchildren and future generations work? If in doubt, ask: . . . are the alternatives to adopting our new goal for *Health Assurance Development* acceptable? If the possibilities envisioned in this new alliance sound farfetched and unattainable, then please remember: It wasn't too many years ago that a small group of people sat around a table talking when one said, "Let's put man on the moon." Some laughed, some left, but those that believed enough to work it out—won!

So can we if we adopt this new goal: "The *learning environment* of all children, all citizens, in America shall *assure* the *development of* lifelong *health*ful skills, practices, attitudes, beliefs, and habits."

. . . and then energetically forge the new, unique partnership between health and general education to integrate and execute the goal.

What steps will shift our society's focus to induction of health? *Step One:* Most important and urgent, the first step is adoption of the *Health Assurance Development* goal by the Clinton administration. The goal must be added to the present six goals for education, Goals 2000. *Step Two:* The Goals 2000 program should mobilize a National *Health Assurance Development* Board with cultural epidemiology, health cost accounting, auditing and standards definitions capability. *Step Three:* The goal must be adopted by individual states; and by professional and academic education and health leaders, organizations and institutions. Steps two and three must provide leadership, organizational, materials and logistic support for the following steps. *Step Four:* Adoption of the goal together with mobilization of local group dynamic, community based governing committees or boards with federal, state and professional organization support. It is most crucial that the local community have ultimate control, with state and federal backup, over the local general education learning environment (informal education as well as formal education) with at least as much determination as local school boards presently exercise over formal education. This step will require a maximum level of federal, state and local cooperation and committed support, including technical, administrative, instructive, interactive communication, information exchange, legal and legislative, material and other support. *Step Five:* Implementation of informal and formal group dynamic, community-based *Health Assurance Development* education programs. *Step Six:* Evaluation of goal achievement and adjustment through data analysis, feedback and governance at local, state and federal levels, and in preparation of administrators, teachers, materials, education and health professionals, and others whose roles and activities affect the health of citizens.

These steps can be accomplished. The result will achieve optimum induction of health and health care cost amelioration. Success in similar steps is being demonstrated

## Figure 1. Health Assurance Development

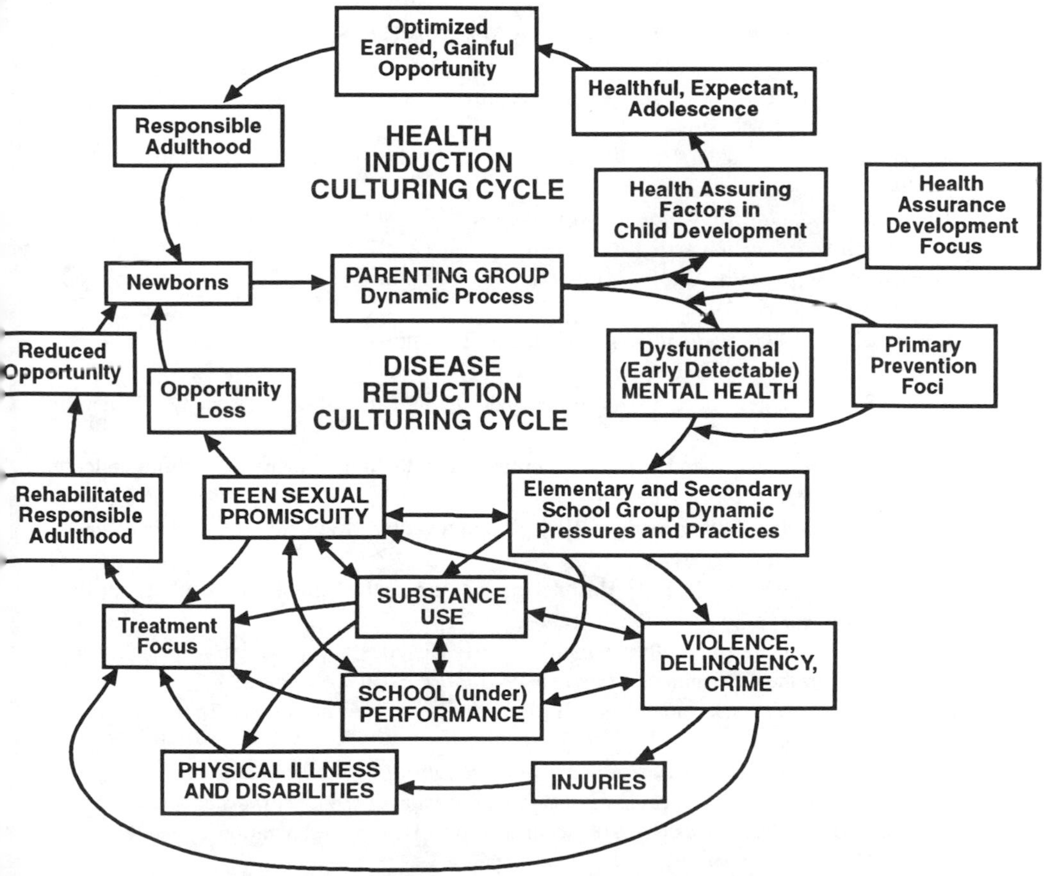

by implementation of the first six goals for education in the America 2000/Goals 2000 program. It is now time to add the seventh goal.

The following natural history diagram illustrates the intergenerational process by which *Health Assurance Development* already occurs naturally within many families in many segments of our communities. The health induction culturing cycle is promoted by learning environments that assure development of healthful skills, practices, attitudes, beliefs, and habits. The disease reduction culturing cycle is a growing cycle reflected by increasing incidence of behavior related dysfunction in society.

Adoption of the *Health Assurance Development* goal will force a positive shift of our focus and our emphasis in health policy and practice to the HEALTH INDUCTION CULTURING CYCLE.

## References

Alexander, L. 1992. *America 2000 community Notebook*. U.S. Secretary of Education; Washington, DC.

Anders, G. March 18, 1993. Canada hospitals provide care as good as in U.S. at lower costs, studies show. *Wall Street Journal*.

Bernstein, C., and Bernstein, H. 1991. *Aging, sex, and DNA repair*. San Diego: Academic Press, Inc.

Dalley, G. 1988. *Ideologies of caring: rethinking community and collectivism*. London: Macmillan Education Ltd.

Emerson, R. W.; cited in: Strain, J. P. 1971. *Modern philosophies of education*. New York: Random House, 55.

Horrobin, D. F. 1978. *Medical hubris*. Montreal: Eden Press.

Illich, I. 1973. *Tools for conviviality*. New York: Harper & Row.

Ingman, S. and Danielson, R. 1976. Toward redesigning national health systems. *Reviews in Anthropology* March/April.

Innis, N. K. 1992. Toman and Tyron: Early research on the inheritance of the ability to learn. *American Psychologist* 47:2:190–197.

Prevention Agenda. 1988. American College of Preventive Medicine. *Presidential health platform position paper*.

Redelmeier, D. and Fuchs, V. 1993. Hospital expenditures in the United States and Canada. *New England Journal of Medicine* 328:772–8.

Reiss, D.; Plomin, R. and Hetherington, M. 1991. Genetics and psychiatry: an unheralded window on the environment. *American Journal of Psychiatry* 148:283–291.

Texas Health Policy Task Force. 1992. *Texas health care * new directions*. Texas Governor's Office, Austin.

Waitzkin, Howard. *The second sickness: contradictions of capitalist health care*.

WHO. 1982. *Prevention of coronary heart disease: report of a WHO expert committee*. WHO Technical Report Series No. 678. Geneva: World Health Organization.

# Chapter 16

## Lessons for Citizen Policymakers
## in Canada and the United States
## on Health Care Policy

*Gerald R. Middents, M. Div., Ph.D.*
Professor of Psychology
Director of Contemporary Policy Studies
Austin College
Sherman, Texas

### INTRODUCTION

How can citizens, policy-makers, professionals and students be educated about the issues concerning health care policies in Canada and the United States? This question is a crucial challenge in reforming health care delivery systems. How do policy-makers and politicians move beyond opinion polls, misinformation, media releases and political slogans into pretested, carefully evaluated policies that are financially feasible, politically possible, ethically sound and scientifically defensible?

Educating citizens, students, professionals and policymakers is a key concern for this paper designed to address macro-issues of health care policy. Interchange among people from different cultures and countries can be helpful in understanding each other particularly in the area of health care delivery. Exchanges between Canada and the United States can highlight similarities and differences, while as an additional benefit better comprehension of each others' strengths and limitations takes place.

Considerable misinformation occurs unless efforts are made to communicate reliable research and accurate findings about the different approaches in health care delivery. Anecdotal information of dramatic and vivid case studies can appeal to media audiences and special interest groups. However, dramatic cases usually make bad policy just as hard court cases can lead to bad legislation and laws.

Americans are very susceptible to advertising, promotion and marketing efforts designed to influence their viewpoints. Canadians tend to be much better informed about the United States than vice versa. Canadians, consequently, have a better capacity to evaluate data about the health care in the United States than U.S. citizens can accurately evaluate information about the Canadian health care system. Moreover,

269

each system of health care is actually multiple systems rather than monolithic national systems. Each province in Canada has unique characteristics and experiences, while each state in the United States has diverse health care programs that cannot be generalized to the whole country. As a result simplistic viewpoints do not consistently represent the complexities of how these multi-faceted health care approaches function in reality.

The dynamics of educating policymakers was vividly illustrated in the United States by contrasting two political leaders, namely former President Bush and President Clinton. President Bush addressed the nation on February 6, 1992, about his administration's approach to health care problems. While major disagreement occurred as to the viability of his solutions, there was one obvious result from one of his most fervent addresses. It illustrated the "educating of the President" on a lesson he apparently did not want to learn. However, his address stimulated intensive reaction by others to come up with better policy solutions during the 1992 presidential election.

President Clinton, as a candidate in 1992, attacked the problems of health care head-on making it a central issue. Immediately upon taking office, he appointed his wife, Hillary Rodham Clinton, as the head of the Task Force on Health Care Reform. In the first 100 days of his administration, he wanted this Task Force to come up with major policy recommendations for reforming the health care system. The lessons that former President Bush failed to learn about reforming health care policy, President Clinton wanted to make a centerpiece of his new administration. He, his wife, and the country became educated on this key issue which he wished to solve by "managed competition." Rather than micro-management which has contributed to many cost increases, President Clinton saw strengths in the Canadian system of macro-management of the health care expenditures. However, different economic mechanisms unique to each country define the parameters of how health care is delivered.

Many efforts have been made before to reshape the health care system in the United States. Some creative thinkers engaged in the process of analysis have concluded that the United States has neither a coordinated nor a coherent system. Rather our current $1,000,000,000,000 annual expenditures (Congressional Budget Office) ironically support an "illness" non-system that is obese, spastic and uncoordinated. Since major consequences are at stake, the public can be unduly influenced by "orchestrated outrage" as conducted by special interests groups such as providers, consumers, payers, lobbyists, citizens, media or policymakers. Since each of these players influence each other and the public in the policymaking process, this chapter has special concern about educating voters as citizen policymakers so that the most informed decisions can be made in a democracy.

This chapter describes an educational program tested for nearly 20 years in educating undergraduate students, policymakers, citizens, lobbyists and professionals in the crucial issues for formulating and evaluating policy alternatives for a viable "health care system." First, key problems will be identified, and secondly, creative problem-solving processes for developing solutions will be presented.

## DEFINING THE PROBLEMS

### History of Problem

Before analyzing the key issues involved in restructuring health care policy, a brief review of historical developments would help set the context for contemporary problems. For over 80 years, efforts have been made to formulate a comprehensive health care system in the United States. Each decade has had unique considerations described by Litman and Robins (1991) in detail. An abridged history from 1910-1990's is attached as Appendix A. This history roughly corresponds to the history of the Canadian system presented in the chapter by Dr. Robert Kinch.

### Current Key Issues

Critical issues are facing "the people" as responsible citizens today that must be considered in identification of health care issues. In contrast to the Canadian system, problems in the United States include access to health care, cost of care, quality of care, and insured users. Each of these problems is discussed in term below.

### Access to Health Care

There is general agreement that over 39 million people have no health insurance and another 50 million are underinsured in the United States. Moreover, there is an assumption that persons who have insurance have adequate access. But there are many exceptions because both those entitled to care and who have insurance coverage do not always have access. For example, under-informed people do not know how and when to seek health services in a system that is not always "user friendly" unless providers and marketing specialists want to promote certain services that may result in over-insurance and utilization.

Moreover, many rural counties and concentrated urban areas do not have primary care physicians let alone hospital facilities due to economic competition plus restrictive regulations of government services for Medicare and Medicaid. Many providers are entrepreneurial in deciding where they can best market their health care services for a profit. The distribution of health providers in a free market economy results in frequent mal-distribution with concentrations of providers in wealthy areas but few if any in inner-city or rural areas. Moreover, some persons with health care needs do not know what is available or where to obtain help. Lack of transportation, ignorance and inaccessibility hamper delivery to numerous segments of the population in the United States.

Another example involves pregnant mothers who need prenatal care but often do not seek or receive it. Impoverished mothers with children are among the most victimized during recent decades. They have few advocates so that preventive services are not pursued in a system that provides disincentives that undervalue preventive services. Rather, the system concentrates on expensive, heroic treatment for acute illness frequently provided in emergency room services.

## Costs

Costs are among major issues reflected in the $1,000,000,000,000 annual expenditures or over 14% of GDP (Congressional Budget Office)—over three time the defense budget for the United States! Employers are becoming desperate in trying to find cost-efficient, managed care. Many employers and companies would like to get out of health insurance coverage. Never before have so many persons in management and executive positions wished that the government would do something to deliver business from the no-win burden of providing health care insurance for employees and retirees. Recently the coalitions of management with unions and government have resulted in collaborative efforts rarely heard of in previous negotiations.

Moreover, private individuals and families are currently feeling exploited by high health insurance which easily runs over $3000 per person or over $6000 annually for a typical family even with higher deductibles, more stringent qualifications and more exclusions that ever before. Some low-wage persons are almost paying half their wages on health insurance if dependents are covered. Employers are wanting to be relieved from providing health insurance benefits not only for current employees but certainly for retired persons. Some large companies would have little profits if they had to state their liabilities incurred for health expenses of retired persons as they are now required in the United States.

Insurance companies in the United States have often been able to survive because they can deselect underwriting high-risk populations by "cherry picking." Moreover, along with physicians, hospitals and pharmaceutical lobbies, the insurance industry collectively has very powerful lobby efforts in Washington (Kemper and Novak, 1992). In addition, persons with prior illnesses may not be able to obtain insurance due to "pre-existing conditions" or "experience ratings." The nature of insurance has been jeopardized when high-risk persons are excluded as being "outside the camp." The metaphor of leprosy from earlier centuries is among us again but with statistical sophistication that marks certain populations with AIDS or other pre-existing conditions as uninsurable.

Moreover, administrative costs range from 20-24% of health care expenditures in the United States. With 1500 payers mostly in the form of insurance companies with a myriad of different forms, paper work and administrivia plague this system with overhead that eats up health care resources. In contrast, the Canadian system spends a fraction of this amount on administrative costs and is much more "user friendly."

## Quality

Quality of health care is conversely correlated to access and positively related to costs in the general picture. Expensive high-tech health care may or may not contribute to quality of care although the myth prevails that technology can produce miraculous results. High-tech medicine may create some of its own problems such as the side-effects of medications in which the cure is almost as great a problem as the disease. The exploitation of in-patient hospitalization for mental health care may be to the benefit of stockholder profits, but may be detrimental to effective treatment as found recently in Texas and a number of other states. Children, families, alcoholics and drug addicts may not always find in-patient hospitalization the treatment of choice.

Moreover, high-tech treatment is so expensive in many cases while low-tech preventive services may be the most cost effective. Consider the benefits of pre-natal and pre-conception preventive care compared with the expense of later high-cost treatment or pre-mature births, impaired infants and other childhood diseases that could be prevented or at least reduced. Cost-benefit ratios range from $1 to $3 and as high as $1 to $10 in the long-run. The Canadian system provides for universal health care for persons of child-bearing age plus childhood vaccinations. In the United States, President Clinton has had to confront the pharmaceutical industry about the outrageous inflationary increases in the cost of vaccinations for children.

## Ethical considerations

Ethical considerations open up difficult major issues that confront health care. At a time when every criminal in the United States is entitled to a court appointed attorney if the criminal cannot afford their own lawyer (Wofford's campaign for the Senate in Pennsylvania), does not a child or helpless persons have as much right to access for health services? Can the citizens of the United States continue to consider access to health care a privilege rather than a basic right of a citizen?

Conflicting interests are rampant in health care delivery. Vested special interests by hospital associations, insurance firms, pharmaceutical industry and health providers provide an inertia that makes it almost impossible to change in the current unmanaged system. Ethical considerations are in critical need of attention from providers, consumers, professional groups as well as legislators. Obviously, there is a need in the United States for universal access to quality health care at a reasonable cost as provided in countries like Canada.

There is a crying need in the United States to set priorities and limitations in view of conflicting demands and limited finances. There is also a myth that market competition will reduce or at least contain costs. Demand for services is not the only factor that drives costs up. Capacity for health care also drives costs according to Rachilis, the author of *Second Opinion: What's Wrong with the Canadian Health Care System*. Rachilis' finding is consistent with Romer's hypothesis that the increased costs of health care have less to do with illness than the excessive capacity of the system to provide additional services.

Rationing is one of those difficult issues which must be faced by any equitable system. In the United States, health care is rationed by a variety of processes largely determined by mechanisms of the free market and regulations. In Canada, rationing largely occurs when annual budgets do not cover the demand for health service. The Canadian system exemplifies macro-management of the total national and provincial costs, whereas in contrast the United States can be characterized by micro-management by third party payers in the federal and state governments plus private insurers and employers. A major complaint of both providers and consumers of the health care system in the United States is the interference of "managed care" which emphasizes micro-management of decisions by providers and consumers. In the process, little attention is given to the macro-issues and expenditures for health care in the United States, whereas the overall national and provincial budget for health care is a major focus in the Canadian system.

## CREATIVE EDUCATIONAL APPROACHES

Now that major issues have been identified and the problem tentatively defined, secondly, this creative problem-solving model involves deliberate steps for developing solutions as part of educating citizen who are the ultimate policymakers in a democracy. As in most problem-solving models, defining the problem is at least half of the solution. Students, professionals and policymakers have also become better informed as well as concerned voting citizens. Educating these various target audiences will now be described from the educational philosophy of the Contemporary Policy Studies program.

## Contemporary Policy Studies Program

Twenty years ago, this undergraduate program was originally pioneered at Austin College as an inter-disciplinary, capstone course for liberal arts students. Over the years, the following ingredients have been incorporated into this educational program:

1. Foster civic and social responsibility in learners who are citizens of a democratic society.
2. Develop competencies in creative problem solving.
3. Address pressing and urgent public policy issues.
4. Involve participants in processes of collaborative learning of self-directed teamwork and group processes.
5. Engage learners in ethical analysis and critical thinking processes.
6. Co-opt policymakers in the educational processes at various stages such as:
   a. identifying and defining problems at an early stage.
   b. providing resource persons and research.
   c. evaluating the policy recommendations of student teams.
7. Develop skills in policy research, creative thinking plus communicating findings in oral and written expression. Teams communicate their policy recommendations to review panels composed of policymakers, public interest citizens and professionals.
8. Evaluate normative policy processes, educational approaches and public policy cycles.
9. Improve the program with the findings of research and feedback.
10. Provide an alternative educational option through student-originated-studies and policy internships.

Since 1972, over 60 topics have been studied in over 110 semester courses. Health Care Policy has been the focus topic for eight courses with numerous health-related topics covered in others courses on bioethics, AIDS, cancer, sexuality, impaired infants, prenatal abuse, abortion, and gender issues. In addition, global policy studies have been addressed on such topics as nuclear issues, development strategies, peace-making, disarmament, terrorism, violence, National Model United Nations, environmental issues, etc. Revisions of the program have occurred in 1979, 1985 and are now in the process with curriculum revisions.

Faculty members find this to be a non-traditional educational program that involves them more as a curriculum planner, learning, coach, facilitator, group dynamics processor, coordinator of learning, and obviously a bridge person between the real world and academia. Numerous elected officials, lobbyists, public interest citizens and professional have been co-opted as resource persons, panel reviewers, and learners. Many persons have indicated that participation in the program is an exciting educational experience as they interact with other learners. Policymakers and elected officials have found the research findings and alternative policy recommendations helpful in their decision-making responsibilities.

The most consistent findings from 20 years of feedback from learners are:

- —awareness of the complexity of health care issues that do not lend themselves to simplistic solutions.
- —the benefit of collaborative teamwork that parallels community participation and professional teamwork.
- —transfer of creative problem-solving competencies to other issues besides health care.
- —experience in communicating with public officials, lobbyists, and legislators.
- —engagement in civic and social responsibilities as voters who are the ultimate policymakers in a democracy.

## Course on Health Care Policy

Initially, this Contemporary Policy Studies course was taught in 1973 at Austin College. It was repeated in 1974, 1976, 1986, 1989, 1992 and twice in 1993. Nuclear issues, war, domestic violence, international terrorism and disarmament issues received more focus in the decade between 1976–86.

The course is limited to juniors and seniors and is taught on an inter-disciplinary model. Naturally many pre-health professionals enroll, but there are also students from the arts, economics, business administration, psychology and the humanities. After an initial orientation to the issues, students are organized into teams of four to eight members to address health care problems related to such groups as 1) infants and parents, 2) children and adolescents, 3) young and middle adults, and 4) young and old elderly. A creative problem-solving model is introduced to analyze problems and issues. Students are guided in understanding ethical conflicts of vested interests, health care systems of other countries, plus distinction between symptoms and causes. Policy processes, players and cycles are introduced including the role of lobbyists, policy researchers, elected officials and of course the role of active, voting citizens.

Public policymakers such as elected officials and professionals with wide public interests are co-opted to help identify problems, unresolved issues, possible directions for solutions and resources. The first half of the course is focused on problem identification and definition plus comparison with systems in other countries such as the Canadian and nations in Western Europe.

In the second half, creative problem-solving energy is focused on developing policy alternatives, evaluating solutions for economic, political and scientific feasibility. Student teams refine their policy recommendations into executive summaries which are then presented in an oral defense to panels of policymakers from diverse perspectives. Students teams are graded on their written reports and oral defense open to the campus and community. Reports are refined and distributed to policy-making officials who have indicated interests in the results of this research. These include congressional leaders, state legislators, legislative aides and local officials.

The details of the course are described in copies of the syllabus which is available upon request. Creative assignments for research papers, self-directed teamwork processes and educational resources are also available to interested educators and professionals in health care fields.

## CONCLUSIONS

This Contemporary Policy Studies program was designed to help bridge the gap between academia and the political realities of public policymaking in our closely related democratic societies. What happens in the United States influences Canada, and vice versa, what happens in Canada influences the United States. There are lessons to be learned from each other.

One paradoxical dilemma in health care policy is that politicians do not want to identify a problem for which they do not already have a solution (Wildavsky, 1979). Otherwise they run the risk of losing votes and elections as illustrated by the defeat of President Bush in 1992, and likewise in the change of government in Canada. However, once politicians have a promising legislative proposal to address a difficult problem, they take the role of the hero or heroine to save their constituency and the nation. President Clinton potentially illustrates this latter direction.

By engaging citizens, talented-but-detached students, policymakers, politicians and professionals in an educational processes, they all benefit while also serving to improve the sophistication and social consciousness of society. Educating politicians, students and the public who are the ultimate policymakers is a critical predicate to developing viable solutions to the health care crisis. Obviously, these bridges need to be built in addressing the urgent problems involved in formulating and restructuring health care policy in our democracies.

APPENDIX A: HISTORY 1910–1990s

1910s:    The Flexner Report condemned existing medical education and
          proposed transformation from a guild apprenticeship model to a
          university-based enterprise. The AMA proposed principles for
          government health insurance.

1920s:    The AMA reversed its position and declared its unequivocal
          opposition to compulsory health insurance calling it "socialist"
          and a "German" invention (Kemper and Novak, 1992). The
          cottage industry model for providers of health care continued.
          While Western European countries had some form of national
          health insurance, little policy research was conducted in this
          country on this topic. President Coolidge called for massive
          increases in federal spending on health care which was at a level
          of 3% of GNP.

1930s:    While social security legislation proposed by President Roosevelt
          passed during the Great Depression, there was neither a political
          will or social vision to pass national health programs. Piece-meal
          programs were designed to react to emergencies.

1940s:    Wartime emergencies dominated an all-out national effort to
          defeat the Germans and Japanese. Wages were frozen, but em-
          ployers discovered perks could be given through employee health
          insurance. Tax legislation permitted deduction of health insur-
          ance as a business expense. Private health insurance continued to
          develop as a measure to assure dependable payment to providers.
          All but the Veteran's Hospitals and public health measures
          proposed by President Truman for universal coverage were
          defeated by powerful vested interests of insurance and providers.

1950s:    President Eisenhower had interest in a more comprehensive
          health care system. The Hill-Burton Act provided federal support
          for hospital expansion and additional legislation laid groundwork
          for federal involvement in health care programs. Employers,
          unions, employees and providers became addicted to hospital
          insurance.

1960s:    After President Kennedy's assassination, President Johnson's
          Great Society Legislation was rapidly passed. In 1965, Medicare
          and Medicaid was legislated to cover elderly and impoverished.
          Initial opposition from health care providers and private insurers

was co-opted politically and economically. Supplemental insurance flourished as did most health insurance firms.

1970s:    Five major health care programs were proposed before Congress by both parties including one by President Nixon based upon promoting Health Maintenance Organizations. The Watergate fiasco arrested a concentrated focus on health care legislation along with a recession.

1980s:    Incremental programs developed further such as the "disease-of-the-month" approach started in Congress in earlier decades. Inflation continued with cost control reaction from the federal government. Cost shifting and "managed" care by third party payers, providers, consumers and employers was the game plan without coordinated effort. The health care system became more spastic with DRG's (Diagnostic Related Groups), and other tinkering devices to manage costs of a "patchwork quilt." Health planning was cut and then further deregulation resulted in over-expansion of hospital facilities, expensive technology and heroic measures with only limited attention to preventive measures.

1990s:    Cost-shifting nearly paralyzes the system as free-market tactics exploit health care "commodities." New alliances develop among employers-unions, providers, consumers with major gaps in private and government insurance coverage. Vested interests hamper the development of comprehensive or credible legislation. Total annual expenditures threaten to reach 17% of GDP or over $1,600,000,000,000 (Faltermeyer, 1993) in a medical "arms race." President Clinton attacked the problem by appointing Hillary, his wife, as head of a Health Care Task Force.

## References

Faltermeyer, (Ed.) 1993. Price control possibilities. *Fortune* March 22.

Kemper and Novak. 1992. What's blocking health care reform? *Common Cause Magazine* 18(1).

Litman, T. J. and Robins, L. S. 1991. *Health politics and policy.* 2nd edition. Albany: Delmar Publishers, Inc.

Rachilis, M. 1989. *Second opinion: what's wrong with the Canadian health care delivery system.* Collins Publishing.

Wildavsky, A. 1979. *Speaking the truth to power: the art and craft of policy analysis.* Boston: Little, Brown and Co.

# Chapter 17

## The Canadian Health Care System: Implications for Nursing in the United States

*Patricia Nottingham Dzandu, MSN, MA, RN, CNAA, CS*
*Chief Executive Nurse*
*Peninsula Center for Behavioral Health*
*and Assistant Professor, Nursing*
*Hampton University*
*Hampton, Virginia*

### INTRODUCTION

Uncompensated care in the United States has become the focus of attention because if not resolved will lead to a health care disaster both short and long-term. Illness costs are exceeding our ability to pay with increasing numbers of citizens without health care. While attempts are being made to pay for health care, uncompensated care, according to Perkins and Perkins (1992), and uncollected accounts were simply spread throughout the system as a way of doing business. Nearly 40 million Americans have inadequate coverage and many families have had to make hard choices between food, clothing, shelter, or health care. This problem of uncompensated care has forced hospitals closing, changing to exempt specialties, trauma units withdrawing from trauma systems, and overloading of public systems.

Eighty-nine percent of Americans in a study by Schell (1989) say that the U.S. health care system needs fundamental changes, 61 percent prefer a system like Canada. Canada has provided access to care for the medically necessary services for its entire population through a national system of health insurance. The Canadian system has consistently viewed their system as effective. Quality of measures have according to Vayda (1988), lowered the rise in health care spending. Lower infant mortality rates and general mortality and morbidity rates equal or out perform U.S. Even though Canada has problems such as physician dissatisfaction, long lines in waiting rooms, and concern with health care cost, the Canadian system has out-performed the United States in important areas, and thus can be a useful model.

## The Canadian Model

What is the model? The passage of the Hospital Insurance and Diagnostic Services (HIDS) Act in July 1958 was the milestone in the evolution of national health insurance in Canada as described by Manga, *et al.* (1987). This act enabled the federal government to reach agreements with each of the ten provinces and two territories, but also provided the legislative bases for implementing publicly and provincially administered health insurance plans which covered acute, convalescent, and chronic care in hospital facilities. Four main principles and conditions had to be fulfilled as summarized by Manga *et al.* (1987):

1. Comprehensiveness—plans must provide all inpatient and outpatient services to all residents of jurisdiction;
2. Universality—provinces must make insured services available to all residents of the province;
3. Accessibility—the provincial law must make services in a manner that does not impede or preclude any one to reasonable access;
4. Portability—a province must make provision for the payment of amounts to hospitals in respect of the cost of insured services and the payment for insured services to all those entitled who are owed and operated by Canada.

In 1968 the Medical Care Insurance Act was approved which adapted the above principles with the added principle of all provincial hospital plans being publicly administered. The costs of hospital care are financed by publicly funded national health insurance scheme that employs principles of prepayment to provide necessary care to insured beneficiaries.

From 1970 through the 1980s, the Established Programs Financing Act shifted an increased share of cost of insurance programs to the provinces. The federal government became responsible for only one-half of its previous burden with provinces assuming the remainder.

## Payment System

Laschinger and McWilliams (1992) has summarized the Canadian system as a model reflecting U.S. free enterprise system and the British socialized medical. The private sector component of health care is limited to consultant services, for-profit management of a few traditionally funded organizations and private operations, nursing homes, private hospitals, and pharmacies. The services are planned, regulated and extensively funded by government. However, the services are not government delivered as they are in the United Kingdom. Health care administrators and their boards manage provincially funded global budgets and decide and deliver as they see fit.

Payments of health care cost in Canada as stated previously is by global budgeting. Global budgeting becomes a basis for a lump sum of money given to hospitals based on previous cost histories. The merits of proposed increases are considered by a central provincial committee and awarded on basis of ability to meet community needs. Canada does not face the current U.S. problem of excess bed capacity. Global budgeting can provide incentives for hospitals to control cost by controlling volume of resources used. Global budgeting also saves administrative cost by eliminating time item review of hospital budgets.

Physician services are paid on a fee for service basis according to scales negotiated by the provinces with physician groups. Costs are controlled by fee schedules and caps on the volume of services in some provinces. Further examples described are general practitioners who, upon exceeding a certain volume of service per pay period, are reimbursed at 25 percent of fee schedule.

## Canadian Nursing Viewpoints

> *"Often called a sleeping giant, the nursing profession in Canada is awakening to the unique skills and insights it contributes to the delivery of health services and the quest for an economically sustainable health care future."* (Baumgart and Larsen, 1992, p.2)

The current status of nursing in Canada and the predictions for its future as described by Baumgart and Larsen (1992) has provided nurses in the U.S.A. a realistic picture of what to expect, predict, implement and evaluate during health care reform. In that the entire blueprint is not replicable, a common thread that binds us all is that nurses are an adaptable **force** to assist in the shaping of the public policies of the 21st Century. The awesome task at hand is to meet the patients individual needs in the midst of the turmoil.

The Canadian health system has provided universal coverage for hospital and medical care regardless of age or health status. The affordibility and effectiveness has been debated but to understand further this issue, nursing assessments of needs is vital. In the mid-1980s, the nursing workforce in Canada faced a weak economic growth, and high expenditures due to the new health care service provisions. Baumgart and Larsen (1992) describe the work setting as unsettling blend of new opportunities with increases in supply of and demand for nurses. The practice demands shifted to high technology and a demand for community oriented programs. Treatment of the elderly overwhelmed the system. The changing health care needs were further influenced by an increased elderly population, fewer young people and advances in technology which increased longevity. Consequentially, a high incidence of chronic degenerative conditions, including heart disease, cancer, diabetes, forced care givers to question certain practices. Consumerism increased and scrutiny of the provisions of the healthcare system were debated.

The mental health services reform started after 1960s and 1970s with psychiatric nurses having to develop more community support networks with gaps in acute care, chronic care to the community, and home care. Disparities have been noted by Baumgart and Larsen (1992) in children, adolescents, the poor, homeless, seniors, First Nations and urban centers, those incarcerated in criminal justice systems, the disabled, and the dual diagnosed.

It is well stated that Canadian nurses form the backbone of the system with majority of nurses (72 percent) working as salaried employees in acute care centers. Laschinger and McWilliams (1992) state that only 10 percent of the nurse population work in community health and the remainder in long term care, physicians' office and educational institutions. Although community health nurses provide health promotion, these services only represent 1.6 percent of the Canadian health care dollar.

Despite the legislation under Canadian Health Care Act of 1985 to allow nonmedical service, the physician continues to be the gatekeeper with focus on illness care. However, Canada is facing high cost issues due to expansion of service need, and decline in economic environment. Baumgart (1992) describes a strategy of freezes on hospital budgets, wage restrictions, capping of physician fees and adoption of new hospital funding formulas. This climate within last two years caused ethical dilemmas in delineation of the nurse accountability, balancing quality and cost to match new hospital funding formulas, and increased stresses due to a cost cutting environment.

The other viewpoint that is on the table is differentiation from generalists and specialist role in nursing. Chalmers and Kristjanson (1992) state that with the pressure to decrease health care cost, with increases in early discharge, home care with high acuity factors, the generalists role is needed because of the need for nursing care diversity. They also cite the importance of specialists because of increased need for l.ealth promotion and wellness.

Lastly, the nurse as a primary health care practitioner deserves a lot of attention. The provision of primary health care to Indian and Inuit people in rural and northern Canada are done solely by nurses in isolated and semi-isolated communities. The educational backgrounds vary from diploma to doctoral degrees. There is concern for preparation, training and cultural sensitivity in the education of nurses. However, this role is the future for nurses and its value may be underestimated as urban nurse practitioners have difficulties in establishing independent practices as described in the writings of Laschinger and McWilliams (1992).

## Canadian Lessons

As the role of the nurse faces changes due to morbidity patterns fluctuation, technological advances and need for both generalists and specialists in all areas of nursing, the need to keep educational and training current has been overwhelming. As changes in consumer expectations, technology and practice settings occur, nurse education must respond rapidly to curriculum changes in nursing schools. The Canadian nursing educational system (Bajnok, 1992) needs to develop a historical analysis model so as to reach a logical prediction of nursing education and subsequently portray accurately the new systems in health care services for the practicing nurse.

In terms of barriers to independent nurse practitioner practice, Laschinger and McWilliams (1992) have described how both national and provincial nursing associations have tried to remove barriers in direct reimbursement of nurses under health insurance plans arguing that nurses provide a viable and cost-effective alternative to physicians for many types of health care services.

It is also evident that promotion programs and community health care cost benefit analysis are lacking in the Canadian model and this service is not receiving the attention that is needed. Difficulties appear to exist in shaping new paradigms of professional nurses as primary health care providers and having the skills to manage continuity of care, educate, and serve as gatekeepers for patient access. According to del Bueno (1993), nurses are experts at prevention and early primary intervention and it makes sense to expect nurses to be asked to provide consultation, direction, and policy formation to any health care redesign. The nurses, however, in the rural northern stations are providing the most important lesson there is in a conceptual framework of primary health care.

The Canadian nursing literature does reveal a proactive stance or issues surrounding nursing economics. Glass and Dick (1992) identify several major issues for nurse administrators. They are:

1.   Current reporting structures hamper nursing input.
2.   Cost benefit research is minimal with regard to nursing value and costeffectiveness as a service profession.
3.   Redefinition of staffing mix must be quick and responsive.

4. Redefinition of community nursing services is needed.
5. Multidisciplinary research is needed on application to particular settings.
6. There is no clearing house of nursing economics information.
7. There is a need for lobbying strategies to influence economic policy decisions based on nursing economics research.
8. There is a lack of nursing economics in nursing education curriculum.
9. Revenue generation for all purposes related to nursing economic research is lacking.
10. There is a need to clarify roles on all levels of nursing in practice setting.
11. Patient education must increase.
12. There is a tendency to respond to systems or procedural problems with overcrowding in emergency, surgery or clinics.

King (1992) supports a case management system as providing cost effective care at the patient provider level in their health system. The case management model was adapted from New England Medical Center in a 1,400 bed tertiary care hospital in Toronto. Staff members were expected to work together to coordinate patient care within appropriate time frames and use resources effectively. All departments were expected to look for opportunities to reduce cost, optimize resource efficiency, and to improve practice patterns within program. King (1992) also describes the managed care model of care maps. In essence, the care of the patient by all health care professionals are outlined day by day with key events such as tests, procedures, and consults. Teaching occurs to achieve the prescribed goals within the designated length of stay. Over time, the care maps are analyzed to look for patterns and deficiencies that can be corrected and which can form the basis for quality improvement programs. Effective patient outcomes were described by King (1992) as related to examples in transurethral resectioning prostate surgery. There was a five percent incidence of readmission due to post-discharge bleeding. With regard to other procedures, length of stays were reduced effectively without compromising the care of the patient.

Sandhu, *et al.* (1992) have been able to cost out the differences in a case management approach to nurses at Logan Regional Hospital, findings showed an average loss of $824 per case. Introducing the care coordination program reduced the cost to $540 with a savings of $284 per case. Logan Regional was able to save $94,572 on 10 DRGs. Another study was cited by Sandhu et al. (1992) in comparing length of stay with non-care managed and care managed cases with total hip replacement or respiratory DRGs. In total hip replacement, the case managed patients had an average of 8.1 days, the non-care managed was 10.2. Similar results were obtained for respiratory patients who were case managed a (6.0 days average stay) compared to non-managed cases (9.5 days). Sandhu *et al.* (1992) further contends that in restructuring care delivery models, it is important for the nurse to be a specialist of nursing care first before being a specialist in costs or coordinator of activities of other professionals.

**Nursing Implication For The Future**

Quebec has been cited by Baumgart (1992) as the farthest along in reorganizing services for the future. The development of local community service center provides medical care, home care, health education, general social services and outreach programs. Nursing associations have been advocating World Health Organization concept of primary health care with shift from curative medicine to health promotion and disease prevention.

The Canadian nursing community has clearly validated its worth in terms of access to care. There appears to be a shift toward cost effective nursing care approaches as demonstrated in the case management and care map models which are now becoming a part of many health care delivery models in the United States. Canadian nurses want primary prevention, and health promotion programs especially in a community based system. The tertiary model will not address the long-term problems with preventing disease especially since life spans are increasing. This will trigger the age-old problem of overcrowding in hospitals with chronic diseases which can increase cost. The global budgeting concept must address these issues up front as opposed to being succumbed to extra fee for service component.

It will also be important for nurses in the United States to continue to push for the independent nurse practitioner status in health care delivery. Canada has not reached a consistent point of allowing advanced nurse practitioners to hold an integral role in assisting clients to access the system. While physicians in Canada hold this place, it is important for nursing to look at this barrier. More than ever is the need for insurance companies to approve consistently third party reimbursement for nurse practitioners in the United States so that if a national health plan is finalized, the transitions will be viable.

Nursing administrators must continue to support cost benefit analysis of nursing system especially in a case management and managed care maps. Staffing systems must always be updated and shifted with new paradigm thinking with participation from line staff on all the changes that may occur. Nurses must build on a collaborative practice model with physicians as their practice patterns may change. These are exciting times for nursing as systems are refined, but nurses must be visible and vocal to evaluate the hard choices that will have to be made in health care reform.

It will be increasingly important to define roles more clearly especially between the specialist and generalists nurse. Whereas Quebec was cited to be able to blend effectively primary and secondary care, there appears a need for both roles. In Dallas, Texas, a major public hospital has developed community primary care centers utilizing the physician, clinical nurse specialist (advance nurse practitioner), social workers, nutritionist, lab, etc., in satellite areas of Dallas communities. The health promotion model is evident as oppose to disease model but this is not the norm in the United States. Canada has had years to graduate to the community model after their transition to national health plan. Perhaps the United States can look at our primary care physician, who at a cost of $150,000, could be replaced by three nurse practitioners. The patient ratio increases with increase in health promotion and teaching, prevention and crisis stabilization.

Lastly, education and training in nursing schools and continuing education must respond quickly to the health care change ultimately sharpening critical thinking in public health policy formulation by nurses.

## Summary

Lessons from Canada for Nurses in the United States:

- Maintain cost benefit analysis on any nursing system redesign. Prepare for global budgeting and be active in operational planning.
- Strengthen case management approaches on multidisciplinary levels.
- Introduce and evaluate care maps as strategy to direct daily care. Track variances and seek improvement continuously.
- Heighten primary prevention and health promotion. Develop longitudinal studies to measure outcome.
- Upgrade awareness and efficiencies of community based and educational programs for patients. Track outcome.
- Lobby to further maintain and improve reimbursement of advanced nurse practitioners. Demonstrate and validate cost benefit analysis for patient care and be at a lower cost than physicians.
- Develop and maintain collaborative spirit with physicians in managing patient care. Enhance the position that physician are partners in practice. Prepare for their practice patterns changing, and their reduced income.
- Develop and maintain collaborative spirit with all disciplines. The smooth flow of patients through hospital and community system is team work and not turf fighting over roles. Look at how one assesses the patients as the primary focus in team development. Strengthen ethics committee procedures to work out common dilemmas.
- Keep education and training components in schools current with emphasis on historical analysis model.
- Include consumer satisfaction polls in strategic long range planning.

# References

Bajnok, I. 1992. Entry level educational preparation in nursing. In *Canadian nursing faces the future,* eds. A. Baumgart and J. Larsen. Toronto: Mosby Year Book,Inc.

Baumgart, A. and Larsen, J. 1992. In *Canadian nursing faces the future*, A. Baumgart and J. Larsen. Toronto: Mosby Year Book, Inc.

Chalmers, K. and Kristjanson, L. 1992. Community health nursing practice. In *Canadian nursing faces the future*, eds. A. Baumgart, A. and J. Larsen. Toronto: Mosby Year Book, Inc.

del Bueno, D. 1993. Paradigm shifts—what's good and not so good for health care. *Nursing and Health Care* 14(2):100–101.

Glass, H. and Dick, J. 1992. Nursing economics in Canada. *The Canadian Nurse*, 46–47.

King, M. 1992. Case management. *The Canadian Nurse*, 15–17.

Laschinger, H. and McWilliams, C. 1992. Health care in Canada: the presumption of care. *Nursing and Health Care* 13(4):204–207.

Manga, P., Broyles, R. W. and Angus, J. 1987. The determinants of hospital utilization under a universal public insurance program in Canada. *Medical Care* 25:658–670.

Perkins, C. and Perkins, K. 1992. Uncompensated care: the millstone around the neck of U.S. health care. *Nursing and Health Care* 13(1):20–23.

Sandhu, B., Dugette, A. and Kerovac, S. 1989. Care delivery modes. *The Canadian Nurse*, 18–20.

Schell, E. 1989. Lessons from the Canadian health care system. *Nursing Economics* 7(6):306–309.

Vayda, E. 1988. Universal medical care insurance in Canada: are there lessons for the United States? *Health Care Cost Management* 1(3):3–6.

# About the Authors

**Ralph J. Anderson**, M.D., is chairman of the Department of Obstetrics and Gynecology Residency Program at John Peter Smith Hospital in Fort, Worth, Texas. Dr. Anderson is a native of Canada. He received his degree in medicine from the University of Western Ontario in 1964. He became a Fellow of the Royal College of Surgeons in Canada in 1969, and a Fellow of the American College of Obstetrics and Gynecology in 1984. He has held research and/or faculty positions at the University of Western Ontario, Texas Tech University School of Medicine, M. D. Anderson Hospital and Tumor Institute in Houston, and Parkland Memorial Hospital in Dallas. Dr. Anderson's publication include articles in *Cancer Research, Journal of Reproductive Medicine, American Journal of Obstetrics and Gynecology*, and *Adolescent Pediatric Gynecology*.

**Ron J. Anderson**, M.D., is President and Chief Executive officer of Parkland Memorial Hospital, the general public hospital for Dallas County, and the primary teaching hospital for the University of Texas Southwestern Medical Center at Dallas. Dr. Anderson is on the faculty of the Medical School as Professor of Internal Medicine and continues to see patients and teach house staff physicians at Parkland. He has authored or co-authored over 200 articles on medicine, ethics, and health policy issues. A native of Chickasha, Oklahoma, he received his medical degree from the University of Oklahoma and his pharmacy degree from Southwestern Oklahoma State University where he was selected as a Distinguished Alumni in 1987. Dr. Anderson has received numerous awards for his contributions to public health including the James E. Peavy Award from the Texas Public Health Association (1988); the McGovern Award from the Texas School Health Association (1989); Health Care Profession of the Year from the Texas Nurses Association (1990); the Safety Net Award from the National Association of Public Hospitals (1990); the Earl M. Collier Award for Distinguished Hospital Administration from the Texas Hospital Association; Distinguished Human Service Professional of the year from the Community Council of Greater Dallas; an honorary doctorate of Public Service from the University of North Texas; and the John P. McGovern Award for humanitarian medicine from the Association of Academic Health Centers (1994). Dr. Anderson was actively involved in health care reform in the State of Texas. He served on the State Task Force on Indigent Care in 1985, co-chaired the Attorney General's Task Force to study not-for-profit hospitals and charity care in 1988; and served as a member of Governor Ann Richards' Health Policy Task Force in 1992. Dr. Anderson is the past chairman of the Dallas-Fort Worth Hospital Council, the Texas Association of Public and Non-Profit Hospitals, the Texas Board of Health; the National Association of Public Hospitals, and the National Public Health and Hospital Institute. In 1990 he initiated the Community Oriented Primary Care Program at Parkland Hospital. This innovative concept in preventive medicine was instrumental in Parkland being honored as the 1994 recipient of the Foster G. McGraw Award for community service.

**Patricia Nottingham Dzandu**, R.N., M.S.N., is currently Chief Nurse Executive for Peninsula Center for Behavioral Health, Hampton, Virginia, and is an adjunct professor at Hampton University School of Nursing. She has fifteen years experience in Nursing Administration. She received her B.S.N. from Hampton University, her M.A. in psychology from the University of Connecticut, and her M.S. in Nursing from Texas Woman's University. She has received numerous awards, including Woman of the year in Fort Worth, Texas, Texas Nurses' Association Leadership Award, and Hospital Corporation of American's Humanitarian Award.

**Tracy L. Dietz**, M.A., is a research associate in the Minority Aging Research Institute at the University of North Texas. Her research interests include aging, medical sociology, the family, and race/ethnic relations. She received her Bachelor of Arts in sociology from Stephen F. Austin State University and her Master of Arts in sociology from the University of North Texas and is currently pursuing a Ph.D. in sociology there.

**Susan Brown Eve**, Ph.D., is currently professor and chair of the Department of Sociology at the University of North Texas. She received her doctoral degree in sociology from the University of North Carolina in Chapel Hill. Most of her research has been focused on health needs of older adults. Publications include articles in the *Journal of Gerontology*, *Sociological Focus*, *The Journal of South African Aging*, and *Research on Aging*. Dr. Eve was Editor of *Clinical Sociology Review*, 1992–1994.

**Frank C. Fedyck** is currently a Senior Analyst with the Aging Policy Section, Health Policy Division, Health and Welfare Canada.

**Derek G. Gill** is the chair of the Department of Sociology and Anthropology, University of Maryland, Baltimore Campus. Previously he was with the Medical Sociology Research Unit, University of Aberdeen, and Chief, Section on Behavioral Sciences, University of Missouri, Columbia. He is the author of two books, *The British National Health Service: A Sociologist's Perspective*, and *Illegitimacy, Sexuality and the Status of Women*. In addition, he has published 40 articles in the areas of sociology of health, human sexuality, the social correlates of pregnancy and comparative health care systems.

**Ms. Betty Havens** is the former Assistant Deputy Minister Continuing Care Programmes Division and Provincial Gerontologist. She has been affiliated with the University of Manitoba, and in October 1994 became Professor, Department of Community Health Sciences, and a Research Fellow with Statistics Canada. A founding member of the Canadian Association of Gerontology, who served as President 1979–1983, she is a Fellow of the Gerontological Society of America. She has held office in the International Association of Gerontology, the International Sociological Association's Research Committee on Aging, the American Sociological Association, the Midwest Sociological Society, and the Midwest Council for Social Research on Aging.

**Stanley R. Ingman** is currently director of the Texas Institute for Research and Education on Aging, a joint program of the University of North Texas and the University of North Texas Health Science Center. Dr. Ingman has written more than two dozen journal articles, and authored or edited half a dozen books and special issues of journals. His most recent book, with Derek Gill, is *Eldercare, Distributive Justice and the Welfare State: Retrenchment of Development* (SUNY, 1994.)

**Robert L. Kane**, M.D., holds an endowed chair in Long-term Care and Aging at the University of Minnesota School of Public Health. Dr. Kane has studied health care systems for older persons in Europe and Canada. An earlier book, co-authored with his wife, *A Will and A Way: What the United States Can Learn about Caring for the Elderly*, has been widely cited. A health services researcher, he has done research on various aspects of care for older persons including geriatric manpower studies and the quality of care. He has written or edited 15 books and 200 journal articles and book chapters, mostly dealing with aspects of care for older persons.

**Robert A. H. Kinch**, M.B., B.S., F.A.C.O.G., F.R.C.S., came originally from England and emigrated to Canada in September 1948. He graduated from the Middlesex Hospital Medical School, University of London, England in 1943. Subsequently, he completed his residency at Middlesex, Queen Charlotte's Hospital, Central Middlesex Hospital, and the University of Toronto. He was appointed Clinical Tutor at the University of Toronto, working out of Toronto Western Hospital in private practice and part-time teaching. In 1957, he was appointed Professor and Chairman of the Department of Obstetrics and Gynecology at the University of Western Ontario, London,

Ontario. In 1968, he was appointed Professor at McGill University and Chief of Obstetrics and Gynecology at the Montreal General Hospital. From 1979 to 1984, Dr. Kinch was Chairman of the Department of Obstetrics and Gynecology at McGill University. In 1987, he became visiting Professor and Director of Maternal-Fetal Medicine at the University of Texas medical Branch at Galveston. In 1990, he became Director of Maternal-Fetal Medicine at John Peter Smith Hospital in Fort Worth. He has been actively involved as Treasurer of the Royal College of Surgeons of Canada and the Association of Professors of Obstetrics and gynecology of Canada. He has also been involved with Reproductive Health Committees of the Federal government of Canada and the World Health Organization.

**Joseph Mensah** received his M.A. in geography from Wilfrid Laurier University, Waterloo, 1989, and his Ph.D. in geography from the University of Alberta, Edmonton in 1993. He is currently teaching quantitative and urban geography at the Malaspina University College in Nanaimo, British Columbia.

**Gerald R. Middents**, Ph.D., is currently professor of psychology at Austin College in Sherman, Texas, Director of Contemporary Policy Studies, and a Registered Organizational Development Professional. He has a B.S.C. and M.Div. degrees, as well as M.A. and Ph.D. degrees, from the University of Minnesota. Previous publications are included in the journals of *Medical Education*, *Organizational Development*, *Scalpel*, and *Religion and Health*. He is a member of the American Psychological Association, a licensed psychologist and health services provider in Texas, and an ordained Presbyterian minister. He has lectured in China, Russia, former Yugoslavia, Poland, and Ghana. He teaches cross-cultural psychology, religion and psychology, ethics, personality, law and psychology, health care policy, and violence, illness and health.

**Joseph R. Oppong** received his M.A. and Ph.D. in geography from the University of Alberta, Edmonton, in 1986 and 1992 respectively. Dr. Oppong is an assistant professor at the University of North Texas where he teaches medical geography, location-allocation modelling and quantitative techniques. His previous work has been published in *Geographical Analysis*, *Canadian Journal of Regional Science*, *Professional Geographer*, and *Social Indicators Research*. His current research pursuits center on rural-urban disparities in access to health services and the geography of cancer incidence and mortality.

**Vijayan Pillai** is an assistant professor of sociology and social work at the University of North Texas. He is currently engaged in examining the impact of modernization on the transition to motherhood among teenagers in Zambia. In addition, he is modelling the differences between Zambian men and women in terms of reproductive goals and ideals. He has published a number of articles on Asian, African, and American fertility, in journals including *Demography*. His most recent publication is an edited volume, *Developing Areas: A Book of Readings* (with Lyle Shannon.) He is currently conducting a longitudinal study of the association between welfare spells and teenage fertility in the State of Texas.

**Michael M. Rachlis**, M.D., M.Sc., F.R.C.P.C., graduated from the University of Manitoba Medical School in 1975. He practiced medicine for eight years and then completed a residency in community medicine at McMaster University in Hamilton, Ontario, in 1988. Dr. Rachlis is an assistant professor in the Department of Clinical Epidemiology and Biostatistics at McMaster University and a staff physician at the Hassle Free Clinic in Toronto. Dr. Rachlis is the co-author of two books on Canada's health care system, *Second Opinion*, published in 1989, and *Strong Medicine*, published in 1994.

**Mark W. Rosenberg**, Ph.D., is an associate professor in the Department of Geography and a member of the teaching staff of the School of Policy Studies at Queen's University, Kingston, Ontario. Dr. Rosenberg holds a B.A. from the University of Toronto and M.Sc. and Ph.D. degrees from the London School of Economics and Political Science. His most recent publications on the Canadian health care system can be found in the *Royal Commission on New Reproductive Technologies*, *Prenatal Diagnosis: Background and Impact on Individuals*, *Social Science and Medicine*, and *The Canadian Geographer*.

**Daniel J. Schneider**, M.D., conceived the features of Health Assurance Development over the past 30 years, commencing while Commissioner of Health for Micronesia where he observed the learning dynamics that result in healthful and unhealthful behavior while attending natives displaced from Bikini and Eniwetok following American atomic bomb tests. Later foci have included health development learning in Native Americans. Dr. Schneider is currently a member of the faculty at the University of North Texas Health Science Center in Fort Worth.

**David R. Smith**, M.D., became Texas Commissioner of health in March 1992, having served as Senior Vice President of Parkland Memorial Hospital in Dallas and CEO and Medical Director of Parkland's Community Oriented Primary Care Program. Previously, Dr. Smith was Deputy Director of the U.S. Special Populations and Program Development in Washington, D.C. A board-certified pediatrician, Dr. Smith Was Medical Director of the Brownsville Community Health Center in Texas' Rio Grande Valley. He holds an undergraduate degree from Cornell University and a medical degree from the University of Cincinnati. He has done postgraduate work at Johns Hopkins University and completed his pediatrics residency at Children's Hospital of Philadelphia. He serves on the faculties of the University of Texas Southwest Medical Center at Dallas and the University of Texas' LBJ School of Public Affairs. He has held teaching positions with George Washington University and the University of Pennsylvania School of Medicine. Dr. Smith's special interest and experience in two critical health issues, childhood immunizations and U.S.-Mexico border health, are recognized in his being named to the U.S. Department of Health and Human Services National Vaccine Advisory Committee and to the U.S. Environmental Protection Agency's Good Neighbor Environmental Board.

**Rex Taylor**, Ph.D., is professor of social policy at the University of Glasgow since 1987. Previously he was a researcher in the Medical Research Council's Medical Sociology Units. He is the author of numerous scientific papers on health services and long term care of the elderly. His chapter for this volume was written while he was a Visiting Scholar in the School of Community Service at the University of North Texas.